SECOND EDITION

A MAGICAL ENCOUNTER

LATINO CHILDREN'S LITERATURE IN THE CLASSROOM

ALMA FLOR ADA
University of San Francisco

Boston   New York   San Francisco
Mexico City   Montreal   Toronto   London   Madrid   Munich   Paris
Hong Kong   Singapore   Tokyo   Cape Town   Sydney

Series Editor: *Aurora Martínez Ramos*
Series Editorial Assistant: *Beth Slater*
Executive Marketing Manager: *Amy Cronin Jordan*
Production Administrator: *Annette Pagliaro*
Editorial Production: *Omegatype Typography, Inc.*
Composition Buyer: *Linda Cox*
Manufacturing Buyer: *JoAnne Sweeney*
Cover Administrator: *Kristina Mose-Libon*
Text Design and Composition: *Omegatype Typography, Inc.*

For related titles and support materials, visit our online catalogue at www.ablongman.com.

Between the time Website information is gathered and then published, it is not unusual for some sites to have closed. Also, the transcription of URLs can result in unintended typographical errors. The publishers would appreciate notification where these errors occur so that they may be corrected in subsequent editions.

Library of Congress Cataloging-in-Publication Data

Ada, Alma Flor.
    A magical encounter : Latino children's literature in the classroom / Alma Flor Ada.
       p. cm.
    Includes bibliographical references and index.
    ISBN 0-205-35544-7
      1. Literature—Study and teaching—United States.   2. Children's literature, Latin American.   3. Hispanic American children—Education.   4. Children—Books and reading—United States.   I. Title.

LB1575.5.U5 A345 2003
372.64—dc21

                                                    2002071198

Printed in the United States of America

10 9 8 7 6 5 4 3 2   07 06 05 04 03

For my great-grandparents, Lorenzo Lafuente Garoña and Virginia Rubio Sierra Ladrón de Guevara, innovative teachers.

For my grandparents, Medardo Lafuente Rubio and Dolores Salvador Méndez, teachers of teachers and sources of daily inspiration.

For my father, Modesto Ada Rey, and my mother, Alma Lafuente Salvador, always teachers, whether in or out of the classroom.

For my aunts, Virginia, Mireya, and Lolita Lafuente Salvador, and my uncle Mario Ada Rey, teachers all.

And for my daughter, Rosalma Zubizarreta Ada, whose students include her grateful mother.

CONTENTS

CHAPTER 3

Once upon a World: The Diversity of Literature   59

CHAPTER 4

Using the Magic: Literature in the Classroom   69

LIST OF FIGURES

The generous reception of the first edition of this book, as attested to by its numerous printings, has prompted the development of this new edition. In the time since the initial publication of the book, the evolution experienced by Latino literature for children and young adults has inspired the ample revisions incorporated in this new edition.

The debate, now centuries old, about the teaching of reading has not faded away; if anything, it has become more acute as it becomes politicized by forces external to the classroom that infringe on teachers' decision-making powers, work against the democratic process, and limit teachers' innovative creativity and reflective capacity. We even witness the unfounded proposition that speaking, reading, and writing in only one language are better than having the opportunity of functioning in two, contrary to the basic nature of education: enrichment.

Yet in the midst of this climate, which is detrimental to many children, certain truths remain unquestioned: Reading is a basic intellectual activity necessary for academic development, and the better a reader a student is, the greater the potential for academic success. There continues to be a direct correlation between the extent of vocabulary and success in reading; therefore, the richness of vocabulary continues to be a clear predictor of academic success.

There is no question that literature is the best expression of a language. It is through authentic literature in its varied manifestations—narrative, poetry, drama, folklore—that the creative potentials of a language are fully expressed. Furthermore, it is in high-quality literature that the profound quests of the human experience are explored and life issues are looked at in depth and from diverse perspectives. Literature is a medium for questioning behavior, for the discovery of alternatives, and for finding hope for new beginnings and reexamined attitudes.

Children and youth should have access to the best of their culture and the universal human culture. To be meaningful, their education needs to include the best of what has been created specifically for them, and high-quality literature, rich and diverse, needs to have a central place in the education of children and youth.

If literature remains a treat for after-school hours provided by parents, many children and youth will continue to lack equal opportunities and the promise of a better future. It is the schools' responsibility to ascertain that each and every child is exposed to the best literature and that these books remain forever accessible to them. It is not a matter of making literature prescriptive and robbing it of its magic by treating it as a subject of instruction;

it is about developing creative ways in which children encounter literature and have multiple opportunities for interacting with books until they become lifelong friends.

WHY LATINO LITERATURE?

The suggestions for the uses of literature in the classroom presented in this book are indeed applicable to any classroom and with any books the teacher may prefer. In the first edition of this book, all the examples referred to books in Spanish. To make the book useful to the widest possible number of teachers and children, the examples in this edition include books in English and books in Spanish. The examples are primarily of books written in English by Latino writers. When a Spanish edition of the book exists, it is also noted. Occasionally, when a corresponding Spanish edition is not yet available or when a Spanish title seems particularly appropriate, a Spanish book may be offered that may be different from, but comparable to, the English title.

The majority of the examples in the book have been purposefully selected from Latino writers for three reasons: First, although literature for children published by Latino writers goes back to the nineteenth century and although there always have been good Latino writers, few of them ever found the means to be published. As with other minority authors in this country, breaking into the mainstream publishing world has been very difficult. Even today, the larger number of books by Latino writers are published by only a few imprints. Therefore many of the titles included in this book are of recent publication, mainly after 1990. Most of them will be unknown to many classroom teachers. Highlighting these books here is an invitation to become familiar with them.

Second, Latino children in the United States have suffered a great deal from the ways in which their culture, particularly in its most creative and representative aspects, has been rendered invisible by the mass media and within the school curriculum. The culture of the Hispanic world is vast and rich in creative aspects: architecture, painting, sculpture, music, ballet, philosophy, theater, and literature. Latino children seldom have an opportunity to see these representations of their culture. This silence not only erodes their self-esteem, but also precludes them from imagining themselves as part of a continuum of creators. Facilitating their encounter with the books mentioned here will be honoring them, their families, and their communities as well as providing them with significant role models.

Third, all non-Latino children in the United States would benefit from the books mentioned here, both for the books' intrinsic value and because they can help the children develop an appreciation for the culture of a large segment of the U.S. population. A strong, united nation can be born only out of respect and understanding among all of the diverse groups that compose it.

To bring a greater awareness of the existing Latino writers and to assist the reader in placing the books cited in the activities within a wider context, a new chapter on Latino literature for children and adolescents ("Words of Jade and Coral") has been added to this edition.

GENESIS OF THIS BOOK

The inception of *A Magical Encounter* was the moment during the first class I taught as a very young classroom teacher when I felt dismay that my young students had not read as many books as I had read at their age, even though at the time, there were not too many years separating us. I realized that I had had the immense privilege of being given wonderful books to read at an early age by my parents. I knew that some of the greatest joys of my life had come out of reading but also that reading had enlarged my view of life, made me a citizen of the world, allowed me resources to cope with difficult situations, and given me a vision of possibilities for generosity, kindness, courage, responsibility, solidarity, and beauty. I wanted my students to have the same opportunities, and I set out to discover ways in which I could bring about the magical encounter between children and books.

Pursuing this goal has been part of my life quest to facilitate the best educational opportunities for all children. I have had the privilege of visiting thousands of classrooms throughout the United States and in Latin America, Micronesia, New Zealand, and Western and Eastern Europe, and I have had the joy of seeing extraordinary teachers sharing their joy of books with children.

I have seen every activity suggested in this book implemented in classrooms. Sometimes I learned an activity from teachers, and sometimes I was the proponent of the activity and then saw it implemented, but none of them has just simply been thought of and not tried. The development of the twelve-part structure within which the activities in Chapter 4 have been organized was in itself an organic process that grew out of numerous workshops, seminars, institutes, and courses over a period of more than twenty-five years. Although the structure has continued to be refined and enriched, the basic principles have been validated by teachers over and over again.

USING THIS BOOK

A Magical Encounter is addressed both to classroom teachers who would like to enhance the presence of literature in their classrooms and to teacher educators who would like to make sure the next generation of teachers will feel comfortable bringing literature to the classroom as a vehicle for language and concept development, creative expression, and the development of higher thinking skills while at the same time promoting the joy of reading.

The book is divided into four major parts:

- Chapter 1 sets out the theoretical principles that ground the practices suggested. The first section offers some reflections on the role of literature for children and adolescents in the language arts curriculum. The second presents the basic tenets of Transformative Education as they relate to books for children and adolescents. The third describes the Creative Reading methodology and explains its applications. The fourth is a description of a very special project, the "One Thousand Book Classroom." Whenever I have shared this authentic experience in a presentation, I have been asked to write about it. The time has come to bestow public recognition on this extraordinary classroom. Finally, the fifth section describes what a transformative language arts classroom would look like, presented as a composite of multiple classroom experiences and real teacher practices.

- Chapter 2 is an overview of the evolution of Latino literature for children and adolescents in the United States. It is complemented by an extensive bibliography of books published by Latino and Latina authors.
- The roles of the various literary genres in the classroom are described in Chapter 3.
- Chapter 4, divided into twelve sections, offers suggestions for the application of the theory. The activities suggested for the exploration of literature in the classroom are accompanied by examples using specific books. Most activities are exemplified through two or more books, one for the lower grades (K–3) and one for the upper grades (4 and up). None of these suggestions involve hard-and-fast rules. The intent is not necessarily that they be imitated with the specific book used as an example, but rather that they become inspiration for similar activities the teacher can imagine, always with the hope that they act as a beginning point rather than an ending.
- Finally the appendixes, bibliographies, and indexes facilitate the use of the book as a reference. Appendix A presents a list of traditional Hispanic sayings, and Appendix B is a list of traditional phrases for beginning and ending stories. The References include cited and recommended academic works, and an extensive bibliography of books for children and adolescents by Latino and Latina authors organized by genre, language, and some significant themes is also provided.

ACKNOWLEDGMENTS

My gratitude goes to those who have supported the development of this book during its long life and growth: Bernice Randall, editor extraordinaire, who translated and edited the first edition; Rosa Zubizarreta, whose insights and editorial assistance with diverse sections of the book have helped to fine-tune many concepts; Isabel Campoy, who in sharing this work with teachers has added valuable dimensions to it; Sherrill Brooks, who carefully edited the revised edition; Aurora Martínez, Acquisitions Editor at Allyn and Bacon, who nurtured the realization of this second edition; Anne Rogers, Karla Walsh, Mary Young, and the rest of Omegatype Typography, Inc., who gently and effectively guided the manuscript to its present book format; and the innumerable teachers and teacher educators who have made this book a friendly companion in their teaching and have requested this new edition.

This book reflects my deep appreciation for and recognition of the work of teachers. During my long career as a teacher educator, I have met countless dedicated and creative teachers who carry out their tasks responsibly and enthusiastically in constant pursuit of new ideas and methods and, above all, in a never-ending process of self-questioning.

Indeed, this book is addressed to those professionals, whom I value both as intellectuals and as teachers. As I have already said, its pages do not contain directives or rules, but instead offer reflection and suggest various ideas, tried in the classroom by me or others, that I hope will validate those teachers' experiences and concerns. I hope too that they will encourage the teachers—and the teachers-to-be—to continue building on their own creativity.

I would also like to express my gratitude to all the teachers who, year after year, have inspired and enriched me with their comments, who have invited me to their schools or welcomed me into their classes, and who have attended my classes, lectures, or training sessions.

All ideas in this book are the product of that continuing dialogue. I cannot, of course, mention all the school districts to which I have been invited, but I would like to single out a few with which I have interacted extensively, both during the time the initial version of this book was being written and since. First, in California: ABC School District, Alum Rock, Bakersfield, Calexico, Fresno, Hayward (particularly Glassbrook School), Kerman, Los Angeles Unified School District (and in particular Project MORE), Oxnard, Pájaro Valley, Salinas, San Diego County (particularly Migrant Education Region IX), San Ysidro, San Mateo County, Santa Ana, Santa Barbara, San Francisco (particularly Marshall and Buenavista Schools, and the Language Academy Program teachers), Watsonville, Windsor, and Willits. Second, in Texas: Austin, Brownsville, Dallas, El Paso, Houston, Laredo, Pharr–San Juan–Alamo, and San Antonio. Third, in the rest of the United States: Alaska, Boston, Cambridge, Connecticut, Chicago, Miami, Milwaukee, the New York State Bilingual Program, Orlando, Philadelphia Bilingual Program, Phoenix (in particular Sunnyslope School), and West Palm Beach. Finally, outside the United States: the Department of Public Instruction and the Catholic schools in Puerto Rico and the schools in Guam, Micronesia, and Saipan in the Northern Mariana Islands. I would also like to recognize the Secretaría de Educación Pública de México and the Open Society Institute. The latter provided the opportunity to work with educators in several Eastern European countries, in particular Bulgaria, the Czech Republic, and Hungary.

I would also like to thank the schools that have invited me to visit them as an author or that have developed authors' study projects based on my work. From these visits and studies have evolved some of the ideas mentioned in this book. The schools are too many to list here, but I want to acknowledge the creativity of the teachers involved and thank them for having shared their projects and their students with me in encounters that I will always treasure.

To them all, I extend my sincere thanks and best wishes. May they, as well as you, dear reader, enjoy the deep satisfaction of knowing that the seeds you generously sow today will bloom, enriching the lives of your students, their families, and those who, in their turn, they reach.

ABOUT THE AUTHOR

Alma Flor Ada is the director of the Center for Multicultural Literature for Children and Young Adults at the University of San Francisco. She teaches and lectures internationally and guides research of doctoral students in the areas of Transformative Education, Education for Social Justice, Family Literacy, Literature in the Classroom, and Students as Authors. A widely published author, her books for children and young adults have received numerous awards, including the Christopher Medal (for *The Gold Coin*), the American Library Association Pura Belpré Award (for *Under the Royal Palms*), the Museum of Tolerance Once Upon a World Award (for *Gathering the Sun*), the Marta Salotti Gold Medal, Argentina (for *Encaje de piedra*), Parent's Honors Award (for *Dear Peter Rabbit*) and many others.

Throughout the United States, Latin America, and Spain she has lectured, provided in-service education and classroom demonstrations, visited schools as an author, and worked with teachers in bringing the magic of children's literature to the curriclum and an awareness of the richness of the Hispanic culture.

1

A MAGICAL ENCOUNTER
CHILDREN AND BOOKS

Whether in nature or in human relationships, few images are more compelling than that of an encounter: a butterfly and a flower blended together in a brief burst of color, the sun's rays and a raindrop joined in a rainbow, a mother reaching out for her newborn child, two pairs of eyes held in a deeply felt gaze, two hands clasped in friendship—and surely, among the most meaningful encounters, the one between a child and a book.

There are several reasons for the extraordinary importance of the magical moment when a boy eagerly opens a book or when a girl loses herself in the lines on a page. For one thing, we know that children who learn to read with ease, who love books and are comfortable with them, are likely to be successful at school because schoolwork centers largely on the printed word.

Yet however significant, academic success is but one of the benefits that good readers enjoy. Books provide moments of joy and healthful constructive entertainment. For those of us who share José Martí's belief that "children are born to be happy," this is a vital aspect of reading.

Books are faithful friends, never withholding their companionship. They can thus be a source of comfort for children at moments in which they feel sad, isolated, or misunderstood. Indeed, storybook characters who undergo similar experiences and have similar feelings often provide valuable emotional support to children in such moments.

Stories invite children to give free rein to their fantasy, to let their imagination run free. Without such stimulation, children are less likely to realize their creative potential, which not only makes their daily life fuller and more satisfying, but may even ensure opportunities in their future as inventors, discoverers, or developers of new concepts or ideas.

Then, too, books broaden young people's view of the world and enlarge their experience. Books enrich the children's minds while strengthening their spirits.

Many children are, on their own, able to discover books and the wealth they offer. Yet many more need guidance in becoming good readers, whether because they lack role models at home or because they lack the self-assurance needed to pick up a book and establish a direct connection with it.

The activities that are suggested in this book not only stem from a conviction that the magical encounter between children and books is of enormous value, but also are designed to make that encounter smoother, more pleasant, and more enduring.

LANGUAGE ARTS AND CHILDREN'S LITERATURE

The search for a solution to the ever-growing problem of illiteracy, whether it is due to an actual inability to read and write or to the gradual loss of these skills through disuse, has focused considerable attention on the teaching of the initial reading decoding skills and the literal comprehension of text content. Yet the danger of such a focus is that even if the discrete reading skills are learned, this does not guarantee the development of readers and authors.

The use of children's literature in the classroom ought to need no defense. Good literature embodies not only the breadth of human experience—as if this were not enough—but also language at its best, at its most creative, intuitive, and precise. Good literature delves into the human soul, expressing its feelings and emotions, its hopes and its dreams. And good literature gives life to the full range of human relations.

Books for children and children's literature are not necessarily the same. This distinction needs to be stressed, because it has received scant attention from educators and has been overlooked in the training of many teachers.

Defining good literature is not easy, as the countless attempts to do so attest. A book becomes good literature in various ways: because of the ingenuity of its plot, the telling psychological portraits of its characters, its ability to re-create reality, the novelty of the world it brings to life, the creative use of language. Good literature may win the reader over because it has a compelling plot, because it sheds light on a minor event in such a way as to give it far-reaching relevance, or simply because it is funny, engaging, or moving. But whatever the devices it employs, good literature aspires to more than mere communication of information or just to be an entertainment: Good literature moves the readers. It broadens the readers' horizons, validates their experiences, invites reflection, and awakens an aesthetic sense.

One of the best ways of bringing children and books together is by oral reading. We know that there is no more effective means of helping young people become good readers than by reading to them. Many children do not have anyone at home who reads to them; that is why it has become so important for elementary school teachers to read good literature to their students every day. This need not demand an inordinate amount of time; a few minutes a day will suffice, provided that the reading has integrity: A poem, a picture book, or a chapter of a book will be very appropriate. This reading does not require discussion afterward. Although the fourth part of this book does present suggestions for interactive use of literature, at this point I am advocating an additional form of reading, that which is given to the children simply as a gift. This reading can be done throughout the elementary school years, even while children are already independent readers. There is a particular pleasure in listening to a good reader; and reading to someone is reaching out with one's own voice, is sharing one's interests and emotions—is indeed a true gift.

Teachers choose different moments for this reading aloud. Some like to use it to begin the day, as a way of focusing the students' attention. Others do it in the middle of the day, as a way to change activities. Others prefer to do it immediately after recess, again to help the students settle down. Finally, there are those who do it at the end of the day as their parting gift to their students, to send them home with a pleasant experience and warm feelings of expectation for a new school day.

Of course, children should be encouraged to become independent readers, to make reading a daily habit, and to treasure every moment they are free to read; thus, another general guideline for teachers is to include in the daily schedule a certain amount of time for recreational silent reading. The teachers themselves would do well to recognize and convey the special importance of this daily period both by serving as role models—reading their own books for pleasure while the students read theirs—and by expressing enthusiasm at being able to spend time reading.

Finally, teachers ought to see that their students have access to as many books as possible, some within the classroom itself. Teachers can make a point of mentioning new books that might be of interest; display book jackets, posters, and other book-related materials in the classroom; and encourage the students to visit the school and public libraries regularly—in short, take every opportunity to foster the students' interest in and love of books.

Besides following these general suggestions, teachers can carry out a language arts program that is specifically based on children's literature or make children's literature a significant part of their language arts curriculum. How to do so is the subject of this book.

Developing a literature-based unit raises multiple considerations:

- Deciding on ways to motivate the students to read or listen to the reading of a book and how to introduce the book
- Accessing the students' previous knowledge and recognizing the importance of students' own experiences
- Choosing among the different ways in which the book can be read to the class
- Engaging in the enriching dialogue that can ensue from reading the book
- Making the best use of the many language development opportunities that ensue from the literary selection
- Honing the students' discovery and research skills

- Promoting creative expression in all areas: oral, written, dramatic, and visual
- Ascertaining that there is family involvement and facilitating home dialogue about the literary selection
- Expanding on the development of multiple intelligence activities and culminating activities that will reach outside the classroom boundaries
- Preparing an author's visit or engaging in an author's study
- Evaluating the process

Within any given unit, of course, not all of these areas will be emphasized to the same extent. It will be up to the teacher to determine which warrant special attention. In the fourth chapter of this book, the activities have been grouped in twelve steps, which are all explained and exemplified. In the classroom, the way in which each area is treated depends on a number of factors, which only the teacher can determine for each specific situation—for example, (1) the type of book selected, (2) the grade level and the students' reading abilities, (3) the particular skills the teacher wants to develop or reinforce, and (4) the overall curriculum of which this unit is a part.

A wide range of suggested activities for making children's books an important part of their language arts program are offered here, and teachers are invited to draw on these proposals whole or to feel free to adapt them to their needs.

The full development of all language abilities—listening, speaking, reading, and writing—needs to be at the core of the educational process if our students are going to be able to move up the academic ladder to develop their potential fully. Traditional schooling tends to give more attention to listening and reading than to speaking and writing. All aspects of language need to be given full attention. Although this book addresses writing as part of the creative expression that should be an integral part of any language arts unit, I would like at this time also to call the attention of the reader to the book *Authors in the Classroom*, by Alma Flor Ada and F. Isabel Campoy (2003), which focuses specifically on the development of authorship. The objective of *Authors in the Classroom* is to facilitate the unveiling of the author within each teacher and to guide teachers in discovering their own ability to create books, through well proven activities and structures, so that they will become the model of authorship in the classroom. In this way, the writing process takes on a new dimension of authenticity and joy. We encourage readers to look on *Authors in the Classroom* and *A Magical Encounter* as complementary to each other.

TRANSFORMATIVE EDUCATION AND CHILDREN'S LITERATURE

Everything that goes on in the classroom reflects the teacher's approach to education. This is true whether we intend it to be so or not. Indeed, failing to question one's approach, like a conscious determination not to adopt one, is in itself a choice.

In developing my understanding and philosophy of education, I have drawn from many sources that have inspired me and guided me in my own transformative process. The synthesis has become my own Transformative Education.

Teaching is never neutral (Freire, 1970, 1982). We express our attitudes in the language we use, in our gestures and movements, in the way we maintain discipline, in our pacing of instruction, in the subject matter we cover, in the books or stories we choose to present, in the amount of time we speak and allow the students to speak, in the kinds of questions we ask, and in the extent to which we involve parents and the community.

The following observations should not ever be taken as criticism of teachers. If they cause anyone a moment's feeling of guilt, they will have defeated their purpose. True, they seek to invite reflection, but not with the intent to blame for deficiencies or errors. Instead, they are designed to help each of us achieve a liberating self-awareness as we look into the future.

Transformative Education is based on a concept of *social reality in the making, a never-ending work in process.* The individual as a historical entity emerges against the background of society.

Education is thus seen not merely as a tool for transmitting information, but as an ongoing process of reflection that uses information to analyze reality and to create new information that was previously unknown. Instead of an omniscient and omnipotent being who doles out equal amounts of information to all students according to a curriculum that bears no relation to the individual class, the teacher is a facilitator of the learning process, in which he or she engages along with the students.

This implies neither chaos nor disorder, nor does it mean a lessening of the teacher's responsibility. On the contrary—by consciously taking an active part in the decision-making process, the teacher assumes a larger role, no longer functioning as a mere presenter of material conceived and prepared by a publishing house.

Transformative Education is *joyful* and *empowering,* for it recognizes that there is no greater good than knowledge and that true knowledge leads to the joyous feeling of intellectual awakening and opens the way to becoming more generous, kinder, more courageous, more creative, and more responsible.

Transformative Education is *humane,* for it recognizes the uniqueness of every individual, student and teacher alike. It is *multicultural* and *antibias* at its core, because it is based on the principle that every human being—regardless of origin, ethnicity, religion, mental or physical health, abilities, gender, sexual orientation, class, culture, or language—deserves respect and appreciation and that a society is enriched by its diversity as the human family is greater because of its multiplicity. In Transformative Education, multiculturalism is seen not as a celebration of food and holidays, but as a firm appreciation of human diversity and a need to unlearn any racist or biased attitude that society may have imposed on us.

Transformative Education is *liberating.* It does not call for grading on the basis of "correct" answers, with the negative consequences of labeling and tracking each student in terms of rigid categories. Instead, it views the learning process, like life itself, as constant reflection leading to action. Because every act lays the groundwork for future reflection, there is no room for helpless inactivity growing out of feelings of guilt or failure—quite the opposite, as invigorating renewal is never-ending.

Transformative Education is *constructivist.* It promotes the construction of meaning, rather than the transmission of information. Every student brings to the classroom a wealth of knowledge and experiences. These individual experiences cannot be a part of a preestablished curriculum, but when the student enters them into a dialogue with the curriculum, they take on new meaning. When a community of students share with each other, new knowledge can be generated. For example, we might know that several students in a given classroom are immigrants, but does anyone know the experiences of immigration of all the students in the classroom? Where were their parents, grandparents, and great-grandparents born? How long ago did the family arrive in this country? What prompted their immigration? What have their experiences been since then? Information generated from a community of students can take on numeric, graphic, and/or verbal expression. It can generate a research process and teach students how to investigate, synthesize, draw conclusions, and identify additional questions to research. Essentially, this pedagogy teaches that knowledge is not static but is constantly being generated, that learning is not receptive but active, and that teaching is not limited to the transmission of information but embodies the facilitation of learning (Vygostsky, 1962, 1978; Freire, 1985; Ferreiro & Gómez Palacio, 1986; Smith, 1995).

Transformative Education is *rooted in critical theory.* It aspires to help students understand that social reality is a human construct and therefore imperfect. As students understand their role as members of communities—their family, their classroom, their school, their neighborhood—they can increase their sense of belonging and of responsibility and share in the liberating experience of being able to construct a better world (Adorno & Horkheimer, 1972; Marcuse, 1968, 1977; Gramsci, 1971; Freire, 1970, 1982, 1997; Habermas, 1981; Giroux, 1983, 1988a, 1988b).

Transformative Education is an expression of *critical pedagogy.* Most educational systems have profound contradictions between what they propose and what they do. For example, although our national educational system might declare that it has an egalitarian goal, wishing to teach all students to the best of their abilities to help them become lifelong learners and productive members of society, in truth, the enormous inequalities between schools (Kozol, 1991) and the inability of the system to overcome social differences perpetuate those differences, resulting in marginalization of whole groups of people who remain outside the greater social benefits. Even worse, the system manages to convince the learners that it is their own fault if they did not do better in school and that the limitations in their lives are of their own doing (Freire, 1970, 1997; Freire & Macedo, 1987; Poplin & Weeres, 1992; Shor & Freire, 1987; Frederickson, 1995; Walsh, 1991a, 1991b, 1996; Wink, 1997).

Transformative Education recognizes as inherent to good teaching the need to provide *aesthetic experiences* as part of the core of the learning process. By acknowledging that the search for beauty in all its forms has been inherent in every culture in the world, Transformative Education recognizes the strong human drive to surround life with aesthetically pleasant realities. Every culture has aspired to make creations beautiful, no matter how utilitarian their purpose. Whether the creations were woven baskets, clay pots, birch-bark canoes, or feathered arrows, people throughout the world have made sure that what they made was pleasing to the eye, the touch, and the ear. This natural inclination toward beauty produces a relaxed attentiveness that is conducive to learning while fostering the sense of value of self. Our students deserve the best. They deserve to be taught in aesthetically beautiful environments, surrounded by inspiring music, creative visuals, and excellent literature (Greene, 1995, 1996, 1998).

As sustained by *feminist/womanist* theory, Transformative Education emphasizes the equality of all human beings, regardless of their gender. Furthermore, it fosters a nourishing, supportive, safe, caring environment as a better place for everyone to learn and grow (Gilligan, 1982; hooks, 1984, 1989, 1994; Lorde, 1984; Pincola Estés, 1997).

Transformative Education is *multicultural,* as it extends the sense of respect to all human beings beyond gender equality, emphasizing the need to know, understand, respect, and celebrate people of all ethnic, cultural, and linguistic origins; of all religions and sexual orientations; and of all repertoires of physical and mental abilities (Nieto, 1992, 1999; Takaki, 1987, 1990, 1993; Delpit, 1995). Even further, because ethnocentrism is a very extended disease and biases and oppression (e.g., racism, linguicism, homophobia, ageism, ableism) are very prevalent in most societies, Transformative Education takes the stand of *Antibias* education. Even though to pronounce oneself as "anti" might sound negative, when there is something that can be very harmful to many, it becomes useful to acknowledge its presence by stating one's position against it (Sherover-Marcuse, 1981; Derman-Sparks & the ABC Task Force, 1989; Derman-Sparks & Phillips, 1997; Lee, Menkhart, & Okasawa-Rey, 1997; Tatum, 1992, 1997; Reza, 2002).

Finally, Transformative Education recognizes the principles and value of *bilingual education.* Language is one of the strongest elements in one's self-definition as an individual and a social being. Respect for a child's home language is needed to show respect for the child and his or her family, community, and culture. All children would benefit from learning two or more languages, and a good education should provide the means to do so effectively. All children have the right to retain, develop, and enrich their heritage language while learning a national language. Education is about addition and enrichment, not subtraction or reduction. When a child abandons, rejects, or loses the home language from lack of appreciation of that language on the part of school and community, full communication between parents and children may be impaired. This in turn may alienate the child from the family, with all the resulting negative effects. Speaking two languages offers many more opportunities for human growth and certainly greater opportunities to work on behalf of humanity. (Ada, 1997a, 1997b; Ada & Campoy, 1998b, 1998c; Baker, 1997; Baker & Jones, 1998; Brisk, 1998; Brisk & Harrington, 2000; Cummins, 1996, 1999, 2000; Cummins & Sayers, 1995; Fishman, 1972, 1976, 1989, 1996; Krashen, 1984, 1993, 1999; Skutnabb-Kangas, 2000; Skutnabb-Kangas & Cummins, 1988; Skuttnabb-Kangas, Phillipson, & Rannut, 1994; Wong-Filmore, 1991). For an example of the Transformative Education process involving teachers, students, and parents, you may want to read *Authors in the Classroom* (Ada & Campoy, 2003).

The activities suggested in this book are inspired by the tenets of Transformative Education mentioned above. They reflect in particular the six principles described below. By themselves, of course, the activities would be meaningless. They take on meaning as each teacher gives them shape and direction and incorporates them into his or her educational principles.

1. *Every child needs to reclaim and revitalize his or her sense of self.* One's personality is shaped by life itself. The process begins at an early age. By acquiring attitudes, beliefs, and values from the models they see at home, small children start developing their potential and defining their personalities.

School presents a major challenge in that it increases the possibilities from which the children can choose. Unfortunately, some schools fail to recognize and appreciate the various lifestyles, attitudes, and values that prevail in the home environment, thus making it difficult for the students to reconcile different views toward life.

Many children mistake this duality for a defect in their own still vulnerable, still evolving personalities. As a result, the three kinds of negative attitudes described below may develop. Although any child whose home environment is not validated by the school might develop one of these attitudes, they tend to become prevalent among language minority or ethnic minority children or children coming from an economically deprived environment.

- The children may retreat into themselves, becoming excessively introverted or passive. Their classroom behavior is above reproach, despite—or perhaps because of—the fact that they rarely speak. They seek acceptance through passivity, not daring to communicate or to expose their own identity, about which they feel insecure. Silence is their protection.

■ The children may develop a second personality in the hope that it will be more acceptable than their own. They change their name, shed their home language and traditions, and emulate what they see as the dominant behavior. Although it is to be expected that children will adopt some new attitudes once they come into contact with other people, excessive shifts are not beneficial, especially if they reflect insecurity and low self-esteem and if they result in alienating children from their family or developing a poor self-concept of the parents, family, and community of origin.

■ Feeling rejected and thus rejecting the system that excludes them, the children may enter into open rebellion. This attitude leads to problems at school, absenteeism, misconduct, and extremely high dropout rates, and dropping out of school is likely to lead, in turn, to membership in gangs and even to juvenile delinquency.

If teachers believe that every child should be given a chance to develop a strong sense of self and that the benefits accruing from such self-esteem are considerable, they would do well to match their teaching to that conviction. The way they arrange their schedules, their choice of activities and subject matter for the lessons, the books chosen for the classroom library and to be shared, the presence in the classroom of students' photos and work, wall space devoted to recognition of the students' cultures and languages, frequent communication with the home, and the public display of words and thoughts from the students' parents are some steps teachers can take to help achieve the desired goal. Not only will teaching thus become student-centered, but each child will finally be recognized as the protagonist, not a secondary character of his or her own life.

2. *The personal and social value of language deserves full recognition.* To be a real protagonist in our own life, each of us must be in control of events; that is, we must take action on our own instead of merely following others.

Few tools are more essential to a leadership role than mastery of the language, both oral and written. Language makes it possible to express our thoughts, to persuade and motivate others, to undertake negotiation, and to arrive at decisions and agreements.

When teachers recognize the importance of language as a social tool and want to help their students become leaders instead of followers, they take advantage of every opportunity to develop language skills. We learn how to read well before an audience of strangers by first reading before an audience of friends. We learn to express ourselves well by speaking at meaningful occasions. We learn to converse and debate well by conversing and debating in a nurturing non-threatening environment. We learn to write well by reading and by writing down our ideas as often as possible. And in the process of speaking, reading, and writing, our own thinking process continues to develop.

3. *Unless consciously approached, technology can increase inequality instead of decreasing it.* At the beginning of the twenty-first century, the United States has become a society with a large and growing gap between rich and poor. One of the great promises of democratic societies is that schools will help children gain equal access to the benefits of society. The greater the class distinctions, the greater is the challenge confronting the schools—yet the greater, too, is their potential for good.

Today's society depends strongly on technology. It follows that the greatest benefits await those who are able to use and manage that technology. Teachers who want to help even the odds between students who come from socioeconomically disadvantaged environments and those who do not need to consider using the classroom as a means of providing technological tools that are now available only in homes that can afford them and know how to use them. Whatever their socioeconomic background, students can acquire much-needed communication skills and produce their own publications by using cameras, tape recorders, duplicating machines, and overhead projectors, all of which are inexpensive, easy to handle, and readily available to teachers. Somewhat more sophisticated equipment—computers, video recorders, digital cameras, and scanning devices—are all important to learn to use. If they are not readily available, their absence should not preclude students from using what is at hand.

It is excellent when teachers use technology to enhance their own classroom presentations, but it is even more important to allow students the opportunity to use technology tools in producing and presenting their own ideas and their original creations.

4. *Children deserve to see themselves as protagonists and authors.* All students can benefit enormously from interaction with high-quality literature. Within the framework of Transformative Education, the teacher stands ready to help them reaffirm their dual roles as protagonists of their own lives and authors of their own books.

Reading lies at the heart of the dialogue between the text and the reader, between the storybook characters and the child, protagonist of his or her own life. Books provide models for what children can do when faced with difficult life situations, the need to make a moral decision, the necessity to make a choice, or the opportunity to make their own decisions and thus create their own path. Books also provide models for the books the students can author.

5. *Cooperative learning facilitates growth while developing solidarity rather than competition.* Although standardized tests and other educational measures promote competition within the classroom, experienced teachers recognize that children learn better not through competition but by working with peers to solve problems, pool information, and get feedback on how they are progressing with their learning tasks. The concept behind cooperative learning reflects an important social value: appreciation and respect for other human beings, which in daily life takes the form of friendship, collaboration, and solidarity.

Children's literature offers a wide range of opportunities for cooperative group work. Many of the activities suggested in this book lend themselves to use by cooperative groups.

6. *Effective home–school interaction is essential for students' well-being and full growth while also increasing academic achievement.* Students live in two worlds: home and school. If these two worlds do not recognize, understand, and respect each other, students are put in a difficult predicament. For many, the consequence is an internalization of shame about their parents or caretakers, who are perceived as inferior to the models presented by the school.

This sense of shame frequently continues to grow in the students and becomes a belief that parents have nothing to teach, nothing worth learning from. This may be compounded by the parents' own sense of inadequacy in relation to the school. As a result, students may lose their confidence in their parents' guidance. A few may find partial role models in teachers or even in literary characters, but many will find substitutes for parent figures in gang leaders who will lead them to the abandonment of school and the beginning of a life of violence.

Although teachers can be very effective role models, it is not their place to substitute for the parents, but rather to collaborate with them. It is important to help students see how much they can learn from their families, encouraging them to tap into the parents' or caretakers' life learning experiences or, in those painful cases in which the model at home may contain negative elements, to learn to respect and love their family while knowing that they themselves can choose to be different.

When students share meaningfully with parents at home regardless of the parents' level of schooling, students gain in their language development, in their sense of self, and in their academic achievement (Ada & Zubizarreta, 2001). Promoting dialogue in the home will result in more successful students and, in consequence, a better classroom environment.

Parents entrust their most valuable treasure to schools. They do not deserve to be disregarded or discounted. Although it might seem that many parents are not interested in their children's schooling process, this is seldom the case. This topic will be explored further in the section on home–school interaction in Chapter 4.

The foregoing principles, as has been pointed out, inform many of the activities proposed in this book. They have been set forth here not to urge teachers to accept each and every one, but to suggest that creating suitable activities is relatively easy if their underlying principles are clear. Once teachers know where they want to lead their students, figuring out which path to take becomes a welcome creative process.

THE CREATIVE READING PROCESS

The question of why some children evolve into lifelong readers, lovers of the printed word and fascinated by books, and others see reading as a task to be performed only under request or duress has been constant throughout my practice. As a fifth-grade teacher, I could tell within the first week of classes who among my students were the readers. As a high school teacher, I found invariably that a small group of my students came with a baggage of wonders and discoveries acquired through reading the best children's books but many had lost the opportunity of enjoying wonderful literature during their childhood. As a college professor, although many of the nonreaders had been left outside the world of academia, I again found the same discrepancy between students who loved books and those who saw them only as tools and not necessarily friendly ones. At all these levels of teaching, I have tried to help my students discover the joy of reading while searching to learn from them what had cemented their friendship with books or their estrangement from them.

After researching exhaustively for answers in professional literature about reading, I resorted to introspection and observation. After all, I have been an avid reader all my life. If I had to list my abilities, the things I know how to do well, and the things I enjoy doing, reading would unquestionably head all the lists. And I have surrounded myself with people who read and have devoted a great deal of my life to motivating reading.

So what does an effective lover of books do in the process of reading? It became clear to me that reading the text is only one element of the process. This is why the same reader can read the same text differently.

As a twelve-year-old, plagued with measles, prevented from going out, and having read every one of my own books multiple times, I laughed my heart out with the only book new to me I could find at home, an old unabridged edition of *Don Quixote*. I must have skipped many words that bore little meaning to me, and I missed many social references to life in sixteenth century Spain and the subtleties hidden behind Cervantes's words; I was simply fascinated by the adventures of the unfortunate knight and full of admiration for his noble intentions, and I could not put the book down until I finished the last chapter. It was a delightful experience—but of course a very different reading from the one I would do at the age of twenty-one when, searching for life's meaning and determined to unravel it, I reread *Don Quixote* in Spain, this time with the enrichment of Unamuno's *Life of Don Quixote*. Reading a chapter at a time from each of the two books, I found extraordinary revelations in Cervantes's prose and Unamuno's reflections, all the time inwardly smiling at the twelve-year-old girl sweating out her measles in her bed in Cuba. A few years later, while doing postdoctoral research at Harvard under the direction of such great Hispanicists as Raimundo Lida and Stephen Gilman, I read *Don Quixote* as a literary masterpiece, stopping at each sentence, looking up footnotes to clarify word usage at the time of Cervantes and for historical and sociological references. What a different reading! And what a different reading still later when I was preparing selected chapters to share with my high school students in Perú, intent on enabling them to enjoy the book from all the many perspectives that had enriched me.

The text had been the same in all my encounters with it, but my readings had been very dissimilar. How could these different readings of the same text by the same reader be possible unless we see the reading act as a dialogue between reader and text?

Having reflected, then, on how much the reader brings into the reading act, the question for me moved beyond "How do we get the reader to decode what the text says?" to "What needs to happen in that dialogue between reader and text for the act of reading to become meaningful, engaging, capable of charming the decoder and transforming her or him into a true reader, a lover of books?"

Again I looked at my own reading process and at the process of experienced readers around me. What I discovered was that the reading act is a complex one; the dialogue is not limited to "What does the text say?," "What do I like (dislike) about it?," or even "What did I know before and what do I know now?" but encompasses far more.

For the sake of clarity and to be able to best describe the process, I would say that in effective reading, the dialogue with the text follows four phases. These phases are neither separate nor linear, but they are clearly distinct.

Each reader approaches each text with a particular degree of anticipation, with certain information, and at a specific moment in his or her own life, all of which will have a bearing on the reading process. Once the interaction with the text begins, the reader finds out what the text says. I have chosen to call this first interaction with the text the *Descriptive Phase,* the moment of discovery of what the text provides. But as the reader approaches the text with unique previous knowledge, personality, and personal history, more than just finding out what the text says takes place. Unfortunately, much too often, schools have focused on ascertaining that students indeed understand what the text says and, as a consequence, rather than facilitating the ensuing dialogue have stalled it. The effective reader, on finding out what the actual words say, naturally reacts to them. They can inspire concern or provide a calming effect, or they can provide answers or bring about more questions, but whatever the reaction may be, there will be a reaction, even if it is one of boredom or disinterest. Just as education is never neutral, reading is also not neutral.

Imagine seeing a memo posted on the school bulletin board, opening a letter or an email from a friend, looking at the newspaper headlines, or beginning to read a book; whatever the text may be, there will be reactions on your part. The information on the memo, the news from your friend, the events on the headlines, the content of the book will make you interested, happy, enthusiastic, concerned, saddened, or intrigued. You will react to the words from your previous knowledge and experiences with your own feelings and emotions. The reading has ceased to be just about the words; it is about the words and their effect on you. I have called this moment of the dialogue the *Personal/Interpretive Phase.*

Much too often, in the school approach to reading, this personal presence in the dialogue with the text is ignored or limited to the likes and dislikes of the student rather than being recognized as essential to the significance of the process. In which ways does what we are reading validate our previous knowledge and experiences? In which ways is it giving us new information that challenges our assumptions? What memories does it bring forth and how do those memories make us feel? What concerns, fears, anxieties, expectations, or hope does it stimulate?

Students who have not seen themselves in the role of interacting with the text may need our support to place themselves in the reading dialogue. Otherwise, reading may continue to be for them something distant and alien that does not truly pertain to who they are.

Of course, our reactions to the text are not limited to feelings, emotions, or the comparison or contrast of the content of the text and our experiences. As reasoning adults, we look for the author's intentions, for the consequences of what the text implies. Our questions, of course, will reflect our own values and worldview. If our motivating forces are centered on justice and equality, we will ask ourselves whether what we are reading is realistic, logical, equitable, just, kind, and generous. We will ponder the universality or particularity of the ideas exposed: Would this be appropriate for all, for some, for whom? Are some voices ignored, silenced, or discriminated against? Do the ideas perpetuate inequality, prejudice, bias, or discrimination? This becomes the *Critical/Multicultural/Antibias Phase* of the reading act.

Effective reading is not merely an intellectual and aesthetic experience; it is also an empowering act that has profound effects on our consciousness. Therefore it moves us to action. Even the reader comfortably sitting in a quiet place, book in hand, apparently removed from the demands of everyday life or the social concerns of the moment, is actively making decisions during the process of reading. The most immediate decision we all make with regard to the text is "Do I continue reading this? Is it sufficiently engaging, informing, interesting, documented, inspiring to deserve my time and effort?" This is a quiet decision, probably not explicitly formulated in most cases but unquestionably responded to. Either we continue reading or we do not.

If the content is indeed valuable, we might begin to make other immediate decisions related to the process itself; for example, we might look in the back of the book to find out more about the author or look in the front of the book for other titles by the same author. We might decide that we want to get an additional copy of the book to give as a gift, or we might include the reference in our reading list to our students, bring the copy to class, mention it to friends and relatives.

But the dialogue with the text may inspire even greater decisions. In the process of reading, we discover things about ourselves and others that will inform, motivate, or transform our future actions. We will become more understanding, kinder, gentler, more generous, more compassionate, and more socially responsible. This is ultimately the great gift of reading: that it helps us grow as human beings.

It is arriving at decisions of this kind that gives meaning to the reading process, a process that does not truly end, because if our dialogue with the text was profound, it will resurface over and over again through the years. I have named this last, open-ended aspect of the process the *Creative/Transformative Phase*.

Throughout my long life of working with children and young adults, I have had the opportunity to see their responses when they have been given the opportunity to discover the fullness of the reading process. It has always been a very rewarding experience. Although this process develops naturally in some readers, it is important to model it for students who might otherwise never discover the full power of reading on their own and might go through life thinking that reading is a painful imposition. The third section in Chapter 4, "The Creative Dialogue," provides specific examples of questions to facilitate the dialogue following the principles of Creative Reading.

For teachers who will raise the legitimate issue of the time involved in awakening this understanding of reading as a transformative process, I would like to emphasize that the time spent at the beginning of an authentic process frequently gives us multiplied results at the end. We already know how much time is wasted in education repeating over and over things that never get assimilated because they are never fully internalized. Although developing in students an awareness of the richness of the interaction between reader and text and getting them used to asking meaningful questions might take some time, once this awareness is grasped, it remains with the students forever, and all their future learning benefits from it.

To conclude, I would like to share one experience in which a very young child reaffirmed once more that this apparently complex process can be grasped by the very young. It invites us to reflect on the conventional sequence in the teaching of reading. When the learning of meaningless isolated skills is placed at the beginning of the process, many students simply lose their interest in reading forever. They experience too many failures and frustration for very little reward. When children are helped to understand the powerful significance of reading to their own lives by letting them first and foremost decode meaning, before they are even faced with learning to decode text, the interest in the process suffers a substantive shift.

Here is the story. I have told it elsewhere, but it deserves retelling.

Some years ago I had the joy of participating in a family literacy project, using children's literature, in a rural area in northern California. The full details of this project, which has since been replicated in multiple ways, can be read in "The Pájaro Valley Experience" (Ada, 1988). For additional information and the description of another extraordinary program, "Familias y Libros/Family and Books" see Keis (2002a, 2002b). For specific guidelines on how to conduct a family literacy process based on Transformative Education see Zubizarreta (1996).

In Pájaro Valley, migrant parents met monthly, in the high school library at night, after having worked in the fields all day. First, I would speak with the parents about topics of importance to them: the relationship with the school, the best ways to help their children succeed, the importance of good communication at home, and the value of continuing to develop their children's first language. Later, several picture books were introduced, and parents could join a small group of their choice. There, a book would be read aloud collectively. The reading would be followed by a Creative Dialogue. The parents then dictated their thoughts, which were recorded in writing on chart paper and later transcribed and self-published as a book to be given to the participants during the following meeting, along with blank books to encourage their children to write with them at home.

Most participating parents chose to have their children attend the special concurrent sessions for children, but a few children remained in the room while I spoke. One of them, Ceci, was barely six years old. She always sat with her mother at the front of the room and looked attentively at me, not losing a word during the whole session.

One time, she brought a book she had just made. Because she could not write yet, she had dictated it to her fifth-grade sister, who had faithfully transcribed all that Ceci had said. Ceci had made the illustrations.

The cover of the book showed a man in cowboy clothing with a large lariat in his hands. He occupied half the page lengthwise and had most likely been traced from a magazine, perhaps from a Marlboro ad. On the other side of the page was the title, which translated from the Spanish would read "The Tired Man and His Little Girl," a drawing of a chair, and a drawing of a little girl so small she didn't even reach the man's knee.

Ceci's mother was very hesitant to read the book to the group; she was afraid it contained language that should not be read. But after some encouragement, she stood in front of the group to read us the story.

She began:

There once was an old man, who came home every day very tired.

At this point, she interrupted herself and, with trembling voice and some tears, told us, "This is all so true! My husband is much older than me, and he does come home very tired from working in the fields." She added sadly, "If the children are noisy, he gets upset and scolds them." Then she continued reading the story:

> But one night, when the old man got home his little daughter said to him: "Daddy, sit on this chair. I have a medicine to take your tiredness away." The old man sat on the chair and said: "Well, let's see what is that medicine." And the little girl brought him the book of *The Pony, the Bear and the Apple Tree.* And she read it to him.

The book *The Pony, the Bear and the Apple Tree* was one of the books families had received in the program, and it is written in rebuses, so even though Ceci could not decode words yet, she certainly could tell the full story with the help of the rebuses.

The mother continued:

> When they got to the part where the Bear and the Pony had eaten so many apples that their tummies were about to burst, the old man laughed, and then he said to his little girl, "You were right. This is a good medicine. I don't feel so tired any more."

The mother concluded reading with some embarrassment, because here was the word she was concerned about—in Ceci's final words, which her sister had copied and incorporated into the story as Ceci dictated it, even though they were actually directed to the older sister:

> And, haven't you figured out yet, dummy, who that old man is? Well, he is our daddy. And, haven't you figured out yet, who the little girl is? Well, it's me, your sister Ceci. And, haven't you figured out what I'm going to do when he is tired?

Little Ceci had discovered the power of story and, like a modern-day Scheherazade, was determined to charm her father with it. Delightful as this is, the most valuable thing the child is telling us is that even very young children can apply the creative literacy process. This six-year-old child had wonderful parents, but when her father got home at night and was tired, the children had to stop playing. Ceci had been listening to me say, "Let's invite children to see in which way, no matter how small, they can begin to transform their own reality," and she decided to do so. That the tool she chose was a story adds delight to the process. The fact that she chose to write about it and created a book for her mother to share aloud just proves how significant and empowering the whole process was to her.

All children deserve to know that they are the protagonists of the most valuable story: their own life—that as protagonists, they will face multiple circumstances and will have the freedom to choose how to react to them. They deserve to be reminded that protagonists face difficulties, reflect about them, and finally respond to them, with more or less success but always trying to do their best and learning from the process.

THE ONE THOUSAND BOOK CLASSROOM

The story described here is a real-life story. In my long career as an educator and a teacher educator I have been privileged to witness or to participate in many significant educational experiences. This was one of the most extraordinary. My part of it was as the mother of one of the students involved. The experience has had lasting effects on my life: It has contributed to keeping alive my faith in teachers' creativity and has reinforced my conviction that the best learning process for children is to participate in highly meaningful projects that will allow the development of multiple integrated skills. It also had such a personal impact on me that it contributed to my decision to change my career from the college professor of Spanish and Latin American adult literature that I was at the time to that of a teacher educator deeply involved in children's literature.

At the time, although I was fascinated by what was taking place, not being a teacher educator, I did not recognize its far-reaching merit and never thought to obtain the data that could have allowed me to do a rigorous study of the process. Yet even though many years have passed since this experience, its impact was such that it has remained vividly in my mind. I tell it here because many teachers who have heard me talk about it have asked me to share it in writing because they have found it very inspiring. The credit for all the valuable ideas goes to Ms. Yvonne Larin, the teacher who created the project, and I take responsibility for any limitation or modification of the details that I may unwittingly have made in telling what happened a long time ago. It is offered here as an invitation to teachers who wish to have a most exciting year and turn their students into passionate readers.

The One Thousand Book Classroom Project took place at Vetal Elementary School, an urban school in Detroit, Michigan, in a neighborhood that was beginning to become integrated. The third-grade teacher, Ms. Larin, decided on her own initiative to do something different that school year. She was not involved in any specific research but was motivated by her own intuition that her students could benefit greatly from this experience.

At the time, I was a college professor teaching Spanish language and literature courses to English-speaking undergraduates at Mercy College of Detroit. I had recently moved to Detroit, and this was my children's second year at Vetal Elementary. My two older children, who had learned to read first in their native language, Spanish, were doing very well in school, but the third, who would be Ms. Larin's student, was having extreme difficulties learning to read. Miguel had not learned to read in Spanish before coming to the United States. Unaware then of what I know today, I had thought that the best thing I could do for him would be to allow him to be introduced to reading directly in English, which he seemed to be picking up so quickly. But although he could indeed use playground English, he failed dramatically when faced with the task of learning to read. We were living in Atlanta, Georgia, at the time, and my children were the only Spanish-speakers in the school. No one at school had any awareness of second language learning or the difficulties a child with a home language other than English could experience in learning to read. A young, inexperienced teacher who left the classroom when she got married at Christmas and a succession of substitutes for the rest of the year didn't provide a good first-grade environment. Though certainly not the cause, these were contributing factors to Miguel's failure to learn to read.

In second grade, at a new school in Detroit, Miguel encountered a very structured teacher who did not know what to make of the only Spanish-speaking student she had ever had, who was the only child in her class who was excellent in math but was not reading at all. Remedial reading classes at a reading clinic at the college where I taught were prescribed. Unfortunately, the only result was a child who refused to learn to read, who declared that he hated books, in a household where books were the only possession, and who began to develop for a whole year all kinds of sicknesses on school days out of fear of going to school.

Then it was the beginning of a new academic year, and all I could do was dread what third grade would be like for this bright boy who could not read and for whom even math was losing its joy, since he could not read the word problems.

My surprise was enormous when on the first day of classes, Miguel returned from school filled with enthusiasm. "Mother," he asked eagerly, "have you ever read *Charlotte's Web?*" The truth is that at the time, I didn't even know what he was talking about. When I told him so, he proceeded to narrate to me the *whole* story. He followed me into the kitchen as I prepared supper, continued through the meal, and was still giving me details of the story as we washed the dishes: "Miss Larin read us the whole book today!"

I was certainly amazed and internally blessed Ms. Larin for making Miguel's first day of third grade such an adventure. Of course, my fear did not disappear. What would the next day be like, once they got into the real teaching? But Tuesday held another surprise: "Do you know, Mother, that *Charlotte's Web* is not the only book written by E. B. White—that's the author, you know? He also wrote *Stuart Little,* and Miss Larin read it all to us today!" Our evening was devoted to listening to Miguel tell us the story of *Stuart Little,* which on Wednesday was followed by *The Trumpet of the Swan.*

Filled with gratitude now not only toward Ms. Larin but also toward E. B. White, someone I was by now determined to learn something about, I waited to see what Thursday would bring. There were, I was told by Miguel, no more books by E. B. White, but how many other authors there were!

Ms. Larin had just been to the library and now had a cart filled with books in the classroom, and she had just spent the whole day reading another book to the class.

By now I was convinced that Ms. Larin probably had decided to make this wonderful introduction to the school year—of doing nothing all day but read books to the kids—last through the first week and that I could leave my fears at rest until the next Monday.

But what a surprise! The following Monday, Miguel announced with great enthusiasm that Ms. Larin had asked the students whether they wanted to be, this year, the One Thousand Book Classroom, and they all had said yes. She had then explained to them that while she would continue borrowing books from the library to read to the class, they would all be writing letters to ask for book donations until they could have one thousand books in their own classroom.

Tuesday, Miguel produced from his pocket a very crumpled paper and, with an expectant face, asked me whether I would help him write a letter. He had painstakingly copied the model Ms. Larin had written on the board. Now he needed to make it his own, and could I possibly give him also a stamped envelope? Ms. Larin would be providing addresses the next day.

The task was not easy for Miguel, and the letter was restarted many times before it could finally be produced with no holes from erased marks. This was the first time he really wanted to write something well. How triumphantly Miguel shared the next day that every child in the class had sent a letter, all addressed to publishers, all asking for the donation of a book to their class!

Letter writing became the one activity of the students, and Ms. Larin continued to read them books. Every student was encouraged to explain why he or she liked books, which book the class had recently heard their teacher read, and what particular aspect of the book the student had enjoyed. They were also invited to tell something about themselves and their favorite topics.

The letters had initially been addressed to publishers and authors. But very soon, Ms. Larin began discussing with the students who the other people were who cared for children. When one suggested that teachers did, Ms. Larin explained the structure of the educational system, she assisted students in finding in the telephone book the number for the school board. She had one child call for a full address, and then the class wrote a letter requesting the names of the superintendent and the school board members. These in turn received letters requesting the donation of a book, as did the state superintendent and state school board members.

When the children decided that police officers, firefighters, and park rangers were among those who care for children's safety and well-being, new inquiries were made to find out the names and addresses of the chief of police, firefighters' captains, and park and recreation officials. Ms. Larin then instructed the students on the governmental structure of the city and state, and they addressed letters to the mayor and the governor, the city supervisors, and the state legislators.

Soon, the first packages began to arrive. This meant that now each child would be writing two different kinds of letters daily: one asking for book donations and another thanking the donors. The first few donors received letters from all the students, but as the packages multiplied, each child was asked to respond to an individual donor, making specific reference to the book sent by that person.

The books received were of diverse nature, and although many were children's books, there were also all sorts of nonfiction and reference books. To make the presence of the books in the classroom a full learning experience, Ms. Larin invited a librarian to visit the class and explain to the students the Dewey Decimal System of classifying books. The children then made signs with the categories to place on top of the bookshelves that were beginning to line the classroom walls.

The librarian also explained to the children how to make index cards, by author and by title, as well as lending cards. Subsequently, the students were assigned to groups. Each group received a number of books, and the children would paste pocket envelopes in the back of the books and create the lending card to be placed in the envelopes as well as the author and title cards to be placed in alphabetical order in the index card files provided by Miss Larin.

But the teacher did not think that just deciding the category—biography, geography, historical fiction, etc.—was enough to determine the appropriateness of the book for the children; she decided to try a most daring idea. She gave each of the students a reading level according to the results on their reading tests. Then she pasted on the inside cover of the book a lined paper with columns for the student's name and reading level, followed by three columns titled Easy, Fine, and Hard, where the students, after reading a page or so, would rate how easy or difficult it was for them to read the book.

Of course, there is more to books than author, title, categories, and level of reading challenge: Ms. Larin explained to children about the literary and artistic awards books can receive. As she continued her daily reading of a book, she made a point of making references to the book's awards or to other awards the author had received and the year of the award. One day, to my surprise, I realized that Miguel and his brothers were talking about these awards, their recipients, and the year they had won the award with the same ease—and enthusiasm—with which they talked about the sport careers of their favorite players.

The award idea culminated in something entirely novel. Ms. Larin suggested to the students that each could have his or her own award to grant to their most favorite book. The students then made medallions for the Susan, Karen, John, Seth, Miguel, ... Awards. Of course, she emphasized, before granting an award the juries have to read many books, so she distributed pages on which the students would write the titles of all the books they had read, and rank them. After reading at least fifteen books, they would be able to decide which one would be most deserving of their medal. It was wonderful to see the value given by each student to his or her medal and how reluctant the students were to finally part with the medals. There always seemed to be one more book that could perhaps deserve it.

The name One Thousand Book Classroom had awakened the children's imagination, but could they really achieve a goal of obtaining that many books? Ms. Larin funneled the expectation that was created into a number of mathematical experiences. Keeping a line record on the wall of how many letters had been written and how many books received was a very direct beginning.

As soon as the library categories were explained, the line turned into a bar graph showing how many books were arriving for each category. This activity then lent itself to determining percentages. The initial queries to be answered were questions such as "Of the first hundred books received, what percentage are fiction and what percentage are nonfiction?" and "Within the nonfiction category, what percentage are books on science and what percentage are social studies?" The answers were shown numerically and in pie charts.

The math grew more and more complex as new questions evolved: "How much time passed between sending the first batch of letters and receiving the first book?" "On the average, how much time passes between writing and receiving a response?" "What percentage of the people had responded so far?" "If we have sent x number of letters and received y number of books, how many letters should we send to receive the books we still need to reach our goal?" Most of these calculations would have been beyond the scope of third-grade math, and these children were not even having a math class! But they were legitimate, important questions, of great significance to all, and the students were able to arrive at their answers, to constantly update them, and to create visual representation for them.

The classroom soon became too small for the project, and some of the graphs were displayed in the hallways, where they contributed to awakening an interest in the project throughout the whole school. Along with the weekly updated graphs, the students began to display creative posters advertising some of their favorite titles.

As the radius of letters was expanded to include the governors and legislators of all fifty states as well as members of the U.S. House of Representatives and Senate, the books that were received became more numerous, and Ms. Larin and the students felt as though they ought to share this wealth with the whole school.

The students then visited other classes to talk about their favorite books and to extend lending privileges. It was a joy to see, at recess and lunchtime, lines of students from the rest of the school wanting to borrow books and the enthusiasm of Ms. Larin' s students in recommending their favorites as well as the responsible manner in which they went about filling out the lending cards and filing them appropriately.

There is no question how much the students learned that year. They surpassed their goal of one thousand books after having written to every representative of the United Nations as well as to each president of the nations represented. Each book implied two letters: one requesting it and one thanking the donor for it. Although the students were told the parts of a letter and were supervised in the process, each letter was individually crafted by one student. The letters of request made reference to the project and to the student's interest in books and made specific mention of a book the student had particularly liked, explaining why. It also made specific reference to the public function of the person to whom it was addressed. The thank-you letter made specific reference to the book received and to some of the students' reading experiences.

The children wrote a great deal, and because they were writing personal, original letters for a specific purpose, they made great efforts to write carefully, to be mindful of spelling and punctuation, and to work neatly.

The students learned how to use the telephone directory, including accessing government agencies, and learned how to request information both in writing and by phone. The latter implied being able to address someone on the phone, stating clearly the information they needed, and writing down answers, which many times included proper names they needed to have spelled. Above all, they learned that there are many steps to finding information and that sometimes different avenues must be used. They also began to become familiar with the services of the public library and other public offices.

Some time into the project, when it was clear that it was indeed a workable idea, the parents were invited to visit the classroom. We were all delighted to collaborate. A book fair was organized to raise some money to buy shelving for the books, and parents were willing to donate time to build the shelves. Initially, parents were asked to donate stamps; as the volume of letters increased, the class organized different projects for fundraising for the postage, such as collecting small empty jars from home to grow plants for sale. As I type these words, I still have in front of me my favorite pencil holder, companion of all these thirty-odd years: a small juice can covered by heavy paper on which Miguel had drawn his favorite animal, a parakeet. Because it was thoughtfully laminated, it is still holding on. Although the cellophane tape has become somewhat yellowed, the parakeet's colors are still bright, as is my memory of this wonderful experience, which changed my reluctant reader into a voracious lover of books.

Perhaps one of the most important gains for children that year was to discover that it is possible to conceive a project, to work firmly to carry it on, to collaborate with each other, to introduce new ideas as one moves on, and to search for information, using as many resources as needed, and that there is joy in sharing one's privileges. That the project contributed to their awareness that books are a treasure and reading and sharing them an enormous pleasure made it twice as valuable.

The long-term effect of a project of this nature is hard to measure. My son Miguel, the fortunate participant in this experience, has continued to be an avid reader. When he started college, he confided in me that many of his classmates felt dismayed at the amount of reading they had to do, while for him, reading the books before the courses began so that he would better understand what the professors were talking about was a simple, natural thing to do. It is true that he comes from a family of readers, but his early experiences with school in English were very traumatic, and he had arrived in third grade without being able to read the simplest of texts independently. Through this experience, he became a most effective reader. While his classmates experienced that the initial reading level assigned to them had to be increased several times during the year, for Miguel, it meant moving from not knowing how to read at all to reading at the sixth-grade level. Above all, during that year, he changed from fearing school to being enthusiastic about it.

But how do we measure the effect of one educational experience in the overall development of a person who will undergo so many? As my children finished high school, I asked each of them which was their best school experience in elementary school. All three boys independently said that it was Ms. Larin's One Thousand Books Classroom—even the two who were not Ms. Larin's students.

I still smile when I look at the few children's books belonging to my children that have not yet passed into the hands of the grandchildren. They all have little handmade pockets and handmade index cards, which my children devoted hours to doing the summer after this experience.

There is no way for me to know whether Ms. Larin's project had any bearing on the fact that before finishing college, Miguel had already produced a software package for graphics like those he created so enthusiastically in her classroom, and on his exceptional career as a designer of software. But I can certainly attest that Miguel's mother, who had been forever a lover of books but who knew very little of contemporary American children's literature and did not know who E. B. White was, developed great respect for this field as a direct result of the One Thousand Book Classroom and that it is not a coincidence that *Charlotte's Web* has become one of her favorite books and that she enjoys teaching, speaking, and writing about E. B. White.

My gratitude to Ms. Larin is enormous for having brought joy to my son's educational experience. I also thank her deeply for having reaffirmed in me the conviction that the best way to teach reading and writing is to read good literature, that all time used in reading aloud to students is time well spent, and that children will do their best to write well when they do it for a valid reason, when they know their words have a purpose. I thank her as well for validating that there is no greater educational experience than one in which teacher, students, and parents join in a common project that can very well be both relevant and fun.

Although Ms. Larin's project was all-encompassing and she did nothing during that school year that was not integrated into it, there are several elements that could be carried out one at a time if one wanted to approach this process slowly. If you replicate any or all of this project, I would very much appreciate hearing about your experience.

THE TRANSFORMATIVE LANGUAGE ARTS CLASSROOM

Frequently, when I introduce the concepts of Transformative Education, I am asked, "But how would this work in an everyday classroom?" In my numerous visits to elementary schools throughout the United States, I have had the opportunity to witness exciting interactions between children and teachers. This text is a composite of several of these experiences. I have chosen to present them here to give a vision of what a transformative everyday classroom looks like. Rather than enumerating them as separate experiences I have incorporated them as if they are occurring all in one classroom. I have a dream of seeing all teachers approach their task with the conviction that they can indeed make a difference in the lives of their students and their students' families and that they can turn their classrooms into safe and nurturing spaces, true democratic spheres, where students are challenged to discover the fullness of their potential both as individuals and as constructors of their social reality.

Because my dream requires that teachers be validated in their innovative efforts and their risk-taking initiatives, I have chosen to present this composite as a reality more than a dream. The teacher described is also a composite drawn from the insights shared with me by hundreds of teachers through both personal dialogue and the journals written by my university students.

All of these teachers, whom I have here rendered as one, have inspired and enriched me, and I will always be grateful for what they have taught me. Although I have created the composite, none of it is a product of my imagination. Every element, to the smallest detail, is something I have witnessed.

I invite you to walk with me into this classroom, a classroom that could be in your own neighborhood, taught by a teacher you know, filled with children from your town.

The classroom is an aesthetically pleasing environment, happy and lively, and not at all confining.   It is rich in printed and handwritten materials; in addition to books, there are newspapers, magazines, and an abundant display of the students' own work, all tastefully arranged. Comfortable rugs and pillows to lounge on while reading line the floor. A live tree stands in one corner, and an old claw-foot bathtub filled with cushions, a favorite place to nestle while reading, rests in the opposite corner. Plants and flowers abound. Book covers and posters of books, which serve to motivate students to read and inform them of special titles, are treated as works of art. During the free-reading period, good music from around the world—Vivaldi, Mozart, Japanese flute, or Andean rhythms—fills the air.

The walls are lined with no less than a thousand children's books, many of them in the heritage languages of the students.   The books, displayed in prominent places, are catalogued and cared for by the students themselves, who have access to the books during periods designated for pleasure reading. The children take books home each night to share with their parents and siblings and read to one another in the classroom in pairs or as a group. They also read books to students from other classes, as well as to elderly members of the community, both those who visit the class regularly as volunteers and those whom the children visit periodically in nursing homes. These books represent the best of children's literature. Books in the various languages represented in the classroom reflect the diversity of this nation.

Many of the books in the classroom have been written by the teachers, by the students, and by their parents.   Some of the books have been recorded on audio cassette. Although some cassettes are professional recordings, most have been recorded by the teachers, by parents and volunteers, and even by the students themselves, who not only have read the stories dramatically, but have also added musical backgrounds and sound effects.

The teacher greets the students at the classroom door. She looks at each young face, trying to establish eye contact with each child, adding a smile whenever eyes connect; but in respect for their cultural traditions and their own individuality, she never forces her gaze on those children for whom making eye contact may not be easy. As the children fill the chairs around the group tables, she looks at them again.

If she were to reflect on the warm feeling that fills her heart, she would probably describe it as a sense of privilege.   For the next few hours, she will have the opportunity to reach these children, giving them the gift of a poem to memorize and hold forever as well as the excitement of a new story. She will encourage them to write and discover the joy of authoring their own books; she will invite them to wonder at the miracle of the diversity of life in a simple pond; she will challenge them to discover their own reasoning abilities as they work on their math problems; and she will delight to see the ease with which they use their classroom computers. At all times it will be important to her to foster camaraderie and solidarity among them, to help them discover the pleasure of working as a team, to contribute to the learning of others, and to recognize the strength that develops when several minds work together.

Regardless of the tasks and the circumstances, she will try not to lose track of her major goals: She wants to see these children become lifelong learners, always surprised at how much there is to learn and eager to know more; she wants them to know that they have the ability to tackle and resolve problems; but above all, she wants them to discover in themselves a deep respect for human beings and all forms of life, their own generosity and kindness, and the richness of their own souls.

Now she is going to begin a class. As she looks at her students, she marvels at the diversity of the shades of their skins and the miracle that two eyes, one nose, and a mouth can produce such different faces, never quite repeated, each one unique. A thought arises in her mind.

Because she is always attentive, ready to embrace the teachable moment generated by a student's comment, she is able to recognize her own intuition. She had come to class prepared to talk about culture. In her class there are four African American students, five Latinos, two Filipinos, one Vietnamese, and one Cambodian student, so she had originally thought to initiate the process by recognizing these children's cultures. But now she has a different approach to get into the topic. She asks all the children to think of how groups of people have specific ways of doing things. These "ways of doing things" help people engage together in social projects for the benefit of the group. To allow the students to discover for themselves the concept of culture, she asks them for examples of how things are done differently at home and at school.

The children are excited to talk about this idea, so close to their own experience. María says, "At school, we always have to raise our hand before talking. At home, I never raise my hand." This remark prompts John to state, "At school, we have to ask for permission to leave the room." The teacher invites them to talk in groups about additional characteristics of the school culture and explains to them how to use graphic organizers to summarize their findings.

After ample discussion, students are encouraged to copy their summaries onto transparencies, using color transparency pens. Then they use the overhead projector to share their observations. They make observations that surprise the teacher and make her reflect on how easy it is to take for granted the norms around us and to cease questioning them. Some of the students remark:

"In school, the kids are divided by age."

"In school, there is one adult in front of many kids."

"In school, we spend most of the time locked in one room."

"In school, you have to stop doing one thing and move on to doing another, even if you haven't finished the first."

"In school, you don't always know why you are doing things."

The teacher realizes that her culture unit has taken a new life of its own. Because the children's observations merit discussion, she now plans to keep the discussion about school culture for the rest of the week. She announces to the students that they will look at different aspects of the school culture: purpose and values, rewards and acknowledgements, entertainment and work, participation and organization.

Then she asks the students to spend some time at home that evening observing their home culture. How is their own specific home culture unique? What is said at their own dinner table that would not be said in other homes? To inspire them, she selects a poem, knowing well the inspirational capacity of poetry. She reads a poem by Sonia Sánchez in which the poet says she has seen an African sunset in her own father's eyes. She is pleased the next day to see how many students are ready to report on their observations and especially to see that those who do not want to report are eager to listen to their classmates. She knows projects of this nature take some time to catch on, but her goal is that eventually every child will participate.

As the students report on their observations, they recognize that each family has some preferred sayings and that some sayings and stories are unique to the family. They also realize that the interactions are unique to each family, although they begin to discover some common trends. For example, in most families, the adults want the children to behave and never to play or fight during meals.

She has each child write on a piece of paper six characteristics of her or his family. Then she has each group tally the responses. Families are described as *good, great, kind, together, supportive, understanding, caring, super, they are there for me, different, OK, normal, the best, like none other, I don't know.*

Although the teacher is young, she has taught for several years, and she knows that some of her students' statements about their family, such as *different* and *I don't know,* may either have little meaning or hide important information and deep feelings. Therefore she is very careful to accept all answers and validate them in their full potential. She says, "Every family is different, because each one is unique. A family can never be repeated exactly. That's what makes it so exciting to be human!"

She acknowledges the child who wanted only to say, "I don't know" by saying, "In reality, it is very difficult to know other human beings, because each person has so much inside. Many times, I also don't know what someone is feeling or wishing for."

Her next assignment is to have the students go back to their families and ask the responsible adult or adults to share with them the best advice they could ever give their own children. She encourages the students to write the advice as well as the name of the person giving it.

Again she needs patience because the next day, only two of the students bring anything in writing. Most of them forgot all about the assignment, and a couple say that they never see their parents at night because their parents work graveyard shifts. The only adults at home are the grandparents, but the grandparents don't speak English. She tells those students that good advice is good advice in any language and that it would be very interesting to know what the grandparents have to say, but both students report that they don't know their grandparents' language. She is saddened by the realization that family stories, traditions, and knowledge continue to die unnecessarily because people don't understand that to speak more than one language is enriching and beneficial.

She knows from experience that some parents prevent children from speaking the home language, trying to shield them from the discrimination and the difficulties that they themselves have experienced. Parents think they will be protecting their children and helping them become full-fledged Americans. But she knows that the loss of the home language is only that—a loss—with no gain. It is for the nation a waste of resources and for the individual an unwarranted personal loss.

Her heart aches from realizing both the pain of the grandparents who will never be able to communicate fully with their grandchildren and the lack of connection for the grandchildren.

Quickly, she makes a note to herself in the journal she always carries with her. This year, she will have a unit on home language; she will treat it as an ecology lesson. She wants to make sure that at least her students and their families understand that knowledge of their home language is a useful skill, one that will be valued in their college applications and beyond—the basis of careers such as interpreter or translator, bilingual teacher, and international consultant and useful in many other professions. She immediately feels a little better. After all, she has chosen this profession so that she can teach, so that she can present ideas, so that she can encourage students to find out more by themselves, and so that she can lead them to become reflective thinkers.

She would like to be able to solve large social problems, such as those that drive a wedge between parents and children by making children feel ashamed of their non-English-speaking parents and/or grandparents and by invalidating a cultural background and therefore the essence of a people. She participates in a number of organizations and their activities, including Teachers for Social Responsibility, subscribes to *Teaching Tolerance* and *Rethinking Schools,* and is even considering sending them a collaboration. She understands that progressive educators need to work at multiple levels and does so. Yet she believes that nowhere can her impact be greater than with her students and their families, and there she concentrates her efforts. This is why now, even though she is saddened to see that errors are unnecessarily perpetuated, she feels hope because she has decided to approach this issue directly with her students.

For the next several days, she encourages students to bring to school the advice from their parents or relatives. As an art project, they make a beautiful blank book with two pages where each child may write and illustrate the saying or advice she or he has brought. They also make banners on the computer with each of the sayings and display two of them a week, one on each of the two longer classroom walls.

A saying from one of the parents touches them in particular. This father had said to his daughter, "We are here to create a better world." The children agree that this saying sums up all the desires of the parents. They decide to make another book, a big book this time, in which each child will write and draw how he or she can make the world a better place.

Although she is gratified by the creativity of her students and their reflections and she sees numerous themes emerging from the sayings project—themes on ecology, on social action, and on better communication—and makes plans to expand on those themes in the future, the teacher is determined to deal first with the issue of cultural identity. She searches for a book, a wonderfully exciting children's book that can motivate a dialogue about identity and the role of the home language in fostering family and individual identity. When she finds nothing on her own shelves, she consults with the public librarian. Going to the library is always a treat for her, entering this world of quietness and richness, and she smiles to herself, remembering what an adventure it was for her to go to the library as a child.

The librarian searches for a while. Although he is a specialist in children's books, he can't quite come up with a recommendation that fits exactly what the teacher is searching for. The teacher is almost at the door when the librarian comes up to her with a small book in his hand. It is not quite about the home language, but it is about the preservation of one's own name in another language. "It might do," the librarian suggests and adds, "and in any case, your students will enjoy it."

That evening, the teacher stays awake late reading the book, thinking about the potential for a number of activities. The book is called *My Name is María Isabel*. The next morning she is so excited with anticipation about the activities she has planned that she tells the children she has a special treat and reads it aloud to them, halfway through.

The students by then have met the book's protagonist, María Isabel Salazar López, and know that her problem is that her teacher has decided to call her *Mary López*. The name sounded so alien to María Isabel that she fails to answer every time the teacher calls on her, and her relationship with the teacher is not doing very well. She is even going to miss being in the Winter Pageant because she failed to volunteer when her strange new name was called. Explaining to her parents why she will not participate is not easy for María Isabel.

The students also know that for María Isabel, her two names are important because she was named after her two grandmothers, just as her two last names are important because they refer to her father's and her mother's families. The children would like to know how the conflict will be resolved and have made the teacher promise that she will read to them the rest of the story the first thing the next morning. She, in turn, has asked them to go home and find out why they have been given their name, who chose it, why was it chosen, whether there is someone else in the family who has had that name, and how they feel about their name.

She has also asked them to find out the naming traditions in their family and whether, in their culture, given names and last names are treated differently than in the majority culture in the United States. She is as eager for their information as they are for the ending of the story, and she is right to be, because as the students share their stories, the true purpose of education is realized. These students are not simply gaining information from the teacher; they have held a dialogue with the information, they have reacted to it with emotions and feelings, and they have contrasted it against their own experiences.

Now they are constructing new knowledge, a knowledge that could not have been obtained anywhere else but in that particular class because it is knowledge pertaining to that community of human beings. The children discover that in several families, it is important to give children the names of other members of the family but that although in some cultures this is done while the family member after whom a child is named is alive, as a way of honoring that person, in other cultures, the name of relatives are given only after the relative is deceased. They learn that people choose names in different ways: that some parents consult the elders, others respect the name of the saint in the Catholic calendar, others choose a name of a movie star or a book character, and others may be searching for a name that is unique, beautiful, or sonorous. Some choose to have all siblings' names begin with the same letter; others will look for a name from their ancestral roots, perhaps in an indigenous language.

But more important, they learn about themselves.

The teacher suggests that they could have a debate based on one aspect of the book. After brainstorming in their cooperative groups, the children choose the issue to be debated: "Do teachers have a right to change children's names?" The students decide that some children will be parents, and other children will be teachers. Four children will represent the school board and serve as moderators.

For several days, the students think of arguments for both sides of the issue and discuss them with a partner in class and at home. Finally, they hold the debate. Some of the students representing teachers explain:

"We are too busy teaching to be worried about names."

"Why do you give your children such strange names, anyway?"

"Your child will do better with a simpler name that anyone can pronounce."

The students representing parents explain that they chose their children's names carefully. When one of the "teachers" suggests that a name is not so important, the parents argue back that it is. Benito says, "You are just wanting to give our children any name. We chose a name with great care."

Eun Mi says, "They changed my grandfather's name when he came to this country, but now we know that people should have a right to keep their own names."

Joshua is representing one of the teachers, but when he hears Eun Mi's argument, he says, "When I told my father what we were discussing, he told me our name didn't use to be Cohen. It was a long name, beginning with a K, but at that time when Jewish people arrived at Ellis Island, they changed their names to either Cohen or Levine. I wish I knew what our real name truly was. I don't think teachers or anyone should change family names."

"You are supposed to be a teacher. You have to defend the other side of the argument," says Betty to Joshua. She has taken her role as chair of the board and moderator very seriously.

"I want my constitutional rights to change my mind," Joshua says, getting up and walking to sit among the "parents."

Everyone laughs, but then they become silent and look at the teacher, who says, "Have we discussed enough? Shall we take a vote?" Then she winks at Josh and adds, "And you all have the right to keep thinking about it."

No one is surprised at the result of the voting. Then Enrique raises his hand and says, "I never really liked my name before. I was always ashamed and wanted people to call me Henry. But when I asked about my name at home, my father talked to me about my uncle Enrique, who died in an accident with a tractor one summer when he was in college. He was the first of our family to go to college. I am going to be the second, and I am going to use my uncle's name. That way, he won't really be dead."

The children are silent for a moment, but very soon, they are eagerly talking with each other. There are still many name stories to share. The teacher relaxes, sitting back in her chair and watching the animated discussions. Then Josie raises her hand. She is a quiet, pensive girl. Sometimes, the teacher worries because Josie does not participate very much in class. She tends to play quietly on the playground, sometimes with another girl playing jacks, often by herself watching her classmates jump rope or play tag.

Now Josie has the teacher's full attention. The teacher raises her own hand to signal the students that all should be quiet. Then Josie says, her voice soft but clear, "Teacher, in our other class we used to study history, but here *we are making history.*" And the teacher's heart fills with joy.

WORDS OF JADE AND CORAL

LATINO LITERATURE FOR CHILDREN AND ADOLESCENTS

Spanish-speaking people and their descendants have lived in the lands that now are the United States continuously since long before any English speakers arrived. The first European-designed city in the United States was Tampa, and the first capital city was Santa Fé.

Contrary to extensive misconceptions, the Spanish-speakers were not all armored men coming to conquer; there were also families who settled on the land and planted, raised livestock, maintained cattle and sheep herds, wove the wool, and tanned the hides. Their genetic and cultural makeup was *mestizo*, a product of the intermarriage of Spaniards with Native Americans and African people.

Of course, the Spaniards themselves are the product of the interweaving of multiple cultures. The closeness of the Iberian Peninsula to Africa as well as its long stretch of Mediterranean coast have made it to this day a crossroad between Europe and Africa, and many people have conquered and settled it through the centuries. The Spanish culture has strong elements of Arabic culture, which flourished for almost eight centuries, particularly in Southern Spain, and of Hebrew culture. The Jewish people have contributed substantially to the making of Spain, and although many left the Peninsula in 1492 rather than be forced to convert to Catholicism, many others remained and continued to enrich the culture.

The population in Spain is far from homogeneous, as attested by the presence in the country of four major independent languages that are mutually unintelligible. In the northwest region, Galicia, people of Celtic origin speak Gallego. In the northeast region, people speak Basque, one of the oldest languages in the world and unrelated to any other Indo-European language. In the northern Mediterranean region, the language is Catalan, with its several variations, as spoken in Valencia and the Balearic Islands. The Castilian that is spoken throughout the country is the first language for some but the second language for others. It has profound differences in accent and vocabulary from area to area.

This rich diversity was brought to the Americas, where it found an even richer diversity, the Native American cultures the Spaniards encountered being extremely different from each other. The fact that the African people in Spanish-speaking America retained much of their regional African identity and language helped to make the African contributions to the resulting mestizo people very distinct and significant.

It could be affirmed that every Latin American is mestizo either by blood, by culture, or both. Besides the three major groups mentioned—Spanish, Native American, and African, all with their own internal diversity—people from other parts of the world added to the richness: Chinese and Japanese, Italians and Germans, Turks, Middle Easterners, and Indians. European wars brought multiple refugees from Eastern Europe and Russia; others came seeking their fortune. The Mexican thinker Vasconcelos described the people resulting from this confluence as the "Raza Cósmica," the Cosmic Race.

What unites their descendants today is the Spanish language and a worldview that comes embedded in the language. People who hold this worldview among other things have close-knit relationships of family and friendship and many times find their own definition from the way they support their family and the friends they keep: Human needs are placed above abstract realizations like professional success; the concept of honor has a great significance, and people would like to have their word carry as much weight as a document; happiness and joy of life, particularly as expressed through music, song, and dance, are essential; conversation is valued; elders are respected and cared for, and generation gaps are not fostered, so people of all ages celebrate together at every possible occasion.

The food and music of the celebrations are different from country to country and from region to region, and these differences should not be taken lightly. Mexicans, Puerto Ricans, Panamanians, and Cubans are first Mexican, Puerto Rican, Panamanian, and Cuban and then Latin American. Yet in spite of the clear distinctions, a common sense of history and worldview exists among them and a clear link to the Spaniards.

LATINOS AND LATINAS

The richness of the topic becomes clear even in the need for a defining term. Spanish-speaking people and their descendants have been called, and have called themselves, by many names in the United States. These names signify their origin, their closeness to their roots, their language retention, even their political stance.

Hispano, Hispanic, Latino, Boricua, Neo-Ricans, Cuban, Cuban-American, Mexican, Mexican-American, and Chicano all have very specific connotations and denotations. A great deal of the difficulty in finding a defining term comes from the still-open wound of the history of colonization.

The Spanish conquest in the Americas was cruel and inhuman, but no more so than any other European conquest. The major difference was that the British, German, Dutch, and Danes did not intermarry with native populations of the lands they conquered but did their utmost to annihilate them. Now the descendants of those conquered populations are small in number and continue to be marginalized or made invisible and can denounce the colonizers as external to themselves.

The Spanish presence in the Americas resulted in the forming of a new culture and a new people. The Spaniards brought with them all that they had—the bad and the good. They conquered and colonized, but they also settled. They brought families, but they also created families by intermarriage. There were universities in Santo Domingo, Mexico City, and Lima two hundred years before the founding of Harvard College. There were even schools of higher learning specifically established for the children of the indigenous nobility. There were print shops and theaters, orchestras and schools of music, painting, and sculpture, all the way from Mexico to Argentina. The potato brought from South America to Europe changed the face of Europe by allowing populations to grow. The Spaniards in turn brought to the Americas olives and grapes; horses, cattle, and sheep; and the techniques to make olive oil and wine, to weave the wool and tan the hides, and so much more.

An issue that merits exploration is that in harboring negative feelings toward things Spanish, the Latin Americans of today, unless members of indigenous communities, are in a way harboring hatred toward parts of themselves. A deeper reflection here is that the extremely negative characterization of the Spaniards made by others has focused in hating the colonizer of five centuries ago to such an extent that the present-day colonization from other sources may not be apparent.

Many descendants of Spanish-speakers do not want to be called Hispanos or Hispanics because they do not want to be reminded of their connection to Spain. They prefer to be called Latinos, feeling that this places them farther away from the colonizer. This term is less precise, because etymologically it includes Portuguese, Italians, French, Rumanians, and every other population whose language derives from Latin. It is somewhat ironic that to escape from the identification with one conquest, we have chosen to identify with a previous conquest—that of the Romans.

Personally, I have chosen *Latina* as my identification for three reasons:

1. It is a word in Spanish, and for me, my language is, if I can paraphrase Heidegger, "the house of my being."

2. It is a word that has a masculine and a feminine form, as most nouns do in Spanish, so I can call myself and my daughter Latinas, while my sons are Latinos, and I find this affirmation valuable.

3. I feel close to the group of people who have chosen to signify with this word a recognition of our mestizo nature, because that recognition is essential to our acceptance of the fullness of our own selves.

Within this overall Latino denomination, there are many different people. Some have lived in this land for centuries and can trace their ancestors back to Spanish pioneers, as is the case for many people in New Mexico and El Paso, Texas; others may be very recent arrivals. Some Latinos have lost their language. Others have maintained it through generations, and many words that have been lost elsewhere remain vivid in their speech. Some Latino families came as refugees fleeing repressive regimes in South or Central America; others came from the same countries but representing the opposite sector. Although the largest number of Latinos have come looking for work opportunities and to escape poverty, others have been enticed to come by scholarships or work offers or have remained after completing university careers, as part of the "brain drain" that attracts highly qualified people to this country. The look and coloring of Latinos are as diverse as their class, education, language repertoire, or degree of assimilation into the majority culture, reflecting the richness of their heritage. Even within the same family, people can look and think very differently.

A LATINO LITERATURE FOR CHILDREN AND ADOLESCENTS

This chapter focuses on literature written by Latino and Latina authors, whether they write in English or in Spanish and regardless of the topic they address. The goal is to see what a specific group of people, sharing a common heritage, have contributed to the field of literature for children and adolescents in this country and to identify some of the genres, styles, and topics they have pursued. This analysis does not pretend to be exhaustive, because that would require a more extensive venue (a complete book devoted to the theme is currently being written by Alma Flor Ada). The aim is to give an overview of the topic to give the reader a greater understanding of the nature and quality of the books that can be made available to their students.

NON-LATINO AUTHORS WRITING ABOUT LATINOS

The focus selected for this chapter leaves out the many books published about Latinos by authors who are not Latinos themselves. The merit of a book is determined not by the heritage of the author or illustrator, but by their intention, knowledge, sensitivity, responsibility, and artistry. It can be aided by the support given by the editor and publisher. Yet there is an inner look to a culture that is not easily acquired and requires long contact with people of the culture and its environment. The deep experiences of a people can seldom be told authentically from the outside.

It is not helpful to think that because there are still so few books about the very rich and diverse Latino reality, then anything that addresses this culture merits publication. It is inappropriate when someone from outside the culture looks at the insufficient number of titles about Latinos as an opportunity to publish, and too much of this is happening. It is painful to see that while Latino authors have great difficulty finding supportive publishers, many of the books about Latinos, particularly the most lavish books, are authored by non-Latinos. Yet it is not helpful either to publish something just because the writer comes from the culture, without maintaining the same demands of quality that would be expected of other authors. Children deserve the best, they deserve authenticity and truth, and they deserve books of artistic and literary merit.

The two sides of the issue that I support here are as follows: First, there are too few books written by Latino authors. The support of publishers and organizations is needed to correct this imbalance, with books coming from within the culture. Second, there are authors who, without being Latino, are very close to the culture—by marriage (like Arthur Dorros or Elizabeth Borton de Treviño), by having interacted considerably with people of the culture (like Jane Medina), or by having lived for an extended period in a Spanish-speaking country (like Tony Johnston). When these writers have studied the culture extensively, coming to it with authentic respect and admiration, seeking counsel and advice from some well-versed person from inside, they can create books of merit. These books must convey that it is the richness of the culture—not just the available market—that has moved the authors to create them. Yet the warning remains: It is important that the people of every culture study, analyze, and define themselves. There is otherwise the risk that we end up believing that we must look, think, feel, as others outside the culture have interpreted us to be.

There is a cautionary tale to be told here. It was related to me by Dr. Guadalupe Solís, and I trust that you will be able to read it someday as related by him in his own book of memories. When he was eleven years old and growing up in a Mexican farmworking family in the Imperial Valley in California, Lupe's teacher told him and a couple of his friends that for a forthcoming school celebration, they should teach the class how to do the Mexican hat dance. On the way home, Lupe and his friends found that none of them knew how to do such a dance. They decided to ask their parents. The next day, on the way to school, they compared notes. None of their parents knew how to do the hat dance either, so they sadly concluded, "Maybe we are not Mexican after all." Not knowing what else they could be left them with the feeling of a terrible void, which Lupe explains took him many years to overcome. Lupe refers to the experience as "the day I lost my identity."

A PANORAMIC HISTORICAL VIEW

Literature began orally, and Latino children's literature is no exception. The first Spanish-speakers who came to this land brought with them a very rich oral treasury: Lullabies and nursery rhymes, ballads and songs, folktales, legends, and tricksters' tales were all part of a living tradition. This literature flourished in the lands where the ancestors of today's Latinos lived, and it has remained alive to this day.

Like the people, this oral tradition stems from many sources. There are old tales from the Arab tradition that were translated into medieval Castilian and survive to the present, there are old Hebrew stories such as "The Horse of Seven Colors." The medieval *balads* or romances gave origin to the Mexican *corrido,* and the old harvest song from sixteenth century Spain, "De colores," has become the unofficial hymn of the farmworkers. The *Dama blanca* or *Dama del alba* of the old Spanish legends continues to cry at night, looking for her lost children as La Llorona wherever people of Spanish-speaking descent live, just as Juan Bobo, Pedro Urdemales, or Pedro Remales continues to entertain them with his trickster's deeds. In African animal tales, the types of animals may have changed many times, but the stories retain their power.

La Edad de Oro

In 1889, an extraordinary publication transformed forever the way writing for children would be viewed in the Spanish-speaking world. A new conception of the child reader and a new style of writing for that reader was born with *La Edad de Oro* ("The Golden Age"), a literary magazine for children written in its entirety by JOSÉ MARTÍ, a man whose transcendent role in Latin American thought and literature continues to have a growing influence.

It is significant that this publication, whose influence in Latin American children's literature has been constant, was published in New York City, from where it was distributed to all of Latin America, from Mexico to Patagonia. The journal was addressed to all "the boys and girls of the Americas." Although only four issues were published, they were later republished as a book, *La Edad de Oro,* in numerous editions throughout Latin America.

It was a glorious moment for Latino children's literature. Martí, aware of children's vast interests and wanting to make them true citizens of the world, approached writing from a variety of genres and perspectives. The breadth of content surprises the reader even today, because Martí was able to anticipate themes that continue to be meaningful.

A very prolific author, Martí created works for adults in many genres, although he is best known for his speeches, essays, and poetry. In writing for children, he included in *La Edad de Oro* also a diversity of genres: original stories and retellings of traditional tales, poetry, biographical sketches, nonfiction information, and essays. Each page is of outstanding literary quality. It was as if Martí was laying the foundation for a new way of speaking to children—light, fresh, without the moralizing heaviness characteristic of the times, engaging, captivating—and wanted to do this in every possible genre, opening up vast possibilities.

There is a total of twenty-three pieces, besides the introductory page on the first issue and the "final page" of each of the issues. Of these pieces, five are poems, six are stories (three original realistic and three retellings of fantasy stories from Hans Christian Andersen and the French author Laboulaye), two are biographical essays, and nine are nonfiction essays.

Within the poems, there are also diverse genres. A brief lyrical poem, "Dos milagros" ("Two Miracles"), sings the beauty of life. An elegy, inspired by the American poet Helen Hunt Jackson, "Los dos príncipes" ("The Two Princes"), shows how the death of a shepherd's son and a young prince generate delicate and profound expressions of grieving, different in their manifestation but born of similar feelings. "La perla de la mora" ("The Arab Woman's Pearl") and "Cada uno a su oficio" ("Each to His Own Business") are fables, the second one from Emerson. The long story in verse, "Los zapaticos de rosa" ("The Pink Slippers"), continues to be recited, sung, represented, and enjoyed today throughout Latin America. In the United States, it has been published as a book illustrated by Lulú Delacre and has been included in *El son del sol* (Ada & Campoy). It appears also sung, in the accompanying cassette, in an original musical arrangement by Suni Paz.

Although Martí was a modernist writer, intent on delighting with the beauty of the language and its imagery, he took any opportunity to address social issues, many of them prevalent today. The young protagonists, the children whom he considered "the hope of the world," rise to help create the world he envisioned: "the happy time when all human beings treat each other as friends." In "Los zapaticos de rosa," behind all the detailed description of a day at the beach, there are a denunciation of class differences and a generous child ready to give what she treasures to ease someone else's pain. The original story "La muñeca negra" ("The Black Doll") addresses the issue of discrimination as the young girl prefers her old black doll,which others despise, to the fancy blond one she has just received, which everyone celebrates.

Martí speaks to young people about the need for all the children of the Americas, regardless of their own ethnicity, to recognize "our indigenous mother," the indigenous roots of this continent, and our debt to the indigenous people. This is not a romantic claim, but one born of a deep social conscience, the same conscience that led him to his early death on the battlefield. Martí uses a variety of literary tools, in prose and verse, to share with children his values about the respect due to all people, his denunciation of any sort of discrimination and oppression, and his hope that young people will embrace the concept of equality among all human beings and espouse justice as the means to live in a world at peace.

Martí believed that truth and knowledge are the roads to freedom. He wanted the children to know about all human achievements in all fields. In his essays, he tells them about Homer's *Iliad* and the works of the great poets, musicians, and artists of Europe—French, Italian, Spanish, German, and English— as well as about the great achievements of the indigenous populations of the Americas, in particular those of Mexico, the country he loved so dearly.

In a couple of the essays, he talks about the history of humankind as expressed by its houses and by the development through time of simple discoveries. In a magnificent essay, he invites the young reader to walk with him through the World Exhibition in Paris in 1889. Imagining being in France creates an opportunity to talk about the French Revolution and its ideals and to marvel at the construction of the Eiffel Tower. Martí stops to give every detail of the Latin American pavilions, and the descriptions become a piece of history of each country. But history as told by Martí is more like an enchanting tale; he doesn't hesitate to insert his reflections. Describing the murals in the Mexican pavilion, he asserts, "That's how one should love the motherland, fiercely and tenderly."

But even if Martí could love the motherland so fiercely, and the bigger mother, la Patria Grande, as he considered all Latin America to be, he held a respect for all the world, hoping for respect and unity among all people of the earth.

One of his essays is devoted entirely to Vietnam. He describes the land and the people, and he explains to children the teachings of Buddhism with the same respect with which he explained the beliefs of the ancient Greeks or the Aztecs. He describes the art of Vietnam, the beauty of the temples, the theater, and the people ("they are like fine silversmiths in all they do, be it wood, or ivory, armory or weavings, painting or embroidery") and dwells on the historical destiny of this land that had been so many times colonized and conquered, affirming that this peace-loving people who had been repeatedly invaded for centuries would eventually have to rebel against foreign colonizers, bringing about much sorrow. That he chose to write about a land that would later be so significant in American history attests once more to his vision.

Shortly before his death, while in Santo Domingo preparing to go to Cuba to fight for Cuba's independence, Martí wrote some letters to the girl María Mantilla, daughter of his heart. These letters are included in his collective writings, published after his death. There is also a beautiful edition for children, *Cartas a María Mantilla*. Fearing his death, Martí wants to give María what may be his last advice. He takes a feminist stance, insisting on the importance of education for women, telling the young girl that education will not only provide her with personal enrichment and the ability to earn her living, but will also give her the possibility of knowing true love. Only if she is able to support herself can she know love. Free to work and be independent, she will have the freedom to be with someone out of love, not out of dependence like most women of her time. These letters, in which he elaborates on how to translate so that the translation is transparent and how to write for young people so as to bring clarity and honesty to the words, are wonderful reading for anyone who wants to understand Martí's vision of the relationship between an author and his or her young audience.

After *La Edad de Oro*

La Edad de Oro laid the groundwork for a literature covering multiple genres and numerous topics. This literature both looked at the direct heritage of the children and expanded their vision to include the totality of the world. It made sure children would recognize that Latin America has an indigenous mother who deserves appreciation and respect and is made of young nations capable of powerful deeds. This literature extols working people and invites the young people to dare to imagine creative possibilities in all areas of human pursuit.

As a mestizo people, we have inherited an extraordinarily rich oral tradition. Whether in Florida, along the Mississippi, or in New Mexico, Arizona, Colorado, Texas, or California, the old songs, legends, and stories have lived on in the hearts of the people, sometimes taking on new settings and characters. But in spite of the richness of the old traditions and the new myths, legends, and stories that have developed and despite the seminal work of Martí in New York, the amount of published literature for and about children and young adults of Hispanic ancestry in the United States, particularly books written by Hispanic authors themselves, was very limited for most of the twentieth century. For almost a hundred years, with the exception of a very few significant Latino writers, literature published for young audiences on Latino themes was virtually nonexistent. In the few instances in which non-Latino writers touched on Latino themes in the first seven decades of the century, Latino people were, at best, treated in a romanticized manner or as exotic creatures and most often in a very stereotypical and pejorative manner.

Emerging Recognition of Latino Children's Literature

The transition from a rich oral literature to a written literature for children and adolescents was a slow process for Latinos. First, there was the language issue, because publishers in the United States did not see a need to publish children's books in languages other than English, and many Latinos felt insecure about writing and publishing in English; second, there was the social perspective toward Latinos, who suffered from the historical trend of conquering nations to put down conquered people. Because the United States had taken possession of Puerto Rico as a trophy of war after the Spanish-American War in 1898 and of the Southwest after the earlier war with Mexico, there was a tendency to show Spaniards and their descendants as people in the wrong so that having taken their lands could seem more justifiable to the general public. Once such views appear in the mass media and become part of the general perception, they are very difficult to eradicate.

Latino literature for children and adolescents came of age in the decade of the 1990s. Few voices paved the way—among them Pura Belpré, Piri Thomas, Ernesto Galarza, Rudolfo Anaya, Nicholasa Mohr, Hilda Perera, and Alma Flor Ada.

Born in Cidra, Puerto Rico, in 1909, only ten years after the publication of *La Edad de Oro*, PURA BELPRÉ became the first Puerto Rican librarian in the New York Public Library system, after attending the New York Public Library School program and Columbia University. In 1932, after many years of storytelling in the library, Pura Belpré was able to publish *Pérez and Martina*, a shortened English version of a beloved traditional tale that was well known throughout the Spanish-speaking world. This was followed in 1946 by *The Tiger and the Rabbit and Other Tales*, a collection of traditional stories that shows the profound African heritage of Puerto Rico. In 1962, Pura Belpré published *Juan Bobo and the Queen's Necklace.* Juan Bobo is a beloved trickster of Hispanic folklore, who has circled the globe under different names (Juan Bobo, Pedro Urdemales, Pedro Remales). This character, apparently silly and inwardly cunning, has entertained children and adults for many centuries. *Oté: A Puerto Rican Folk Tale* was published in 1969.

After publishing folktales for close to thirty years, Pura Belpré published *Santiago,* a realistic fiction story, in 1961. The transition to realistic fiction is of great significance because it exemplifies what would become a trend among Latino writers: the need first to rescue the roots, recording and celebrating them, as is the case in the folktales published by Pura Belpré and many of us, before beginning to look at and re-create the existing present-day reality.

Santiago is a young boy living in New York who constantly daydreams about his life in Puerto Rico and the pet hen he left behind. It depicts the homesickness and sense of loss of the immigrant and was probably inspired by Pura Belpré's own childhood experiences.

Pura Belpré's last book in English, *The Rainbow Colored Horse,* another folktale, was published in 1978, the same year she received the Award of the Asociación de Literatura Infantil y Juvenil en Español y Portugués in San Francisco.

Pura Belpré's lifelong involvement in children's literature is a true example of the responsibilities faced by our pioneer authors: She kept the old tales alive by telling them in Spanish in the Bronx Public Library, sometimes with the aid of puppets, for three generations. She used to glow when telling how the grandmothers who walked into her library with their grandchildren had heard the same stories from her. She expanded the life and reach of the tales by publishing them in English so that they could be read by all children. Finally, she was able to re-create for us some of the difficult experiences of living in two worlds and the feelings of the immigrant child. She brought them to light not only so that children who are undergoing similar experiences could find themselves in a book, but also to extend to other children an awareness of who these brown children with sparkling eyes and funny accents are, whose inner richness they may otherwise perhaps never suspect and who, for all their external differences, are children no more nor less than themselves. To share her own childhood, she wrote *Firefly Summer*, which has recently been published by Piñata Books.

Pura Belpré received numerous well-deserved awards during her lifetime, and the American Library Association recognized her pioneering work by giving her name to the ALA Award for Latino authors of books for children and young adults.

Determined to provide Latino children in California with high-quality literature that addressed them directly, ERNESTO GALARZA, who had come from Mexico when very young, took on the responsibility single-handed. Just as Martí had written by himself all the pages of *La Edad de Oro*, Galarza created his own books, which he wrote, translated, illustrated with his own photographs, and published. The very humble format of these wonderful little books does not obscure the quality of Galarza's writing.

He called them "Mini-Libros" in reference to the small format and published them under his own imprint, Almadén. The quality of the brief poems is such that many have survived even though the Mini-Libros have been out of print for many years. They continue to be incorporated in anthologies and reading programs in Spanish and English. Galarza's books deserve to be reprinted.

Two of Galarza's most important contributions were, first, singing to the everyday experience of the children of farmworkers and showing them the poetry in the world around them and, second, making the bilingual/bicultural reality a focus of some of his books, particularly of *Mother Goose in the Río Grande*, in which he gives a Mexican flavor to some of the traditional rhymes, initiating a trend that other authors later followed.

HILDA PERERA had a well-established career as a writer, particularly with the book *Cuentos de Apolo*, before she moved from her native Cuba to the United States. She continues publishing in Spain, where she received the Premio Lazarillo, the Spanish equivalent of the Newbery Award, and in the United States. She is highly respected among the Cuban community in Florida.

RUDOLFO ANAYA is a giant among Latino writers for all ages. His book *Bless Me, Última* has remained a best-seller since its publication in 1972. It is a blessing for young readers that Anaya has decided to extend his work to them. His recent *Ballad on the Death of César Chávez* is one of the most inspiring and beautiful books that could be read by Latino youths. Because César Chávez was an American hero, it belongs in the hands of all youths.

The issue of identity, common in adolescence, becomes very significant for bilingual and/or bicultural people. Latino youths growing up in the

United States search for their identity with regard to both their parents and grandparents—who may speak Spanish and maintain many traditions from "back home"—and the general population. They are caught like a hinge, neither fully on one side nor fully on the other. NICHOLASA MOHR was one of the first Latino authors to address this issue through a young protagonist in a book addressed to children. Felita's quest for identity continues to be as authentic today as when the book *Felita* first appeared in the late 1970s.

Literature in Spanish for Children and Adolescents in the United States: The 1970s and 1980s

The development of bilingual education in the 1970s brought about an awareness of the need for materials written in Spanish for Spanish-speaking students in the United States. This had some very significant consequences: Some publishing houses from Spain began first importing and later publishing literature in Spanish, as is the case of Santillana. Publishing houses such as Hampton-Brown were developed to produce materials primarily for this population. Some were born initially as nonprofit organizations supported by federal and private foundation funds—for example, Piñata Books of Arte Público Press in Houston and Children's Book Press in San Francisco. Also, specialized distributors imported children's literature from Latin America and Spain, in particular Iaconi Books and Lectorum.

In the early 1970s, a group of enthusiastic idealists, aware of how little information there was in the field of children's literature and what scarce communication existed between authors, illustrators, publishers, and critics in Spanish-speaking countries and those who work with Spanish-speaking people in the United States, created the Asociación Internacional de Literatura Infantil en Español y Portugués. The founding members included Tim Beard, a bilingual teacher; Mariuccia Iaconi, a dedicated book distributor and pioneer in the identification and dissemination of books written in Spanish; Mary Frances Johnson, a librarian; and Alma Flor Ada, a professor and author. With support from Susan Benson at the Organization of American States, a Title VII resource center (BABEL) in Berkeley, and the University of San Francisco, in 1978 they organized the First Congress of Literature in Spanish and Portuguese in San Francisco. The presenters included children's literature specialists and historians from various countries, among many: Carmen Bravo Villasante from Spain, Efraín Subero from Venezuela, Flor Piñeiro de Rivera from Puerto Rico, and Marta Dujovne from Mexico, as well as Carmen Diana Dearden representing Ekaré-Banco del Libro from Venezuela and Gabriel Larrea representing the Secretaría de Educación Pública de México. That year, the Award of the Asociación was given to Pura Belpré, who was present to receive it and was introduced by Anne Pellowski. This landmark event had multiple repercussions. Its significance was recognized by all attending and moved the Secretaría de Educación Pública de México and the OAS to cosponsor two additional congresses in the following two years, one in Mexico City and Cocoyoc and one in Tucson, Arizona. The important resolutions that came from these meetings motivated the initiation, strengthening, or expansion of the IBBY (International Board of Books for Young People) sections of the countries represented (Spain, Cuba, Puerto Rico, Panama, Venezuela, Peru, Bolivia, and Argentina) and awakened the publishers' interest in this market. In Mexico, a publishing company devoted to children's literature, CIDCLI, was born right after the Second Congress. It took as its logo the one that had been developed for that congress. In the Second Congress, the association awards were given to Ernesto Galarza and Gabilondo Soler "Cri-Crí" and presented by Alma Flor Ada. During the Third Congress, the award was granted *in absentia* to the Puerto Rican poet Ester Feliciano Mendoza and was presented by Flor Piñeiro de Rivera.

The reflections, activities, partnerships, and support that evolved from these congresses are still evolving now, more than twenty years later.

In 1981, Sylvia Cabazos Peña, professor at the University of Houston and an active member in the Asociación, edited *Kikirikí*, which was soon followed by *Cuenta-ca-tún*, both bilingual anthologies of Latino writers published by Arte Público Press. Although the selections included are of diverse merit, as the first anthologies to gather the writings of Latino authors of children's literature, these were a significant effort toward giving recognition to their work.

Courses on children's literature in Spanish in the University of Texas at El Paso, the University of Tucson, Arizona, the University of Houston, the University of Saint Thomas in Houston, and the University of San Francisco, among others, began to give academic recognition to this field. In 1988, Alma Flor Ada initiated a course, sponsored by the Ministry of Education of Spain, on children's literature in Spanish for Latino children, taught at the Universidad Complutense de Madrid. This ongoing summer course has been attended by hundreds of U.S. teachers, who have had the opportunity to listen to some of the most recognized authors, illustrators, and scholars in the field. The professors from the United States conducting the course have included Suni Paz, María Torres-Guzmán, Sylvia Cabazos Peña, and Alma Flor Ada. Some of the many featured speakers have been Carmen Bravo-Villasante, Alonso Zamora Vicente, Elena Catena, Mercedes Gómez del Manzano, Jaime García Padrino, illustrators Ulises Wensell and Viví Escrivá, and authors Monserrat del Amo, A. R. Almodóbar, and José María Merino.

More recently, a similar course has been conducted by F. Isabel Campoy and Alma Flor Ada at the prestigious Fundación José Ortega y Gassett in Madrid under the leadership of María Fernández Shaw and Paloma Varela Ortega.

Although these were some of the first courses in the United States or for U.S. teachers devoted exclusively to the study and analysis of children's literature published in Spanish and of Latino children's literature as distinguished from methodological courses on the use of literature in the classroom, other courses have been developing across the nation.

Presentations on Latino children's literature are becoming more frequent at regional and national conferences, and there is a Center for the Study of Books in Spanish for children and adolescents at the California State University in San Marcos. This center is directed by Isabel Shon, who through the years has published many reviews and annotated bibliographies of books published in Spanish throughout the Spanish-speaking world.

A journal devoted to children's literature *Cuentaquetecuento,* published in Costa Rica by the Fundación San Judas Tadeo, with distribution throughout Latin America, dedicated its volume III, number 3 (1998) to Latino Children's Literature in an effort to bring an awareness to Latin Americans of what Latino authors are producing in the United States. This issue, edited by F. Isabel Campoy and Alma Flor Ada, includes a brief panoramic history of the literature as well as a selection of stories and poems by Latino writers.

The "Little" Boom of the 1990s

The minimal presence of Latino writers in the field of children's literature in the United States began to change slowly at the end of the 1980s. Keeping in perspective that the number of books for children and young adults published by Latino authors is very small in proportion to the total number of books published, it is still noteworthy that most of them have been published since 1990.

Several things seem to have come into play. Latin American literature (with figures such as Gabriel García Márquez, Mario Vargas Llosa, and Carlos Fuentes) as well as Latino literature (with figures like Isabel Allende, Sandra Cisneros, Julia Alvarez, and Esmeralda Santiago) gained great credibility and readership. Some well-established Latino writers (such as Rudolfo Anaya, PAT MORA, and GARY SOTO) began to write for younger audiences, and Latino writers who were publishing and winning awards in Latin America and Spain (such as Hilda Perera and Alma Flor Ada) began to be published and translated into English in the United States. The Reforma group from the American Library Association began requesting authentic literature by Latino authors and lobbied for several years to establish the Pura Belpré Award, which was finally initiated in 1996.

Smaller publishing houses specifically dedicated to addressing the needs of Spanish-speakers (such as Arte Público Press and Children's Book Press) published books in Spanish or bilingually, in many cases with the support of federal funding or grants from private foundations. The "whole-language" movement had emphasized the importance of literature in the teaching of language arts, and educational publishers were looking for materials that recognized the Latino population as well as for books in Spanish for the bilingual market. Some, like Santillana and Hampton-Brown, began publishing a line of trade books alongside their educational materials. As the number of high-quality books produced by African American authors and illustrators increased and became more visible, Latino authors and illustrators were stimulated and inspired by their example. Some specialists in the field began strongly advocating—at meetings of the USBBY, ALA, IRA, NCTE, and similar forums—the need for publishers to search for, and support, Latino writers.

We are very far from where we need to be, but there is now a body of literature that we can share with our students.

GenRes and Themes

The bibliography of Latino authors that is included at the end of this book has been divided by genres to show the publications that exist in the areas of poetry, theater, biography, autobiographical narrative, historical and contemporary fiction, and fantasy. The objective here is to offer a general view of the major trends that appear in the combined work of these authors. Individual portraits of major Latino authors, as well as descriptions of their most relevant books, can be found in the very informative book *Latina and Latino Voices in Literature for Children and Teenagers* by Frances Ann Day (1997); an updated version of this excellent book is forthcoming. Aware of the increasing number of Latinos in the country, Sharon Chickering Moller (2001) has created a useful resource book for librarians interested in providing services to Spanish-speakers: *Library Services to Spanish Speaking Patrons: A Practical Guide.*

An analysis of the books for children and adolescents by Latina and Latino authors when looked at collectively shows the following seven major trends:

- Preserving and continuing tradition
- Telling one's personal story
- Telling original stories of people like us
- Valuing love of family
- Acknowledging social issues concerning Latinos
- Celebrating and transmitting the richness of the culture
- Giving free rein to fantasy

Preserving and Continuing Tradition

Sharing traditional literature—nursery rhymes, legends, folktales—is an important aspect of children's literature in general. All adults are in some way exiled from childhood and may feel profound nostalgia for those years; many want to share with the new generations of children the traditions that enriched their own childhood. For Latino authors, the traditional oral literature takes on a major significance. They may be aware of Latino children's struggle with issues of identity and might like to offer them the confidence of being part of an unending culture by providing traditional literature they can share with their parents. Having experienced the pain of uprootedness, some may want to offer new immigrant children the comfort of the known and familiar. And having loved these traditions, they probably all wish to share them with all children. Among those who have collected folklore and retold the old tales are Alma Flor Ada, Rudolfo Anaya, Carmen Bernier-Grand, María Cristina Brusca, F. Isabel Campoy, Lulú Delacre, Lucía González, Antonio Hernández Madrigal, Nicholasa Mohr, José Luis Orozco, and Suni Paz. Their works can be found in the bibliography.

Occasionally, they may tell a new story incorporating elements of the traditional literature, as does GLORIA ANZALDÚA in *Prietita and the Ghost Woman/Prietita y la Llorona* and ROSALMA ZUBIZARRETA in *The Woman Who Outshone the Sun/La mujer que brillaba aún más que el sol*.

The significance of traditional folklore is also manifested in two other ways. First, experiences with the folklore as a child appears in the authors' autobiographical memories. For example, two of Alma Flor Ada's autobiographical books are centered on folklore: *Pregones* on vendors' callings and *Pin, pin, sarabín* on recollections of nursery rhymes and song games. Second, the familiarity and enjoyment of the traditional tales has led some authors to write original stories with a folktale style, as is the case of Nicholasa Mohr's *La vieja Letivia y el Monte de los Pesares* and Alma Flor Ada's *The Gold Coin* and *Jordi's Star*.

Telling Our Stories: Autobiographical Writing

It seems only natural that authors of literature for children and youth would write their autobiographies or vignettes of their life as a child in a style that is directed to their readers. Children and young people have a natural curiosity to know about an author's life as a child and in which ways it might be similar to or different from their own.

Latino and Latina authors have been particularly inclined to write about the early parts of their lives. The section on autobiographical writing in the bibliography shows autobiographical picture books by, among others, Alma Flor Ada, María Cristina Brusca, Lucha Corpi, Juan Felipe Herrera, Carmen Lomas Garza, Loretta López, and Amada Irma Pérez and more extensive autobiographical narrative by ALMA FLOR ADA, Pura Belpré, Ernesto Galarza, FRANCISCO JIMÉNEZ, Nicholasa Mohr, JUDITH ORTIZ COFER, and Gary Soto. There is even a cassette, "Growing Up Cuban in Decatur, Georgia," by CARMEN AGRA DEEDY, on which the author-performer enlivens her narrative with the accurate rendition of the voices she remembers. In these authentic texts about their own lives, these authors have contributed a most significant chapter to literature for children and adolescents in the United States. These books need to be considered essential in any collection that aspires to be representative of the society of the United States whenever one is choosing and sharing books with the intent of inclusion.

Each individual author's motivation to write is as personal and unique as the individual. One can write childhood memories to preserve one's experiences from oblivion, to honor the people who helped shape one's earlier memories, or to heal wounds and soothe the pain of hurtful experiences. Looking at the proportionately abundant autobiographical writing among Latinos, I can think of three profound motivations to add to the natural desire of writing about what one knows best, one's own life:

1. Having been ignored or silenced, having grown up invisible to the eyes of the media and mainstream writing, we may have a desire to have our lives recognized.
2. Having felt discrimination and disdain from others toward aspects of life that were dear to us and particularly representative of our family and community, we may be determined to validate their significance by making them part of a literary or artistic pursuit.
3. For those of us who have grown up immersed in the literary traditions of the Spanish-speaking world, there are numerous examples to serve as powerful inspiration. The Spaniards Juan Ramón Jiménez (*Platero y yo*) and Alonso Zamora Vicente (*Primeras hojas*), the Argentinian Norah Lange (*Cuadernos de infancia*), the Venezuelan Teresa de la Parra (*Memorias de la Mamá Grande*), and the Cuban Reneé Méndez Capote (*Memorias de una cubanita que nació con el siglo*) all contributed to creating a tradition of literary autobiographical writing about one's early years.

Telling Original Stories of People Like Us

Many good stories are created with bits of reality and large doses of imagination. Writing about people one knows, streets one has walked, and meals one has eaten can contribute to the power of a story. Authors may also have the desire to explain life as they see it and perhaps even to make it have the evolution they would like to see.

Contemporary realistic narrative is an important aspect of literature for children and adolescents. Although each genre has something valuable to offer children, it is in realistic fiction, especially in contemporary narrative, that they can see themselves, their friends, and their quest represented

In the bibliography, contemporary narrative books have been divided according to the setting: those set primarily in Latin America and those set primarily in the United States. Although the need for books in all genres is great, the need in this area is particularly noticeable. There are realistic picture books by, among others, Rudolfo Anaya, Gloria Anzaldúa, Francisco

Jiménez, Leyla Torres, and Alma Flor Ada, and realistic chapter books and young adult novels by, among others, Nicholasa Mohr, Hilda Perera, Gary Soto, and Alma Flor Ada. The work of both Nicholasa Mohr and Gary Soto is substantive and merits special attention and recognition, yet the need to tell many stories from the barrios, the fields, the small towns, and the suburbs, from Latinos on both coasts, the Midwest, the South, and the Southwest continues to be immense.

Acknowledging Social Issues Concerning Latinos

Latinos face some very specific concerns and issues. Some of the ones that appear in the recent literature for young readers are language, identity, issues related to poverty and discrimination, and internal struggles resulting from the internalization of oppression.

Heritage Language and Bilingualism.   One of the most significant issues concerning Latinos is the right to retain and develop the Spanish language. From the moment of beginning school and sometimes even before, Latino children are faced with societal prejudice against their home language. Everyone agrees on the value and importance to children of learning English and learning it well. Conflicts arise when, instead of a societal attitude of appreciation of bilingualism and a fostering of the benefit of acquiring two languages in a situation of additive enrichment, children are faced with societal mistrust and lack of appreciation of their home language. They see themselves ridiculed, discriminated against, ignored, or teased for speaking a language other than English.

Usually, their parents will be putting a lot of emphasis on having the children learn English as quickly as possible for a number of reasons. If the parents themselves are having difficulties getting good working opportunities because they lack knowledge of English, they want to prevent their children from suffering in the same way; if they have suffered discrimination, they tend to believe that it is related only to the language. They firmly believe that the moment their children can speak English, they will be fully accepted as bona fide Americans. Furthermore, if the parents are trying to learn English, they want to practice with their children and have the children help them learn. They also may need the children to translate for them.

Thus the children are getting a push at home to speak English and a societal message that their home language is inferior. And most likely, no one close to the child is fully aware of what will happen once the child stops speaking Spanish. The parents don't suspect that the child will become incapable of using Spanish beyond very simplistic commands or statements of need, particularly if this is a younger child who will be communicating with the parents through an older sibling. One day, when it is already too late, the parents will be faced with the painful reality of not being able to communicate about meaningful themes, to transmit values, to clarify situations, to share the family history, or to reveal to their children their deep feelings and thoughts.

The role of bilingualism and the love for Spanish, whether as a source of full communication or even when reduced to the presence of significant words as gems that carry special meaning even when the communication is mostly in English, have been addressed poetically by several writers, attesting to the depth of feelings involved. Gary Soto inserts Spanish words in many of his poems and addresses the issue specifically in the poem "Spanish" (in *Canto familiar*), in which he expresses the sentiment that by being bilingual, the world is twice as big. FRANCISCO X. ALARCÓN makes a point of publishing all his poetry bilingually, which is in itself a very powerful statement. He addresses the richness of knowing two languages with delightful humor in his poem "Bilingual" (in *From the Bellybuttom of the Moon*). He writes about his bilingual dog, who, if not understood when saying "guau guau," will repeat his greeting by barking "bow wow." Pat Mora incorporates Spanish words in the poems of the book *Confetti*. Alma Flor Ada's poem "Ser bilingüe" (in *Días y días de poesía*) emphasizes that to be bilingual is an unending source of joy. F. ISABEL CAMPOY addresses the importance of the heritage language in several poems. In the poem/song "Hablar como tú" (in *Música amiga*, no. 6) a granddaughter tells the grandmother that she would like to be able to speak like her, to be able to express all her love. In "No, no te olvides, no" (in *Música amiga, no. 10*), the poet encourages children not to forget how to speak Spanish or the valuable words *amigo* ("friend") and *familia* ("family"). This poem, set to music by Suni Paz, has become for many teachers a hymn of inspiration and solidarity in the struggle to defend the right to develop the students' home language.

The children's tendency to internalize shame in speaking a language whose value society often fails to recognize has also been addressed, although perhaps not as much as the issue deserves. One example is *Pepita Talks Twice/Pepita habla dos veces* by OFELIA DUMAS LACHTMAN.

Identity.   The concern for identity, which in many ways may be related to the maintenance of the heritage language, also takes on major importance. Who is the young person in relation to parents or grandparents whose language and traditions may be very different from those the young person is acquiring in this country? How much of the old should the young person retain? At the same time, who is one in relationship to the dominant society? How much does one want to be like others? Finally, how much would one be accepted even if one were to give up many aspects of oneself?

Other significant issues concerning Latino realities are the hardships of the farmworking life, the presence of violence and drugs in the barrios, and the rivalry between the established community and recently arrived immigrants.

These topics appear in many of the books. Sometimes they are the focus of the book; sometimes they appear as marginal topics.

The issue of identity has been explored with magnificent insight by Nicholasa Mohr in *Felita* and *Going Home*. It is also central, represented by the desire to retain one's full name in Spanish, in *My Name is María Isabel* by Alma Flor Ada.

Poverty and In-Group Struggles.   Because some Latinos live in conditions of extreme economic poverty, they suffer from the social illnesses that plague our economically deprived neighborhoods, where people might not see hope of a better future and might internalize a sense of worthlessness society projects unto them. The issue of gangs and the dangers of drugs and violence are powerfully explored by LUIS J. RODRÍGUEZ in *It Doesn't Have to Be This Way: A Barrio Story/No tiene que ser así: Una historia del barrio.*

One of the consequences of internalizing the values of the oppressor is that the oppressed turns against their own people. Newly arrived immigrants many times face discrimination from people of their own culture who arrived previously and are better established. Several elements come into play. Those who arrived earlier may be of a different social class, or they may have made great sacrifices to become established and somewhat accepted and feel that the presence of the newly arrived will have a negative impact on what they have achieved. Sometimes they believe that the newly arrived will be competing for their jobs; at other times, they might fear being identified with the same stereotypes. These negative attitudes from some Latinos toward newly arrived Latino immigrants are the central topic of Gloria Anzaldúa's book *Friends from the Other Side/Amigos del otro lado.*

Within the whole topic of immigration, the disconcertment from being uprooted, the pain of loss of what was left behind, the feelings of alienation, the struggle for survival, the anxiety to become accepted, and the negotiating of identity are very significant issues. Much more needs to be written about them still.

Valuing Love of Family: The Important Role of Grandparents

One of the most constantly recurring themes in the literature we are considering is the expression of love for family, in particular for grandparents and other elders. Although again this is not an uncommon theme in books for young readers, it seems to take on a special poignancy among Latina and Latino authors.

Several conditions of the Latino reality may contribute to this:

1. The grandparents represent continuity in lives where that continuity may have been shattered either because the family has left a homeland

to move to the United States or because the family is a migrant family that needs to move frequently to find work.

2. The grandparents may have played a very important role as caretakers when parents have to work extensive hours or have left the children in their care for prolonged periods.

3. The grandparents or elders as cultural transmitters not only enrich children's lives with their stories, songs, and sayings, but also contribute to giving them a sense of pride in who they are.

A look at the bibliography at the end of this book will reveal many picture books centered on these topics: Rudolfo Anaya's *Farolitos for Abuelo*, Amy Córdova's *Abuelita's Heart*, Pat Mora's *A Birthday Basket for Tía*, Carmen Santiago Nodar's *Abuelita's Paradise*, Leyla Torres' *Liliana's Grandmothers*, and Alma Flor Ada's, *I Love Saturdays y domingos*.

This significant role of grandparents can also be seen in the outstanding poem by Francisco X. Alarcón to his grandmother, "Matriarch" (in *A Chorus of Cultures*); in Pam Muñoz Ryan's historical novel *Esperanza Rising*, winner of the Pura Belpré 2002 Award; in many poems and songs by F. Isabel Campoy dedicated to the family; and in Alma Flor Ada's vignettes "The Teacher" and "Choices" in the autobiographical book *Where the Flame Trees Bloom* and "My Abuelita, My Paradise," included in the anthology compiled by Bonnie Christensen (2003) of authors' stories about their grandmothers, *Across the River and through the Woods: Stories about Grandmothers*.

Celebrating and Transmitting the Richness of the Culture

Sharing the richness of the Hispanic culture has been for Latino and Latina authors both an act of joy and one of duty. On one hand, the culture of the Spanish-speaking world is extraordinary: There are twenty Hispanic countries plus more than thirty-five million Latinos in the United States. The mixed heritage of these people makes the Latino child of today the inheritor of an extraordinarily diverse culture with Spanish, indigenous, and African roots that has contributed achievements in all areas of human endeavor. From the Aztec pyramids and the Inca city of Macchu Pichu to the Arab Alcázar of Granada; from the medieval Cathedral of Santiago de Compostela and the Renaissance Plaza Mayor of Salamanca to the colonial churches of Oaxaca, Quito, or Lima; from the California missions to the revolutionary art of Gaudí; and from the contemporary buildings of Caracas to those designed by Architectonica in Miami, Hispanics have created some of the most beautiful buildings in human history. From the classical paintings of Velázquez, Zurbarán, el Greco, and Goya to the majestic murals of Diego Rivera, Xiqueiros, and Tamayo and the revolutionary creations of Picasso, who influenced the art of a whole century, the joyful art of Miro and Fernando Botero, or the intimate work of Frida Kahlo, Hispanic artists have contributed substantially to the evolution of painting in the world.

Cervantes, Lope de Vega, Sor Juana Inés de la Cruz, José Martí, Gabriela Mistral, Nicolás Guillén, Alejo Carpentier, Jorge Luis Borges, César Vallejo, Pablo Neruda, Carlos Fuentes, Isabel Allende, Sandra Cisneros, Julia Alvarez, and many others have written some of the finest pages of literature. And we could go on.

The majority of our children do not have any idea that this heritage is theirs. The desire to inform them and to give them the message that they too can find a way to contribute to the world is a strong motivator to create books sharing the richness of the Hispanic culture. Another motivator is to share this culture with all children so that they may develop respect and appreciation for those who constitute a significant part of the American mosaic and may, in turn, also be inspired to discover the best in themselves.

The sharing of this vast culture has just begun. Although there are many books and cassettes, they represent only a small portion of what is to be shared.

Some of the books of literary and artistic merit center on celebrations of special festivities; others focus on everyday life. There are collections of poetry, art, theater, biographies, books on specific monumental works, and cultural overviews.

A powerful way to share the immediacy of the culture in all its details is the use of photography. In this field, GEORGE ANCONA has made an invaluable contribution with his photojournalistic books; *Pablo Remembers: The Feast of the Day of the Death, Mayeros: A Yucatec Maya Family, Charro: The Mexican Cowboy, Viva Mexico! The People,* and *Fireworks* are some of his many excellent titles. Another significant book on celebrations is Lulú Delacre's *Vejigante/Masquerader,* about the carnival feast in Loíza in Puerto Rico.

As this literature comes of age, authors are finding inspiration in the past but reconstructing it to fit the present. One of the most significant books in this respect is *My Daughter, My Son, the Eagle, the Dove: An Aztec Chant* by ANA CASTILLO, illustrated by Susan Guevara. Inspired by Aztec poetic chants to give instructions to young people on their coming of age, Castillo and Guevara have created an exquisite book that Latino parents can put into the hands of their adolescent sons and daughters as a message of pride in their heritage and hope for their future.

F. Isabel Campoy and Alma Flor Ada continue to develop and publish *Gateways to the Sun/Puertas al sol,* a collection devoted to the transmission of the richness of Latino culture to children. Published by Alfaguara/Santillana, under the art direction of Felipe Dávalos, this constitutes to date the largest effort to put biographies, art, poetry, theater, and a vision of Latin Americans and Latinos in the hands of children.

Giving Free Rein to Fantasy

No author should feel compelled to write only within the parameters of cultural transmission. Everyone deserves the freedom to explore all fields and all topics, to navigate uncharted waters, and to contribute the product of her or his originality.

No matter what genre or topic authors choose, their work will ultimately reveal their inner self, their experiences, and their worldview. No matter how apparently remote from the authors' historical background the topic may be, if the writing is of high quality, it must have been nourished by the author's own soul.

Although there is an enormous need for more realistic fiction based on the authentic experiences of Latinos, and we hope to see more and more of these books being produced, it is also a symbol of having come of age that Latinos do not feel compelled to remain within the boundaries of folklore and realistic narrative but feel free to open the doors to the imagination and write fantasy.

The fantasy books may sometimes have characters that are very definitely inserted in some cultural aspects, like the Chato books of Gary Soto, which depict a low-riding cat, or *Martí and the Mango* by Daniel Moretón, in which the animal characters are playfully named Martí and Gómez, after the great figures of Cuban independence, José Martí and Máximo Gómez. Or the books may have a more universal flavor, as in some of the books of Carmen Agra Deedy (*Agatha's Feather Bed*) and Alma Flor Ada (*The Malachite Palace*, *The Unicorn of the West*, and *With Love, Little Red Hen*).

LATINO FOLKSINGERS

Songs are an important literary expression and an important aspect of childhood. The richness of the Hispanic folklore has been recorded by numerous singers. Some have not only recorded the traditional songs, but have also added their own creations.

JOSÉ LUIS OROZCO has been singing to children throughout California for over two decades. His selections include traditional songs and some songs of his own creation. His music celebrates the people's struggle for a better life and thoughts of solidarity, freedom, and peace. He has compiled many of these songs in three books with lively illustrations by Elisa Kleven.

SUNI PAZ is a folklorist specializing in children's songs. A composer, musician, songwriter, and singer, Suni has recorded a large number of songs of her own creation, songs from the folklore, and songs whose music she has composed and whose lyrics are poems from various well-known poets from the Hispanic world. The collection of 120 songs in *Música amiga* represent a diversity of folk rhythms from Mexico, Central and South America, and the

Caribbean. The Smithsonian Institution has honored Suni by protecting her recordings in their vaults as part of the selected voices of the twentieth century to be saved for posterity.

Suni, who chose the last name Paz (meaning "Peace") for her stage name has a commitment to preserving the music of the people and to promoting the values of peace, cross-cultural understanding, self-reflection, and social justice through her music.

LATINO ILLUSTRATORS

It is not surprising that a culture that has contributed some of the most important architects and plastic and visual artists of human history would also produce numerous outstanding illustrators of children's books.

Latinos feel pride that DAVID DÍAZ, a Latino illustrator, received the Caldecott Award for *Smoky Night*. Díaz's work, which includes books such as *Wilma Unlimited*, continues to receive the ample recognition it deserves.

LULÚ DELACRE and LEYLA TORRES are both outstanding author-illustrators who have contributed to making Latin American everyday life real to children in the United States. Lulú Delacre's illustrations for Lucía González's rendition of *The Bossy Gallito* uses a noteworthy combination of animal characters in a realistic setting to capture the images and spirit of Miami's Little Havana. Leyla Torres's humanity, transparent in her writing, is powerfully conveyed in her illustrations of people so realistically individualized as in *Subway Sparrow* or *Saturday Sancocho* that they become unforgettable characters from the moment one opens her books.

Author-illustrator DANIEL MORETÓN uses the computer to create his bold and striking art for his original story *Martí and the Mango* and his new version of *Cucaracha Martina: A Caribbean Folktale*. The result, filled with extraordinary humor, is powerfully attractive.

One of the most recognized Latina illustrators, SUSAN GUEVARA is best known for the striking characterization of Chato and his world in Gary Soto's *Chato's Kitchen* and *Chato's Friends*, for which she was awarded the Pura Belpré 2002 Illustrator's Award. Yet her talent has many expressions and a wide range of always alluring styles.

FELIPE DÁVALOS moved to the United States when he was already a world-renowned illustrator acknowledged as mentor by more than one generation of Mexican illustrators. To his extensive academic preparation as an archaeologist, Dávalos adds his reflective experience as art director and book designer. Some of the books he has recently illustrated are *The Lizard and the Sun*, in which his archaeological knowledge of ancient Meso-American cultures is displayed, and the Christmas book *The Secret Star* by Joseph Slate. He has been the art director of Alfaguara's collection of books on Latino culture *Puertas al Sol/Gateways to the Sun* and has contributed some original art to these books.

Dávalos belongs to a select group of Maestros, exceptional Latin-American illustrators, that also includes Antonio Martorell from Puerto Rico and Gian Calvi from Brazil, who see children's book illustration as an artistic expression for the transformation of Latin American and Latino children. Their profound expositions on this topic deserve publication and dissemination.

ANTONIO MARTORELL's woodcut illustrations for Isabel Freire de Matos *ABC de Puerto Rico* were a powerful statement of Puerto Rico's nationalist pride and a source, at the time of publication, of both controversy and an enormous following. Although Martorell's career as a painter who is recognized worldwide and an author-illustrator of books for adults (*La piel de la memoria*) has not allowed him to illustrate many books for children, it is gratifying that he recently illustrated *Where the Flame Trees Bloom* by Alma Flor Ada and *The Song of the Coqui and Other Tales from Puerto Rico* by Nicholasa Mohr.

SIMÓN SILVA has inherited the boldness and strength of the Mexican muralists, particularly Diego Rivera's ability to present the people with tenderness, dignity, and respect. Drawing on his own experiences as the child of farmworkers, Silva has rendered the colors and images of life in the fields in *Gathering the Sun*, his first illustrated picture book. In this ABC of farmworkers' life, his full-spread paintings overlaid by poems in both English and Spanish by Alma Flor Ada, create a powerful rendition of the experiences and feelings of the migrant farmworkers and their families.

The art of two other Latino artists, CARMEN LOMAS GARZA and AMADO PEÑA, has become the basis for children's books. Carmen Lomas Garza developed a primitivist style to depict in full detail the life of her childhood in Texas. Some of these paintings became the basis for two bilingual autobiographical books, *Family Pictures/Cuadros de familia* and *In My Family/En mi familia*, in which the illustrations are accompanied by brief texts elaborating on the experience captured visually by the artist. Amado Peña gathered some of his paintings in the book *Peña on Peña*. Other paintings by Peña were collected by Juanita Alba in the book *Calor*. Using the motif of *calor* (warmth) in its many real and metaphorical meanings, the author wrote simple but poetic bilingual statements to accompany selected paintings by Peña.

In his prolific work, ENRIQUE O. SÁNCHEZ, originally from the Dominican Republic, has created a distinctive style, and his palette gives a Latino flavor to many books authored by Latinos (*Abuela's Weave*) and non-Latinos (*Saturday Market, Amelia's Road*). The tenderness of his renditions of children, the authenticity of the settings, and his playful use of color have made his illustrations very well received.

The art of MAYA CHRISTINA GONZÁLEZ is lively, with the colors and spirit of the barrio muralists. JOE CEPEDA captures the colors of these neighborhoods with vivid oil paintings that have been compared to those of Ezra Jack Keats. STEPHANIE GARCÍA used sculpture clay to create the outstanding scenes for *Snapshots from the Wedding* by Gary Soto.

Some outstanding Latino illustrators have illustrated mainly books by non-Latino authors. This is the case with BEATRIZ VIDAL and with FABIÁN NEGRÍN, who has created a most extraordinary rendition of the Argentinian gauchos and the pampa for the exquisite book *Gauchada* by C. Drew Lamm.

There are a few Hispanic illustrators who cannot be considered Latinos because they do not live and work in the United States, but who have illustrated extensively books by Latino authors and for Latino children and have thus become a part of this movement. They are, among others, LEOVIGILDO MARTÍNEZ, from Oaxaca, Mexico, whose whimsical art has received wide recognition, and VIVÍ ESCRIVÁ, ANA LÓPEZ ESCRIVÁ, PABLO TORRECILLA, and ULISES WENSELL from Spain.

Latino and non-Latino children alike deserve a literature that shares the rich Hispanic tradition of stories and folktales, nursery rhymes and songs, poetry and plays. They should have access to a literature that recognizes the rich Hispanic heritage of art, music, celebrations, and creations in all areas, outside and inside the United States. They need books that explore the complex reality of Latinos in the United States, that portray the many unknown heroes of our communities and show our multiple manifestations of a zest for life, friendship, and solidarity; the diversity of our families; the strength of our creativity; and our ever-varying, always creative approach to life, its hardships and demands, its possibility and hope.

3

ONCE UPON A WORLD

THE DIVERSITY OF LITERATURE

There are many literary forms that should have a well-deserved presence in the classroom: nursery rhymes and other forms of the traditional oral folklore, poetry, songs, plays, and narrative all have something important to offer, and none should be neglected.

Literature should permeate all aspects of the classroom and surround students throughout the day with its richness of thought and information, its enjoyment and inspiration. As was stated earlier, it is important that literature should not always be approached from a teaching mode; books should become good friends of children—always available, always trustworthy.

Many teachers have discovered the power of literature in its many forms as a classroom management tool and as an important element of their classroom environment. Good-quality songs greet the children as they enter the classroom, or the children engage in singing them as they change activities. A poem, a riddle, or a story can mark the end of a task, the morning, or the day or can be given as a reward for completing an individual project.

Chapter 4 of the book discusses how literature can be the cornerstone of the language arts development of students. The activities presented in its twelve sections can be applicable to any high-quality literature, regardless of its genre. In this chapter, some considerations concerning the use in the classroom of oral traditional folklore, poetry, music, and drama as well as the different forms of narrative will be presented.

ORAL TRADITIONAL FOLKLORE

Although the word *literature* etymologically refers to "letters" in every culture, literature began orally, sometimes many centuries before it began to be written. When speakers discovered that words could do more than convey meaning and share emotions, that they could be tools for aesthetic enjoyment, for joyful play, and for the exercise of the imagination and fantasy, literature was born. Myths to ponder the wonders of creation and the origin of life, legends to remember the history of a group or to explain the majesty of nature, ballads to sing heroic deeds, songs to accompany the planting and the harvesting of crops, or stories to help pass the long winter nights or to charm and entertain while handing on wisdom and advice—all these and many other forms of literary creation appeared all over the planet wherever there were speakers.

Originally, all would partake together of the same creations; later, children began to appropriate some fragments or variations as their own. Folktales were tamed to be less frightening for young audiences, fragments of ancient ballads became rhymes to sing while playing or while jumping rope.

The treasury of oral folklore can have many applications in the classroom. We will refer to folktales and fairy tales in the section on narrative and to nursery rhymes in the section on poetry and songs; here, the focus is on briefer forms of oral folklore: proverbs and sayings, tongue twisters and riddles.

These shorter forms of folklore make excellent writing samples. If students are to practice calligraphy and writing for spelling and punctuation, they will be more inclined to pay attention to what they write if it has meaning and is entertaining. Besides, students can be invited to create their own collections if they have notebooks or folders in which to write sayings, riddles, tongue twisters, and rhymes. Through this activity, they will understand the concept of an anthology and the work of someone who collects and edits folklore, as well as enjoy seeing the product of their own work.

Proverbs and Sayings

Because sayings are such an inseparable part of culture, students should come to know them, understand what they mean, and recognize how they are used. If you have Latino students or are trying to create an awareness of the Latino culture in your classroom, you may find useful the list of well-known Hispanic proverbs and sayings that appear in Appendix A.

Be sure to point out that, far from expressing absolute certainties, sayings merely reflect opinions about life stated over a long period of time. This is why some sayings convey the same idea in different words. For example, two well-known sayings in Spanish are *"En boca cerrada, no entran moscas"* ("No flies will enter a closed mouth") and *"El que mucho habla, yerra"* ("Whoever talks too much will make a mistake"). On the other hand, sometimes two sayings might seem to contradict each other—for example, *"A quien madruga, Dios lo ayuda"* ("The early bird gets the worm") and *"No por mucho madrugar amanece más temprano"* ("The sun will not rise earlier just because you get up"). In reality, the first suggests that is important to get up early and to be well prepared; the second, that rushing too much may not lead very far.

To bring an awareness to sayings, you can have a running list on a chart on the wall. Add new ones as appropriate occasions for their use appear or as they relate to a book being shared. You can draw or paste a star or a happy face next to a saying every time someone in the classroom uses it appropriately.

Riddles

Riddles are charming ways of playing with language and imagination. Traditional riddles may be based on the similarity of sounds in different words or in rhyme, thus requiring careful listening.

Some teachers create a treasure chest of riddles, copying them onto index cards and placing the answer on the reverse of the cards. They might have their students draw the answers or cut them out of old magazines and paste them. These riddles can be handed out to students as rewards for a job well done or timely accomplished or simply as treats.

Students can be encouraged to create their own riddles about a specific topic they are studying or about the theme or characters of a book.

Tongue Twisters

Tongue twisters are language games whose main purpose is to bring about laughter. Although they can be excellent for fostering listening skills and for the practice and recognition of certain sounds, they should be treated with caution when used with second-language learners, for whom they may be very difficult. It is important that a spirit of joy and laughter accompany them and that no child be made uncomfortable for not being able to say them right. Usually, if the teacher shows how hard it is for her or him to say a tongue twister and is willing to laugh at her or his own mistakes, they should go well.

POETRY AND SONGS

Poetry and children are natural friends. Poetry requires one to look at reality in a new way, and a child's view of the world is always new.

Very few gifts are as generous as the gift of a poem or a song. They are gifts that last for a lifetime. These gifts do not break or lose their shine; on the contrary, they keep enriching us every time we remember them, just as they did the first time. They accompany us through life wherever life may take us. When we have room to take nothing else, poems and songs, which require no space, will come with us.

Poetry and songs are not simply a repertoire of words and language structure. True poetry touches the spirit, expands and refreshes it. The words of a real poem can be savored. We feel their rhythm inside us, and as we marvel at the images they form, we learn to see life from different angles and we discover new hues in its colors.

Children and youth deserve a new poem and a wonderful new song each day—new poems and songs to savor and memorize, to learn and internalize until the poems and the songs are part of who they are. And so that the ones already known are not forgotten, children also deserve a few minutes each day to repeat and bring the poems and songs back to memory.

Poetry and her sister, the poetic song, are not only good friends of children, they can also be excellent friends of teachers. We all have a passive vocabulary that is much larger than our active vocabulary. This is why we can understand many words we hear or read and yet we might not use those words when we speak or write. Now here come poetry and song to familiarize us with new words and expressions. Once we have recited or sung a new word, phrase, or sentence, it will be much easier to make it part of our active repertoire, and our language will grow in wealth and strength.

Poetry and songs not only enrich our vocabulary and our soul, they can also contribute to learning throughout the day. A poem or a song can awaken a child who is sleepy, tired, or inattentive, and—wonder of wonders—poems and songs can also quiet down students who are too active. Teachers who choose poems and songs to mark the transitions of the day, to initiate or close a subject, find them excellent support.

Poetry can be a tool to practice handwriting, to develop good spelling, and to enrich vocabulary and language in general through the acquisition of new structures. Poems and songs that we have memorized are a language repertoire to which we can constantly return. They can also be very faithful friends.

Reading Poetry

There are very different styles of poetry; therefore, to approximate the poem, the reading needs to respect its form. Some poems require an intimate, delicate tone; others are rhythmic and joyful. Some are playful and filled with humor; others require a certain sobriety. In any case, reading should be natural, never affected or pedantic.

It is essential to explain to children that the pause at the end of a line or verse is a very brief one and should never break a sentence or a meaningful unit. When reading poetry, children should avoid stopping forcefully at the end of each verse; this is not what the rhythm of poetry suggests. The rhythm of the poem will be marked by many elements within the verses, not just the end of a line. To read all lines with the same intonation will sacrifice meaning and feeling.

Some teachers like to give poetry reading a special touch—for example, having a corner of the room dedicated to poetry, with poems on the walls, and using it for poetry readings. Others enjoy taking the children outside to read poetry under a tree. There are others who play instrumental music as a background to their reading; with this, they are also enriching the children's musical background.

Although all of these resources may be valuable, it is important not to make them a requirement, which might deter us from the main objective: ensuring that children have daily access to good poetry and poetic songs. The poems and songs in themselves will be able to enchant the students.

Sharing Songs

Music is one of the most important creations of human beings. Every culture in the world has found ways to make music and has incorporated music into the significant experiences of life. Song is the most essential musical expression, in which the human body itself is the instrument. All cultures have incorporated songs in their ceremonies—as part of their spiritual worshipping, of the planting and gathering of crops, and of ceremonies to celebrate births, coming of age, marriage, and in some cases even death. Songs are also individual vessels for expressing joy, longing, sadness, hope, and caring. The mother entrusts the child to sleep, leaving in the child's ears the soft echo of her lullaby. Children play to the sound of song. Lovers sing to each other and choose their special song.

Songs can convey thoughts and values, and promote action, unity, and solidarity. For the role of songs in the classroom to develop values of solidarity and social responsibility, see Peter Baird (2001). He talked with some of the most recognized songwriters and performers of folk songs for children about their role as developers of a social awareness and transmitters of hope. For the use of songs in Spanish in the classroom, see Ada and Campoy (1998d).

No one should hesitate to use songs for fear that they do not have sufficient musical training or are not good singers. Fortunately, technology enables every teacher to bring songs to the classroom through the use of cassettes and CDs.

Songs and poetry belong in every classroom, every day. They will enrich students' lives with words and images, with thoughts and values, and with the pleasurable experience of sound and rhythm. In making learning joyful, they will also make it meaningful and lasting.

PLAYS AND DRAMATIC GAMES

The benefits that plays can bring to education are innumerable and multifold. Besides the many benefits they bring to the students, plays and dramatic games are excellent tools for the teacher. They can help in clarifying concepts and making them alive, in sharing values and in bringing issues for dialogue and reflection. Furthermore, plays can facilitate and increase a positive home–school connection as parents and relatives come to school to see the performance of their children.

Benefits for the Students

Plays can offer students multiple benefits; some of them are as follows.

Improved Memory. Often, in the process of educational improvement, some changes can also bring about unnecessary losses because false dichotomies are established. Memory is a case at hand. In old-fashioned education, students frequently memorized things they didn't quite understand. This was detrimental. In the process of fostering comprehension, memorization has been discarded almost completely from education. This is a pity, because a good memory is a valuable resource. It need not be pitted against comprehension but should be seen as a complementary skill.

Poetry and theater are excellent ways of increasing memory power with valuable content. Students who exercise their memory in learning the lines of a play or the poem they will recite will later be in possession of a useful resource.

Enunciation, Articulation, and Voice Projection. The skill of speaking effectively in front of an audience is a valuable leadership tool. In any community, social or professional, to be called on to speak in front of an audience is a mark of recognition that the person has something special to offer.

Good public speaking is not reserved for politicians or public broadcasting; in any profession, to be able to address an audience is a way to share knowledge or ideas, to offer and defend a viewpoint, to support or request support for a good cause or a valuable project.

By participating in plays and dramatic games, students will develop ease not only in sharing memorized lines, but also in improvising in front of a group. They will also develop stronger enunciation skills and will learn to articulate clearly, give words adequate intonation, and project their voices.

Increased Self-Confidence. Dramatic games played in the classroom in a cordial and nurturing atmosphere can help even very shy children lose the fear of speaking to a group. When these activities are done on a regular basis, students grow in self-confidence. Teachers who embrace these activities are frequently surprised to see how some of the less outgoing students or some of the troublemakers improve in their behavior when given the opportunity of self-expression.

Development of Multiple Creative Expressions. Dramatic activities give teachers the possibility to motivate multiple forms of expression in their students. Although it is important to take care that all students have the opportunity to play an acting part, in even the simplest of performances, there also will be opportunities to decorate the stage, create posters announcing the play, or design a program.

The performance also provides room to collaborate in finding or creating the costumes and props. Students can also take responsibility for requesting permission from the principal's office to use the auditorium or cafeteria, sending invitations to the community or to other classes, and announcing the performance on the school PA system.

Development of Better Understanding of Self and Others. To perform a play, it is necessary to understand the feelings and circumstances of the protagonists. This offers an opportunity for class dialogue about personalities and human responses to situations as well as a deepening of the understanding of one's feelings and the feelings others may experience. As a consequence, students can grow in understanding, tolerance, compassion, and appreciation of self and others.

Development of a Spirit of Collaboration and Solidarity. Of the many benefits offered by theater, maybe the most important is precisely that it requires the collaboration of many. All students should be able to participate with the assurance that no task is too small and that all are essential for the success of the play.

A major consideration should be that promoting students' academic success does not result in pushing them toward a competitive race in which only some will succeed. Although we wish each child to develop to her or his fullest potential, it is important that this achievement be done not exclusively for personal gain but in solidarity with others, with the intent of facilitating growth and success for all participants.

Every school activity that promotes solidarity and collaboration, as theater does by making everyone feel important and necessary, will be a counterbalance to the selfish competitiveness promoted by a materialist society.

Development of a Creative and Innovative Spirit. Theater is an art in constant evolution, which takes many different forms. Inside the school, it is possible to improvise plays, do pantomime, use puppets, dramatize traditional tales, or turn a story into a play. It is possible to produce plays written by playwrights or to write one's own. It is possible to use a real stage with real curtains or put on the play in a classroom, with children announcing each of the acts. Actors can use costumes, dress in black leotards, or dress in everyday clothes. It is fine to have two or three students represent one character together, if they need that reassurance. Students can pantomime the actions to a recorded song or a series of songs, or they can record their voices and do the actions later. The play can be videotaped as performed on a stage, or a video camera can be used to make the play into a real movie, in which the actors change environment and outdoor and indoor shots are combined. There are really no more limits or restrictions than those one wants to impose.

Better Understanding and Retention of Curricular Materials.   When teachers invite their students to create a play to explain an area of the curriculum, the content takes on new meaning. For the play to be of interest, students need to gather information and understand the topic very well. The process incorporates all learning modalities.

Benefits for the Teachers

All that is beneficial to students will in turn benefit teachers. For example, the language development that is achieved through participating in plays and dramatic activities will contribute to greater comprehension on the part of the students, both in reading and in listening to the teacher.

Teachers also benefit from processes that increase students' sense of worth and well-being, because this is usually reflected in better behavior and higher academic gain.

Students who get used to collaborating effectively to produce a play will be better able to collaborate in other joint class projects.

Benefits for Home–School Interaction

The significance of good home–school interaction cannot be overstressed. An additional benefit of theater is awakening the parents' interest in participating in the school, making them feel welcome, and allowing them to see the validation of their children. If the play is performed in the heritage language of the parents or incorporates their cultural experiences, it will convey a message of dignity and worth.

Narrative and Other Forms of Prose

The first distinction that is essential is that not all books for children and adolescents are literature. Many are informative or entertaining; they have a purpose for existing, but they do not have the literary or artistic quality to be considered literature. In many cases, they are commercial objects directed to a particular market, just as toys or clothes for children and youth can be. It is important to have a clear understanding of this to avoid further confusion.

Although it is not difficult to distinguish books with literary and artistic merit from those that do not reach those standards, the differences between genres are not usually as distinct. Literary books in prose for children and adolescents represent a great diversity of topics and styles. Sometimes they can be easily classified as belonging to specific genres, but the genres are becoming more and more creative, and their limits are not absolute. A general classification that frequently used is fiction and nonfiction; nevertheless, contemporary books sometimes combine fictional and nonfictional content.

Nonfiction books can address every area of knowledge. They can be scientific in nature, presenting animal life, the environment, ecological issues, or astronomy, for example. They can also address issues of the social sciences: portraits of civilizations, the history of human achievements. There is really no topic that cannot be treated with enough care, originality, and quality to make an artistic nonfiction book.

Biographical and autobiographical books, while nonfictional in nature, constitute specific genres of their own. Again, we find that creativity sometimes stretches the traditional limits of these genres.

To make biographies more realistic and engaging, many times the biographer, while adhering to the major historical facts, chooses to imagine dialogues and small daily activities that could have taken place. Multiple literary devices can be used: The biography may be written in first person, presented in the form of letters or a diary, or narrated by a secondary character who was present at the time.

Autobiographical books can take the form of a continuous narrative that tells the full length of a lifetime or can be a collection of vignettes of specifically significant moments.

Within the realm of fiction, books could be grouped into fantasy and realism. The boom of the Latin American novel in the second part of the twentieth century originated a new form of narrative, known as magical realism, that is beginning to find its way into narratives for younger readers. Traditional forms of fantasy include fairy tales and folktales, legends and fables, modern-day fantasy, and science fiction.

In most instances, the realistic narrative is divided into historical fiction and contemporary fiction, the distinction being based essentially on the time of the story. This does not preclude a novel for young readers being set in two times, through parallel stories of a contemporary hero and an ancestor. In this case, the book would remain in the field of realism and yet be both contemporary and historical fiction.

Because many of the activities suggested in Chapter 4 of this book will be centered on narrative text, the previous reflections will assist in the characterization by genre of these texts and in clarifying how this characterization is not always rigid. Literature is an art. As such, it is innovative and ever changing—that is its privilege and certainly a great deal of its charm.

Literature in all its multiple manifestations has an important role in the classroom. The diversity of genres provides the opportunity of finding always what is appropriate for each moment to motivate and facilitate learning, to create a pleasant aesthetic environment that is supportive of growth, to discover new richness in the human spirit, and to make the classroom a lively space for discovery and reflection.

CHAPTER 4

USING THE MAGIC
LITERATURE IN THE CLASSROOM

This chapter discusses how literature can be used in the classroom to enrich all aspects of language development—listening, speaking, reading, and writing—from a Transformative Pedagogy perspective geared to the full development of the individual students and their collective awareness of their role as protagonists of their lives and constructors of their social reality.

To better describe the suggestions and examples offered, they have been grouped in twelve numbered sections:

1. Preparing to Share a Book
2. Reading the Book
3. The Creative Dialogue
4. Promoting Language Development
5. Promoting Discovery and Research
6. Promoting Creative Written Expression
7. Promoting Creative Visual Expression
8. Promoting Dramatic Expression
9. Home–School Interaction
10. Culminating Activities
11. An Author's Visit or Author's Study
12. Evaluation

Clearly, teachers are not expected to carry out all the activities presented in all twelve sections with any one book. The intention is to provide enough suggestions from which to choose those best suited to the book and the occasion.

1 PREPARING TO SHARE A BOOK

There are many ways of presenting a book to a class to awaken students' interest. In theory, no one way is better than another; yet some seem more appropriate for a certain kind of book, while others work for all kinds. Varying the procedures throughout the year will help to keep students' interest high.

Some teachers like to create a ritual around the reading of the book, whether by having a special place in the classroom assigned to reading aloud, by dimming the lights and reading by candlelight, by using a particular song or music, or by ringing a chime to signal that reading aloud time will begin. Others wear a special hat or shawl or hold a magic wand in their hand. A few go as far as dressing up like book characters. There is no end to teachers' creativity and therefore no end to ways to make reading seem and feel special.

Here are some other effective ways of preparing to share a book.

Sharing Experiences

In keeping with the principles of Transformative Education, which recognizes children as protagonists in their own lives, teachers must never fail to acknowledge the validity of their students' experiences.

A good way to bring a book and its readers together is to ask the students to share experiences they have had that are somehow related to the book. It is extremely valuable to have the teacher serve as a model by sharing his or her experiences with the group as well.

Teachers who wish to involve the parents in the totality of the education process, not only at selected moments, might want to announce to the students the topic to be read the next day and invite them to ask their parents to share their own experiences about the topic. The parents' experiences then become part of the students' preparation for encountering the topic.

EXAMPLES

For the Lower Grades (K–3)

- Ada, Alma Flor. 2002. *I Love Saturdays y domingos.* New York: Atheneum.
- Torres, Leyla. 1998. *Liliana's Grandmothers.* New York: Farrar, Straus and Giroux. (Also in Spanish: *Las abuelas de Liliana.*)

Tell children you will be reading a book that talks about grandparents (*I Love Saturdays . . . y domingos*) or about grandmothers (*Liliana's Grandmothers.*) Ask them to talk about their grandparents: *Do they have grandparents? Do the grandparents live close by or far away? Do all the grandparents speak only English or do any of them speak another language also or only another language? What do they enjoy doing with their grandparents? What do they know about their grandparents' history? If any of the grandparents live in the United States, were they born here? When and how did they come?*

Invite the children, either before or after reading the book, to talk with their parents about their own grandparents and the parents' grandparents.

The first of these two books compares two sets of grandparents: one Spanish-speakers and the other English-speakers. The second compares two grandmothers: one living in the United States and the other in South America. The books themselves can be compared with one another, an activity that can later lead to comparing and contrasting the children's own grandparents with the grandparents in the books.

For the Upper Grades (4 and up)

■ Ryan, Pam Muñoz. 2000. *Esperanza Rising.* New York: Scholastic.

Tell students they will be reading a novel about how Esperanza came to the United States from Mexico and about her special relationship with her grandmother. Proceed to elicit their knowledge about their own grandparents and their family history, and invite them to ask their parents for more information.

Recalling Previous Knowledge

Along the lines of the above-mentioned sharing of experiences, it is useful to try to find out what the students already know about a given subject, setting, or type of character. This activity is very appropriate for cooperative groups. The students in each group exchange information about what they know and then prepare a summary to share with the whole class.

EXAMPLES

For the Lower Grades (K–3)

■ Anderson, Joan. 1989. *The Spanish Pioneers in the Southwest.* Photography by George Ancona. New York: Lodestar/E. P. Dutton. (Also in Spanish: 1996. *Los pioneros españoles en el sudoeste.* Translated by Louis de la Haba. Orlando, FL: Harcourt.)

Explain to the students that you will be sharing with them a book that shows how Spanish-speaking people lived a long time ago in the Southwest. *What do they know about how Spanish-speaking people arrived at lands that are today the United States? Do they know anything about how they lived? What things were different then? What are some of the things Spanish-speaking families brought to this land? Animals? Plants? Knowledge?*
After reading the book, you will be able to help students distinguish what they already knew from what they have learned. You might want to read to them the *Josefina* books, mentioned in the following example, to give them additional contextual understanding of the times.

For the Upper Grades (4 and up)

■ Tripp, Valerie. 1997. *Meet Josefina: An American Girl.* New York: Scholastic. (Also in Spanish: *Así es Josefina,* translated by José Moreno.)

- Tripp, Valerie. 1997. *Josefina Learns a Lesson: A School Story.* New York: Scholastic. (Also in Spanish: *Josefina aprende una lección: un cuento de la escuela.* Translated by José Moreno.)
- Tripp, Valerie. 1997. *Josefina's Surprise.* New York: Scholastic. (Also in Spanish: *Una sorpresa para Josefina.* Translated by José Moreno.)

There are a number of misconceptions and much misinformation about the history of the Spanish-speakers in the United States. Engage students in sharing what they know. *When they hear the word "pioneer," who do they think of? Which do they think is the oldest state capital in the United States?*

After reading the Josefina books, the students can contrast what they previously knew with what they now know. You might want to make available the picture book mentioned earlier in this example, *The Spanish Pioneers in the Southwest*, to provide the visual images of the times.

Relating the Book to Previously Read Books or to the Author

Previously read books can be strong motivators to the sharing of a new book. Calling the students' attention to the fact that the book to be introduced has a similar topic, format, setting, or character to that of a well-known book can help set the stage. You might want to invite the students to look for similarities and differences between the two books.

When children are familiar with a particular author, telling them that the book to be read has been written by the same author will awaken their interest. An author's study carried on for a prolonged period or the preparation for an author's visit, whether real or simulated, will be a strong motivator for sharing the author's books. The eleventh section of this chapter "An Author's Visit or Author's Study," offers suggestions on how to do this.

EXAMPLES

For the Lower Grades (K–3)

- Campoy, F. Isabel. 2002. *Rosa Raposa.* Illustrated by Jose Aruego and Ariane Dewey. New York: Harcourt.

Invite the students to enjoy this hilarious trickster's tale by having them talk about other works of F. Isabel Campoy that they already know, whether poetry, songs, plays, or retellings of legends and folktales.

- Ada, A. F., and F. I. Campoy. 1996. *Ecos del pasado.* Orlando, FL: Harcourt.

Spanish-speaking students can read *La leyenda del maguey, La leyenda de Pitá-Morotí,* or *Los pies del inca* also by F. I. Campoy in this collection of Latin American legends and folktales.

For the Upper Grades (4 and up)

- Mohr, Nicholasa. 1994. *In My Own Words: Growing Up inside the Sanctuary of My Imagination.* New York: Julian Messner/Simon & Schuster.

Engage the students in recollections of *Felita* and other books of Nicholasa Mohr that they may have read, or have them read the books now as an introduction to her memoir.

Using Props

Many teachers find it both motivating and instructive to have on hand objects related to a topic or concept that is central to the book. There is virtually no limit to what these props can consist of: films, photographs, drawings, maps, animals, plants, fruit, toys, food, and the like.

You might show an object and then ask the students to describe it, drawing on the five senses. To help them sharpen their powers of observation, you might ask questions like these: *What form does it resemble? What color is it? How is it used? What sound does it make? What does it taste like? What does it smell like? How does it feel to the touch?* Or you might ask more specific questions, such as: *Is it hard (soft, rough, smooth, hairy, woolly, fluffy)?*

Another possibility is to hide the object, perhaps in a bag, before anyone has had a chance to see it. Invite the students to ask questions to discover what it is. They might ask, for example: *Is it natural or human made? If natural, is it vegetable, animal, or mineral? What color is it? What size is it? Where can it be found?* Depending on the grade level, you might limit the questions to one per student or to ten questions in all. You might also choose to show the object to a pair of students and allow them to be the ones answering the questions.

EXAMPLES

For the Lower Grades (K–3)

- Gary Soto. 1993. *Too Many Tamales.* Illustrated by Ed Martínez. New York: Putnam. (Also in Spanish: *¡Qué montón de tamales!* Translated by Alma Flor Ada and F. Isabel Campoy.)

What better way to introduce Gary Soto's charming book than bringing to class some tamales for the students to taste? But if bringing tamales proves to be too complicated, do not deprive the children of enjoying this book. Ed Martínez's pictures are a delight in themselves.

For the Upper Grades (4 and up)

- Castañeda, Omar S. 1993. *Abuela's Weave.* Illustrated by Enrique O. Sánchez. New York: Lee & Low. (Also in Spanish: *El tapiz de abuela.* Translated by Aída E. Marcuse.)

Handmade weavings as well as other handcrafts that could be found in a Latin American marketplace can be wonderful props to introduce this book about courage and a profound relationship between grandmother and granddaughter. Of course, any visual information about Guatemala would be also very appropriate.

Making Predictions Based on the Title

The title of the book itself is a good motivator. The students might discuss the words in the title and perhaps include them in a semantic map. (For suggestions on making such maps, see pages 97–100.)

Once the students have discovered the various meanings and connotations of the words in the title, encourage them to imagine what the book is about. Again, this is an activity that can be extended to the home by sharing the title the previous day and asking children to explore it with their parents or caregivers.

Because of its brevity, a title can only say so much. One of its purposes is to entice the reader to want to read the book. Have the students discuss whether this is better achieved when the title is very specific, when the title is intriguing, when it is unusual, when it has a ringing sound.

You might want to create a list of titles, including some suggested by the students, of books they have read, including some they have chosen on their own. Comment on the titles and invite the students to decide which of the titles are descriptive, which have a nice ringing sound, which would be easy or hard to remember, and which are particularly appealing to them.

Then discuss the title of the book you plan to introduce.

EXAMPLES

For the Lower Grades (K–3)

- Herrera, Juan Felipe. 2000. *The Upside Down Boy/El niño de cabeza*. Illustrated by Elizabeth Gómez. San Francisco: Children's Book Press.

Have the students talk about this title. *How could a boy be upside down? Would the author mean this literally? Have they ever experienced a moment when they felt "upside down"?*

For the Upper Grades (4 and up)

- Jiménez, Francisco. 1997. *The Circuit: Stories from the Life of a Migrant Child*. Albuquerque, NM: University of New Mexico Press.

Elicit students' opinions of what they think "The Circuit" might mean as a title before you give them the subtitle, "Stories from the Life of a Migrant Child." If none of the students are familiar with the migrant experience or the notion of traveling following the crops in a circuit, have them look the word up and ponder its various meanings as a preparation for reading the book. If some of the students have knowledge of the migrant experience, encourage them to share what they know.

■ Ada, Alma Flor. 1993. *Pregones*. Illustrated by Pablo Torrecilla. Beverly Hills, CA: Laredo. Colección Cuentos con Alma. (Other titles in this series include *Barquitos de papel, Barriletes, Días de circo,* and *Pin pin sarabín.*)

Do the students know what *pregones* are? If they do not, invite them to look the word up in the dictionary. Once they know that *pregones* are the callings of the street vendors, can the students imagine what a book with this name could be about? There are five books in this collection, each one a vignette of the author's childhood. Another word that might not be familiar to students is *Barriletes* ("Kites"). They will have no difficulty knowing what *Días de circo* ("Circus Days") and *Barquitos de papel* ("Paper Boats") mean. Can they predict from the title what any of those books may be about? And what about a title like *Pin, pin, sarabín?* Can they guess where it comes from? What effect does this title have?

Examining Illustrations or Text Selections

Another way of awakening interest in the book is to show some of the illustrations or share a selection from the text and then to ask the students, individually or in groups, what the book might be about.

EXAMPLES

For the Lower Grades (K–3)

■ Ada, Alma Flor. 1997. *The Lizard and the Sun/La lagartija y el sol*. Illustrated by Felipe Dávalos. New York: Doubleday.

Have the students look at the magnificent art of this book set in ancient México. *Can they tell by the illustrations where the story is set? Do they recognize this kind of monument (pyramid)? Do they know of a city (Tenochtitlán) where people moved about in canoes?* Because a great part of the story happened while the sun had disappeared, the coloring of the illustrations is very significant. Call the students' attention to it with questions like: *What do the coloring of the illustrations suggest?*

For the Upper Grades (4 and up)

■ Lomas Garza, Carmen. 1999. *Magic Windows/Ventanas mágicas*. San Francisco: Children's Book Press.

Show some of the intriguing illustrations to the students. *Can they guess how they have been made? Are they familiar with "papel picado," the art of cut-out paper?*
To give the students the opportunity to learn how to make papercutting illustrations, see the workbook in which the author explains the process: Carmen Lomas Garza. 1999. *Making Magic Windows: Creating Papel Picado/Cut-Paper Art*. San Francisco: Children's Book Press.

Drawing on Poetry, Song, and Folklore

Poetry and various forms of folklore, including sayings, riddles, rhymes, and tongue twisters, are effective ways of introducing a book. Besides, folklore provides many expressions for beginning and ending stories. You might want to combine these devices with one of those described above.

Songs, Poems, and Riddles.   Songs and poems make a good introduction to a narrative book. In the preceding chapter of this book, a case was made for the importance of presenting songs and poems for their own sake. They can also be wonderful tools to generate interest in a book.

It is a good idea to keep a running list of songs and poems related to the themes you know you would like to emphasize during the year, as well as of those related to the subject matter of books you frequently introduce to your students. You might also want to consider the possibility of making up a new song or poem to suit a particular occasion. It is easy to change the lyrics of a song to match the topic of a book you will be sharing if the students already know the melody. "La Bamba," "Cielito lindo," "Twinkle, Twinkle, Little Star," "Guantanamera," "Row, Row, Row Your Boat," and "De colores" all have melodies that invite new lyrics.

Whatever the song, it need not retell the whole story. All it has to do is introduce the book in such a way as to capture the students' interest. You might divide the song into several parts, singing the first part with the students before you read a portion or all of the book aloud and then going on to finish the song. Or you might make up only the first part of the song yourself, leaving the rest to the students once they have heard the story.

You might want to tell the students a riddle and, when they discover the answer, suggest reading a book whose subject is related to that answer. Or you might ask the students, individually or as a group, to make up and share riddles for which the answer is given. The students then read the book to find out how many of the elements mentioned in their riddles appear in the story.

EXAMPLES

For the Lower Grades (K–3)

- Ancona, George. 1994. *The Piñata Maker/El piñatero.* New York: Harcourt.
- Ada, Alma Flor. 1993. *The Empty Piñata.* Illustrated by Viví Escrivá. English translation by Rosa Zubizarreta. Miami, FL: Alfaguara. (Also in Spanish: *La piñata vacía.*)

To introduce these books about piñatas, present the children with a rhyme like the following:

"It's beautiful and filled with goodies,
but to enjoy it, we must destroy it."

As was mentioned above, songs can also be good introductions. For the topic *piñatas,* you could have the students learn the very lively song "Sube y baja" by

Isabel Campoy. The lyrics are very simple, so non-Spanish-speakers can also sing it. It can be found in Ada, A. F. and F. I. Campoy. (1998). *Corre al coro*. Westlake, OH: Del Sol. Música amiga 4. Book and cassette.

Sayings. You might tell the students a saying and join them in discussing its meaning and most appropriate use. Once they have given several examples of situations to which the saying applies, suggest reading a story to which it relates as well.

This is another approach: Present and discuss several sayings before reading the story aloud. Then ask the students to decide which saying best fits the story and why. The purpose of this activity is not to have them arrive at a single, preselected answer but to encourage them to reflect critically.

Eventually, the students themselves should be able to make up sayings that they believe best summarize the point of a story.

EXAMPLES

For the Lower Grades (K–3)

■ Ada, Alma Flor. 1995. *Mediopollito/Half-Chicken.* Illustrated by Kim Howard. New York: Dell.

Half-Chicken sets out to visit the court of the Mexican viceroy. On his way to Mexico City, he encounters several characters (Wind, Fire, and Water) who are in need of help. Later, when his adventures place him in great dangers, those he had helped will help him in return.

Discuss with the students different sayings that have to do with helping or being kind to others: *"Do unto others as you would like them to do unto you." "Haz bien y no mires a quien." "Hoy por ti, mañana por mí." "Arrieros somos, y en el camino andamos."*

For the Upper Grades (4 and up)

■ Kurusa. 1985. *Streets Are Free.* Illustrations by Monika Doppert. Copenhagen, Denmark: Annik. Translated from the Spanish by Karen Englander. (Also in Spanish: 1983. *La calle es libre.* Caracas, Venezuela: Ekaré/Banco del Libro.)

This highly acclaimed book shows very realistically how a group of children manage to create a playground for their neighborhood with the help of the community. It could be introduced with any saying that implies perseverance, never giving up, such as the Spanish sayings *"El que persevera triunfa"* and *"Quien la sigue, la consigue."*

Story Beginnings and Endings. Folklore provides many ways of beginning and ending stories. They can be used anytime, even if the book being read does not actually include them. Children are fond of such beginnings and endings, which help to create an atmosphere of magic and fantasy in which it is easy to suspend disbelief and enjoy the story to the utmost.

The beginnings and endings listed in Appendix B are among those used most often in Spanish-speaking storytelling. If some of your students speak Spanish, they will welcome the acknowledgment these familiar words would provide. These can also be a treat for non-Spanish-speakers, for whom they will add magic to the moment. Of course, you can also draw on your own repertoire of traditional story beginnings and endings in English.

EXAMPLES

Invite the students to look at the beginning and endings of these books. *Which are familiar to them? Which other forms have they heard when they have been told stories? Would they like to make their own beginnings and endings?* You might want to write all the traditional beginnings and endings the students know on one piece of chart paper and the ones they create on another piece.

Older students might want to research multiple retellings of folktales from various countries to create a multicultural list.

For the Lower Grades (K–3)

- González, Lucía M. 1997. *Señor Cat's Romance and Other Favorite Stories from Latin America.* Illustrated by Lulú Delacre. New York: Scholastic.
- Mohr, Nicholasa. 1995. *The Song of El Coquí and Other Tales from Puerto Rico/La canción del coquí.* Illustrated by Antonio Martorell. New York: Viking.

For the Upper Grades (4 and up)

- Delacre, Lulú. 1996. *Golden Tales: Myths, Legends, and Folktales from Latin America.* New York: Scholastic. (Also in Spanish: *De oro y esmeraldas: Mitos, leyendas y cuentos populares de Latinoamérica.*)
- Ada, Alma Flor, and Francisca Isabel Campoy. 1996. *Ecos del pasado.* Orlando, FL: Harcourt.
- Ada, Alma Flor, and Francisca Isabel Campoy. 1996. *Imágenes del pasado.* Orlando, FL: Harcourt.

Whatever form you use to prepare for the reading of a book, the ultimate goal is the same: to share the double message that reading is interactive and we bring our own life experiences to make the process richer and that reading is always enjoyable. When children have become good friends of books, just announcing that a book is to be shared will bring sparkles to their eyes and fill them with anticipation.

2 READING THE BOOK

There are many ways of reading a book with the class before going on to further exploration. Some external circumstances that will influence the choice are the students' age, level of maturity, and reading ability; the nature of the book; and even the number of copies available. Even more important will be the goals being pursued, because any choice made will have a different impact.

Transformative Education invites teachers to see in each student a protagonist, an author, a leader, and a teacher. Too frequently in the classroom, students are given only the opportunity to be followers, while all leadership roles are assumed by teachers. If the goal is that students see themselves as possible leaders, it is necessary for them to see themselves in the classroom limelight on a regular basis, not just sporadically. Although it is important that the teacher models good reading, it is equally important that she or he shares this important activity with the students.

Oral Reading

Oral reading is quite different from silent reading. Besides being a special skill in its own right, it has considerable social importance. Yet despite its value both as an art form and as a leadership tool, reading aloud in front of a group who do not have the text in front of them has been all but banished from students' practice in the classroom.

There are two main apparent reasons for the demise of oral reading. First, some educators believed that by doing away with it, they would strike a blow against the old-fashioned teaching of reading, which required students to utter mechanically and with little understanding the words printed in their books. Second, some well-intentioned educators wanted to protect students from making embarrassing errors while reading aloud.

The oral reading proposed here has nothing to do with the mechanical utterance of meaningless printed words. Rather, it is an artistic re-creation of the text, and such craftsmanship both demands and demonstrates comprehension. Moreover, those of us who favor the reinstatement of oral reading as a highly important skill are persuaded that the acquisition of reading and writing skills is part of an indivisible development process that stresses meaningful practice instead of toting up mistakes. The students should understand that they are expected to make mistakes, that doing so is a natural part of learning. They need never be embarrassed to read aloud, because achievement, not errors, will receive attention. No matter that the achievement is simply a student's standing before a group, book in hand.

There should be no doubt that oral reading is a leadership skill. Everyone would do well to master this skill; indeed, some professions, such as teaching and television or radio broadcasting, require it. More important, regardless of the field of work, those who are called on to address a group are the achievers, the people with something worth reporting or sharing. The fewer the occasions on which children can carry out socially significant activities away from school, the greater the need for the school to provide opportunities for practice.

Six possible modes of oral reading you might want to consider are described in the following sections. Rather than choosing one, the suggestion is to alternate them as much as possible during the year.

Oral Reading or Tape-Recording by the Teacher.   Few activities are more effective in promoting a love of reading than having the teacher read to the whole class often, daily if possible—to read enthusiastically, knowing that it is a gift and that no student is ever too old for the joy of being read to. What a delight teachers feel when, overcoming their own reticence and thinking only of the joy they can give their students, they dare to create different voices for the various characters, to keep a tempo that matches the narrative pace, and to utter each word in such a way as to convey its full meaning and emotion.

Some books are best read all the way through so as not to break the suspense. Others, usually longer ones, are best read a chapter at a time. In this kind of installment reading, the teacher might ask the students at the end of each chapter what they think will happen next. Then, before reading the next chapter, the teacher might ask the students to recall their predictions. However, it is generally not a good idea to interrupt the reading with too many explanations and comments; literary works have their own integrity, which is worth preserving.

A word about reading in languages other than English may be appropriate here. Many teachers of bilingual students hesitate to read to the students in their mother tongue for fear of not doing it well. This happens frequently with bilingual teachers who are reluctant to read to their students in Spanish. If only they realized that being unable to express themselves more frequently in Spanish is not their fault! If they are Latinos or Latinas, they might well have been subjected to humiliation for speaking their own language and been denied the opportunity to master it. If they are English-speakers, they should feel proud of their efforts to learn a second language, for this is an achievement ordinarily won at great cost in a society that has been very negligent in providing everyone with the richness derived from knowing several languages. Besides, whatever their origin, teachers will find few better ways to improve their Spanish than to read aloud to their students daily. This, of course, is also true of any other language.

Teachers who find themselves in this situation, instead of focusing on thinking that they do not read exceptionally well, can entertain two thoughts of a different kind: first, that practice will make them better readers, able to benefit their students even more later on, and second, that by making an effort to perform a difficult task, they are providing the students with an invaluable model right now. Students who see their teacher striving to acquire a second language will feel both validated in their efforts to learn English and enriched by the message that it is never too late to go on learning.

Some teachers prefer to tape-record the book. This allows them to experiment with different speech patterns and to enhance the text with sound effects, music, or both. The recording can be playing while the students look at the illustrations of the book. Later on, the students can reread the text while listening to the recording. Students are pleased to hear their teacher's recorded voice and to know that he or she took the trouble to make the recording especially for them.

Oral Reading or Tape-Recording by Another Adult.   It is important for students to listen to people other than their teacher. This allows them to become familiar with various speech patterns and styles.

Parents or other members of the community might be invited to read aloud to the whole class. To dispel any doubts about their ability, the teacher might first observe them reading to only one or two students. Many parents are very good readers, and inviting them to class is an effective way of validating their children's origin and culture.

Playing tape-recorded stories is another alternative for bringing diverse voices into the classroom. Commercial cassettes can be used, as can tape recordings made by parents or volunteers.

Oral Reading or Tape-Recording by One or More Students.   One basic objective of everything we do in the classroom is to build the children's self-esteem as much as possible, both to promote their overall growth as individuals and to help ensure their success in school. Another is to give the children an opportunity to develop leadership skills that are not easy to come by in their everyday lives.

It is therefore essential to take advantage of every occasion that allows students to speak individually before the entire class. Having a single copy of a book does not mean that only the teacher can read it aloud. It can mean that a student is given a chance to read the book to others, including the teacher. If necessary, this student might practice with the teacher beforehand. Thanks to the technological tools that can easily be made available, one or more students might tape-record a book before reading it to their classmates.

Students need not always read aloud before the entire class, of course. Cooperative groups can be organized to maximize the opportunities for individual oral reading. In this way, all the students can have a chance to read a book aloud even if only four or five copies are available.

Choral Reading.   When oral reading means choral reading, several readers can take part at the same time. Choral reading generally works best with cumulative tales or predictable stories and with certain poems. You might, for example, read all the narrative passages and let the students read the repetitive ones, whether these consist of a word, a phrase, or an entire stanza.

An alternative is to have all the students read together. In this case, do not allow the students to fall into the habit of mechanical, lifeless reading but instead encourage them to read dramatically, enthusiastically, and emphatically.

EXAMPLES

For the Lower Grades (K–3)

- Ada, Alma Flor. 1993. *In the Cow's Backyard.* Illustrated by Viví Escrivá. English translation by Rosalma Zubizarreta. Miami, FL: Alfaguara. (Also in Spanish: *La hamaca de la vaca.*)
- Mora, Pat. 1998. *Delicious Hullabaloo/Pachanga deliciosa.* Illustrated by Francisco X. Mora. Houston, TX: Arte Público Press.

For the Upper Grades (4 and up)

- Darío, Rubén. *Marguerite.* Illustrated by Waldo Saavedra. Translated by Alice Stone Blackwell. In Alma Flor Ada and F. Isabel Campoy. 2001. *Curtains Up!* Miami, FL: Alfaguara. 2001. (Also in Spanish: *Margarita.* In *Tablado de doña Rosita.*)

The classical poem by the Nicaraguan poet Rubén Darío will leave musical-sounding words resonating in the students' spirit. It lends itself to many types of readings, including choral reading by older students.

Dramatic Reading or Readers' Theater. Although dramatic reading is similar to choral reading in that several readers take part, it is different in that the readers do not read the text in unison; instead, each takes a separate part of the dialogue as narrator or one of the various characters.

It is, of course, possible to combine choral and dramatic reading. This would mean having given sections of the text or dialogue read by a group rather than by an individual student.

EXAMPLES

For the Lower Grades (K–3)

- Campoy, F. Isabel. *The Three Little Goats.* Illustrated by Gloria Calderas. In A. F. Ada and F. I. Campoy, *Rat-a-Tat-Cat.* 2001. Miami, FL: Alfaguara.

This original play will give six students the opportunity to read a part each, or you can divide the students into six groups, and each group will read a part.

For the Upper Grades (4 and up)

- Anaya, Rudolfo. 1999. *My Land Sings: Stories from the Río Grande.* New York: Morrow Junior Books.
- Loya, Olga. 1997. *Momentos mágicos. Magic Moments: Tales from Latin America Told in English and Spanish.* Little Rock, AK: August House Publishers.

Individual students can select different tales and prepare to read them dramatically to the class. Suggest that standing up with the legs somewhat apart for balance, looking into the audience's eyes, and pausing for effect will contribute to the success of their reading. To encourage public speaking, you can ask a different student to introduce the reader and the tale. For that, the student should interview the reader, to be able to tell something about him or her that perhaps most students in the class do not know. Also, the introducer should read the tale beforehand to be able to say something about it to awaken the listeners' interest.

Paired Reading.   The time allocated to reading practice can be maximized if the students are encouraged to read in pairs. Most students feel more comfortable initially reading to a partner than to a large group. Indeed, paired reading can be a very meaningful experience, for each reader has a real listener who is generally well-disposed to be attentive.

Paired oral reading by students from different grade levels can produce good results. First, it allows the older children to read stories that their younger listeners could not read on their own. Second, it gives the younger children a chance to practice reading to listeners whose attention is undivided. Both feel special and important.

Although commercially produced books can of course be read, so can books authored by the students themselves. A nice touch is to encourage each partner to write, and then read aloud, a book in which the other is the central character or in which both interact. For more about authoring and publishing books see *Authors in the Classroom* (Ada & Campoy, 2003).

EXAMPLES

Almost any book could be appropriate for this purpose. Here are some titles the students will surely enjoy.

For the Lower Grades (K–3)

- Moretón, Daniel. 1997. *La Cucaracha Martina: A Caribbean Folktale*. New York: Turtle Books.
- Soto, Gary. 1995. *Chato's Kitchen*. Illustrated by Susan Guevara. New York: Putnam. (Also in Spanish: *Chato y su cena*. Translated by Alma Flor Ada and F. Isabel Campoy.)

Silent Reading

We would like to mention two kinds of silent reading here. Each has its place in the classroom. In the first, students read silently a text—story, poem, play, and so on—that is about to be discussed in class. The second kind of silent reading is recreational. Although the activities presented in this section of the book are focused on books shared by the class, we must never forget that students ought to be given ample opportunities to encounter books on their own by reading books of their own choice. It is a good idea to set aside a period every day for independent reading. At the start of this period, the teacher should remind the students that pleasurable moments await them. Indeed, by silently reading a book along with the students, the teacher serves as a valuable role model. You might want to have classical music playing softly while the students are reading and enjoy your own reading alongside them.

The bibliography on books by Latino writers will give you an ample selection of books to incorporate into your classroom library for students to select quality books for their own enjoyment.

3 THE CREATIVE DIALOGUE

Traditional schooling tends to be text centered. Paulo Freire (1970, 1982) described it as "banking education," because the teacher, relying on information in the textbook, "deposits" facts in the students much as one deposits money in a bank account. The assumption is that the act of reading is completed the moment the reader has absorbed what the text has to say. Reading ability is thus measured in terms of literal comprehension: Can the student repeat what is written in the text?

In Transformative Education, by contrast, the goal is not merely to transmit information but to help students analyze that information in light of their personal experiences, reflect on it critically, and then incorporate it into their own concepts of reality. In other words, reading is far from being simply a conduit of information; it becomes a dialogue, however silent, between the reader and the text.

This approach to reading, which I call Creative Reading (Ada, 1988, 1991) and described in the first section of this book, begins but surely does not end with the text. Instead, the reading experience continues until the reader has reflected on the information provided in the text and, in a sense, has come to a new set of terms with reality. It might indeed continue to inform the growth process of the reader for the rest of her or his life. Accomplished readers, who are likely to view life critically, go through this process almost automatically. However, because they are still unsure of their identity, unaware of their potential, or trapped in passive schooling, some children may never have a chance to discover Creative Reading.

In our effort to give these children access to the full power of reading, nothing is more important than helping them realize the extent to which reading can affect their whole lives. To this end, it is advisable to follow the act of reading with a Creative Dialogue in which the students discover how reading can enrich them by giving them greater self-awareness and greater understanding of others, a more realistic view of the world, and the ability to use what they have learned in making meaningful changes in their own lives.

The Creative Dialogue is carried out simply and naturally. It is a conversation of interest to the teacher and students alike, not a question-and-answer session in which the teacher knows the single correct answer to each question. In the lively exchange of ideas, open-ended questions are raised, various alternatives are suggested, and the conclusions reflect the views of the individual students themselves.

A four-phase series of questions come into play. In a real dialogue, of course, the phases overlap and the questions are interrelated. Here, however, each phase is presented separately in order to identify and stress its importance.

Descriptive Phase

Approaching the text, the readers discover what the text has to say. At this moment, the traditional questions—Who?, What?, When?, Where?, How?, and Why?—find their answers.

The students delve deeper into the text as they are encouraged to find such elements as recurring words, images, and metaphors, as well as to identify the point of view of the narrator.

Personal Interpretive Phase

After assimilating the information given in the text, the readers can be expected to react by expressing their own feelings and emotions. In the Creative Reading approach, the students should be made to feel that they too are protagonists and that their personal experiences are valid and important.

Questions along the lines of *Have you ever seen (experienced, felt) something similar? How would you feel if what happened to the character should happen to you? and What would you do?* are designed not only to validate the students' personal experiences, but also to make it clear that the act of reading, like the act of learning itself, begins when new information is placed in the context of previously acquired knowledge.

At this stage, it is important that students compare and contrast the new information with what they already have and the characters' experience and reality with their own. *How are they similar? How are they different?*

Critical/Multicultural/Antibias Phase

The information that the students have received and viewed in light of their own experience is now subjected to critical analysis. In this phase, it is important that students realize that every situation has different potential outcomes and that they must be aware of the likely consequences of the various alternatives if they are to choose freely among them.

The questions are generally of this kind: *What other possibilities exist? What would their consequences be? Who could benefit (or suffer) from each one? Are they all logical, healthy, just, generous? How would people of a different culture, age, place, time, genre, or social class react to this? Are all points of view, all voices, recognized? Are some silenced or ignored?*

Besides developing critical reflections, such questions will help the students understand that attitudes vary because of people's circumstances and that we should be aware that others may have attitudes and beliefs that are different from ours but equally deserving of respect. These reflections should have a goal of encouraging the students to learn about others and to develop understanding of and appreciation toward them as well as to build solidarity with members of other groups.

Creative/Transformative Phase

The culmination of the reading process is reached when the students see a connection between their own lives and the thoughts and feelings to which the text has given rise and then consider taking actions and adopting attitudes that will enrich and improve their own lives.

EXAMPLES

For the Lower Grades (K–3)
Maurice Sendak's widely celebrated book *Where the Wild Things Are* has been selected to demonstrate the dialogue questions for two reasons. First, because it is known to most readers, it will make the example clearer. Second, it shows that even a book with short text and addressed to the very young child offers the opportunity for rich dialogue.

- Maurice Sendak. 1963. *Where the Wild Things Are.* New York: Harper Collins. (Also in Spanish: 1984. *Donde viven los monstruos.* Translated by Agustín Gervás. Madrid: Alfaguara.)

Descriptive Phase
To lead the students to retell the story and show their understanding of the text.

1. Why was Max's mother upset at him?
2. How did she punish him?
3. How did Max get to the land of the wild things?
4. Why did the wild things choose him as king?
5. Why did he decide to return home?
6. Observe the book illustrations. Notice how they become larger and larger until all the white margins disappear. When does that happen? What does it mean?

Personal Interpretive Phase

To lead the students to become aware of their feelings and emotions and to discuss their own experiences in relation to the text.

1. Have you misbehaved sometimes? What happened? How did you feel afterward?
2. Do your parents ever punish you? Do they punish you in a way similar to the way Max's mother punished him?
3. Have you ever wanted to run away? Where would you go?
4. If you could go in a boat to a wild place, as Max did, what would it look like there?

Critical/Multicultural/Antibias Phase

To lead to critical reflection and examine the book in view of Transformative Education's tenets of justice and equality.

1. Max was sent to bed without dinner. Would your parents send you to bed without dinner? Would they punish you in a different way?
2. Max told his mother, "I'll eat you up!" Do you think Max meant what he said? Why do you think he said such a thing?
3. Max's mother had called him "Wild thing!" So he decided to go where the wild things are. What can happen when we call people nasty things?
4. After two people have called each other names, it is not easy for them to like each other again. What can be done?
5. Max could have remained as the king of all wild things, but he decided to return home. What would you have done? Why?

Creative/Transformative Phase

To encourage students to see themselves as protagonists of their own lives and promote creative transformative attitudes.

1. What are some things you do that upset your parents? What can you do about it?
2. What can you do if someone calls you names? What can you do if you hear someone else calling somebody names? What can you do if you have called someone names?
3. When Max felt wild, he was able to visit the place where wild things are. Later, he felt much better. What can you do when you feel angry or upset? What can you do if you see that someone else is feeling upset or sad?

For the Upper Grades (4 and up)

■ Anzaldúa, Gloria. 1993. *Friends from the Other Side/Amigos del otro lado*. Illustrated by Consuelo Méndez. San Francisco: Children's Book Press.

In this picture book for students of all ages, Prietita, a brave Mexican-American girl, befriends Joaquín, a young boy who has crossed the river with his mother to try to find work in the United States. She defends him from the other children who tease him by calling him "wetback," and she helps him find a place to hide from the Border Patrol.

The book addresses a profound social issue. Many immigrants who have suffered discrimination and difficulties in being accepted and integrated into a society tend to, in turn, oppress the newly arrived immigrants.

As was mentioned in Chapter 2, several reasons may explain this generalized phenomenon: The internalization of oppression causes those who have been oppressed to imitate the actions of the oppressor. Newly arrived people constitute competition for low-paying jobs. The assimilated immigrant or descendant of immigrants might feel embarrassment because the newly arrived immigrant often does not know the language and customs of the place and may besides be very economically disadvantaged. The groups may have immigrated at different times and constitute members of different social classes. The assimilated, feeling themselves superior, might believe they will get "tainted" or that outsiders will consider them the same as the newly arrived immigrants. The assimilated might also feel some unconscious jealousy at the newly arrived immigrants' fluency in the heritage language and closer ties to the heritage culture.

Whichever the reason or combination of reasons, the resulting effect is very detrimental. Harboring feelings of superiority with regard to other human beings is self-destructive, as is the lack of compassion or solidarity. The gang phenomena that are prevalent in some Latino, Asian, Southeast Asian, and Pacific Islander communities are often related to this rivalry between assimilated and newly arrived groups. Gloria Anzaldúa addresses these issues in *Friends from Other Side* at a level appropriate for children.

Descriptive Phase
To lead the students to retell the story and show their understanding of the text.

1. In which ways did Joaquín look different from the other children?
2. How did the other children treated Joaquín?
3. What did Prietita do to protect him?
4. Why do you think she challenged the others?

Personal Interpretive Phase
To lead the students to become aware of their feelings and emotions and to discuss their own experiences in relation to the text.

1. Have you ever been teased for being different in any way? How did it make you feel?
2. Have you ever seen someone else being teased? How did it make you feel? Were you too embarrassed or afraid to stop the teasing?
3. Do you know people who have come to this country very recently? What are some of the difficulties they face?

Critical/Multicultural/Antibias Phase
To lead to critical reflection and examine the book in view of Transformative Education tenets of justice and equality.

1. What causes people to immigrate? What are some of the sufferings connected with immigration? What are some of the things people lose or give up when they immigrate? What are some of their hopes?

2. There are many reasons why people tease or discriminate against other people. Some have to do with the way others look, speak, dress, or show their feelings. Are any of these reasons valid? Why or why not?

3. Who were the original inhabitants of the United States? Could it be said that everyone else is an invader? What is most helpful to the nation: that people cooperate or that they fight with each other?

4. What would be some reasons why it is valuable and important for people to maintain the language of their ancestors?

Creative Transformative Phase
To encourage students to see themselves as protagonists of their own lives and promote creative transformative attitudes.

1. What can we do to interrupt the teasing when someone is being called names or made fun of?

2. Is there someone in the class or in the school who is a newly arrived person? How can we make that person feel welcome and appreciated?

3. Are there students who tend to be picked on by others? Without naming those students, what decisions can we make to get to know them better and discover their good qualities so that we can learn to appreciate them?

4. What would you like other people to know and appreciate about you?

There needs to be time and place in the classroom to lead students to reflections that can open the way to more supportive attitudes toward each other. An excellent demonstration of how this can be accomplished in the class appears in the PBS documentary "Oliver Button Is a Star," featuring Tomie de Paola's beloved book. The video can be obtained from the TCGMC-Oliver Project, 26 Ayers Rd., Monson MA 01057; (www.oliverbuttonisastar.com).

4 PROMOTING LANGUAGE DEVELOPMENT

Good literature is an excellent tool for the development of language at any developmental stage. There is no better way to develop language than to use it. Students need to hear the sounds of words and glean their meaning through attentive listening; they need to read and be read to extensively; they need to play with words, their multiple meanings, their sounds, and the rhythm that can be created with them; and they need the opportunity to develop their own voice in spoken and in written form.

Language needs to be used in real situations, for authentic and meaningful purposes, and in a variety of circumstances if its whole range of possibilities is to be made accessible to the students.

All the activities suggested in this book are, in a sense, activities for developing language. This chapter emphasizes vocabulary building and expressive language skills.

Relating a Story to a Saying

Sayings are pithy expressions of wisdom or truth that have stood the test of time. Because many stories convey a message, a connection can sometimes be made between them and a popular saying. After sharing a story with the students, you might give them several sayings and ask them to choose the one that best fits the main idea. Or you might encourage the students to make up an original saying. For these activities, you might want to draw on the list of sayings included on Appendix A.

EXAMPLES

For the Lower Grades (K–3)

■ Alma Flor Ada. 2001. *With Love, Little Red Hen.* Illustrated by Leslie Tryon. New York: Atheneum.

In this collection of letters between well-loved storybook characters, the story of Little Red Hen takes new, unsuspected turns.

Invite students to identify sayings that could apply to this book. For example, "Birds of a feather flock together" applies to the way in which the characters are divided between hard-working and lazy. "A friend in need is a friend indeed" applies to the help Little Red Hen received from Little Red Riding Hood and her friends.

Encourage everyone to make up a saying to summarize an idea in the book. Because the answers will be the students' own creation, they will vary greatly. Some might be along the line of:

"Whoever doesn't work, doesn't eat."
"If you don't cooperate, don't expect a reward."
"Hard work provides great joy."
"Good friends help each other."

Retelling a Story from Another Point of View

Students often enjoy retelling a story to one or more listeners if they are invited to adopt another point of view. This activity can be done orally or in writing, depending on the grade level of the class and the purpose you have in mind.

The students might want to use the first person, as though they were a principal or secondary character. And they might want to tell the story in the present tense as if it were just taking place.

Deciding who the listener is to be will give greater immediacy to the storytelling.

EXAMPLES

For the Lower Grades (K–3)

Have the students retell well-loved traditional stories from new points of view. For example, Cinderella's story could be told from these points of view:

Cinderella telling her children how she met their father, when he was a prince

The bewhiskered rat telling his grandchildren what happened the night he fell into a trap and ended up an elegant coachman

Two of the gray mice reminiscing about the night they became sleek horses

A lizard telling his friends that he was once a chamberlain dressed in a gold-trimmed robe

The prince telling his daughter how he met her mother and how they were married

One of the stepsisters trying to blame the other for everything that happened

The fairy godmother telling of her joy in helping Cinderella

For the Upper Grades (4 and up)

- Ada, Alma Flor, and F. Isabel Campoy. 2000. *Paths: José Martí. Frida Kahlo. César Chávez.* Miami, FL: Alfaguara. Collection Gateways to the Sun. (Also in a Spanish version: *Caminos.*)

- Ada, Alma Flor, and F. Isabel Campoy. 2000. *Steps: Rita Moreno. Fernando Botero. Evelyn Cisneros.* Miami, FL: Alfaguara. Collection Gateways to the Sun. (Also in a Spanish version: *Pasos.*)

- Ada, Alma Flor, and F. Isabel Campoy. 2000. *Voices: Luis Valdez. Judith F. Baca. Carlos J. Finlay.* Miami, FL: Alfaguara. Collection Gateways to the Sun. (Also in a Spanish version: *Voces.*)

- Ada, Alma Flor, and F. Isabel Campoy. 2000. *Smiles: Pablo Picasso. Gabriela Mistral. Benito Juárez.* Miami, FL: Alfaguara. Collection Gateways to the Sun. (Also in a Spanish version: *Sonrisas.*)

After reading biographies of recognized Hispanic figures, the students can be encouraged to write the biography of a selected figure of the Hispanic world as an autobiography or as if told by a brother or sister or a close friend of the person.

Retelling a Story in Another Setting or Time

The retelling can be done by placing the story in another environment, bringing it to a more contemporary setting, to a different place, or enriching it with cultural elements from the student's own culture.

EXAMPLES

For the Lower Grades (K–3)

- Salinas, Bobbi. 1998. *The Three Pigs/Los tres cerdos: Nacho, Tito and Miguel.* Spanish version by Amapola Franzen and Marcos Guerrero. Alameda, CA: Piñata Publications.

Students of all ages will enjoy finding the numerous details from the Latino culture hidden in the whimsical illustrations of Bobbi Salinas's retelling of the story of the three pigs in a contemporary Southwestern setting.

For the Upper Grades (4 and up)

- Presilla, Maricel E. 1994. *Feliz Nochebuena, Feliz Navidad. Christmas Feasts of the Hispanic Caribbean.* Pictures by Ismael Espinosa Ferrer. New York: Henry Holt.

This nonfiction book describes the various celebrations of Christmas in Cuba, Puerto Rico, and the Dominican Republic through the memories of the author's own childhood.

    Invite your students to write their own description of Christmas or other particular cultural celebrations in their family and their own recollections of memorable moments during the holidays. They could also add memories narrated to them by their parents, relatives, or caregivers.

Retelling Using a Different Literary Genre

Another way of giving originality to a retelling is to change the literary genre or style. The same story or the same topic or characters can be approached from many different perspectives, thanks to the richness of literature and the unlimited possibilities of creativity. Reflecting frequently on this freedom will help to convey to the students that they have the potential to look at life creatively. One of the basic principles of Transformative Education is the idea that whatever difficulties the students' present reality may hold, they have the potential to transform it.

EXAMPLES

For the Lower Grades (K–3)

- Ada, Alma Flor. 1993. *Dear Peter Rabbit.* Illustrated by Leslie Tryon. New York: Atheneum. (Also in Spanish: *Querido Pedrín.*)
- Ada, Alma Flor. 1998. *Yours Truly, Goldilocks.* Illustrated by Leslie Tryon. New York: Atheneum.
- Ada, Alma Flor. 2001. *With Love, Little Red Hen.* Illustrated by Leslie Tryon. New York: Atheneum.

The stories of Peter Rabbit, Goldilocks and the Three Bears, Little Red Riding Hood, the Three Little Pigs, and the two hens—the Little Red Hen and the Little Hen Who Liked to Saw—are intertwined in these books written exclusively in letter format.

After enjoying unraveling all the old stories and seeing their new development and how the characters meet and develop friendships with one another, students can decide which characters they would like to combine in their own telling and which style they would like to choose for it.

For the Upper Grades (4 and up)

- McKinley, Robin. 1997. *Rose Daughter.* New York: Greenwillow Books.
- McKinley, Robin. 2000. *Spindle's End.* New York: Greenwillow Books.

Robin McKinley has created a genre all her own, transforming traditional fairy tales (Beauty and the Beast and Sleeping Beauty) into full-length novels with extraordinary descriptions and profound depth of character that provoke reflection. In the words of *Publisher's Weekly,* she creates a "heady mix of fairy tale, magic and romance that has the power to exhilarate." Because of the universality of the fairy tales, and the uniqueness of her style it is a perfect example here. After reading either of these books, students could attempt to follow McKinley's inspiration and expand a story into a fuller narrative.

- Campoy, F. Isabel. *La Cenicienta—versión desempolvada.* In A. F. Ada and F. I. Campoy. 1996. *Ensayo general.* Orlando, FL: Harcourt.
- Campoy, F. Isabel. *Busco un socio para mi negocio.* In A. F. Ada and F. I. Campoy. 1996. *Saludos al público.* Orlando, FL: Harcourt.

Two traditional narratives, the fairy tale of Cinderella and the fable of the Mouse and the Mountain, have been transformed into plays by Francisca Isabel Campoy. Cinderella is a contemporary girl who wins a radio contest that provides her with a limousine, due back at midnight, to a ball where she meets the "King of Rock." It will not be a slipper that helps him find her again, but being able to repeat the last words she said on leaving the ball. The mouse of the fable has been changed into a little mole who sets up an excavating business threatening the mountain's majesty but remains unassumingly ignorant of his own power.

After enjoying these plays, students can decide what genre they would like to use for their retelling and in which way they might want to change the setting and characters.

Writing about the Same Topic or Character Using a Different Literary Genre

An extension of the previous activity is to look at how the same topic can be approached in different genres by the same author or different authors.

The contributions of César Chávez to the farmworkers' struggle to achieve the basic human rights granted other workers not only resulted in bettering the inhumane conditions of work in the fields, but also became a source of inspiration for all Latinos. It is not surprising that his life should be honored today in many ways, including writings that bring it closer to youth.

EXAMPLES

For the Upper Grades (4 and up)

- Ada, Alma Flor and F. Isabel Campoy. 2000. "César Chávez." Illustrated by Felipe Dávalos. In *Paths*. Miami, FL: Alfaguara. Collection Gateways to the Sun. (Also in a Spanish version: *Caminos*.)
- Ada, Alma Flor. 2001. *Gathering the Sun*. Illustrated by Simón Silva. New York: Harper Collins. (*Gathering the Sun*. CD album. Westlake, OH: Del Sol.)
- Anaya, Rudolfo. 2000. *Elegy on the Death of César Chávez*. Illustrations by Gaspar Enríquez. El Paso, TX: Cinco Puntos Press.

You might want to have the students read César Chávez's biography as it appears in *Paths/Caminos* or read or listen to the poem/song "César Chávez" from *Gathering the Sun* and then read the extraordinary elegy written by Rudolfo Anaya. Invite the students to reflect on how the same person can inspire different authors to create very different works in different genres. Invite the students to see these works as complementing each other rather than in competition, because they are all responses to the same inspiration. Have the students reflect on what each genre and style contributes to each literary piece. Also invite them to look at the work of the different artists: the portrait by Felipe Dávalos; the bold painting of Simón Silva, reminiscent of the Mexican muralists' work; and the very rich art of Gaspar Enríquez, filled with symbolism. Let the students express how each of these artists moves them, again emphasizing that it is a matter not of choosing one above the others, but rather of being able to enjoy the work of each one in its uniqueness.

Building a Word Treasury

A word treasury is a good way of sharpening the students' listening skills while building their vocabulary. After reading a story with the entire class or with a smaller group, ask everyone for a special word that he or she remembers. Write the words on the chalkboard or a sheet of chart paper as they are called out. Once everyone has volunteered one word, ask for a second word and then a third. Continue until the students have given as many words as they can.

To produce all these words, the students must recall the story in detail by retelling it to themselves, and this is an excellent exercise in itself. In the future, they will probably listen to stories more attentively.

By being able to recall and reproduce the words, the students assimilate them into their vocabulary. The words thus become a valuable tool that can be used in a number of contexts.

The words will be easier to handle if you or the students copy them onto cards or slips of paper. For many activities, at least two cards showing the same word will be needed.

To make the cards more attractive, you might cut them out of construction paper in the shape of a recognizable object or character in the book—for example, a green *coquí* (the Puerto Rican tree frog) to represent *The Song of the Coquí and Other Tales of Puerto Rico/La canción del coquí* by Nicholasa Mohr, a basket for *A Birthday Basket for Tía* by Pat Mora, a feather for Antonio Hernández Madrigal's *Blanca's Feather,* or a *farolito* for *The Farolitos of Christmas* and *Farolitos for Abuelo* by Rudolfo Anaya.

You might want to display the cards in the classroom, retaining the original shape of each card but on a larger scale. This way, the words will be visible whenever they are needed for a language activity. (For an example of displayed word treasure cards, see Figure 4.1.)

Students in the lower grades can do the following:

- Match cards whose words begin with the same letter or syllable
- Match cards whose words end with the same letter or syllable
- Match cards whose words are the same
- Match cards whose words rhyme

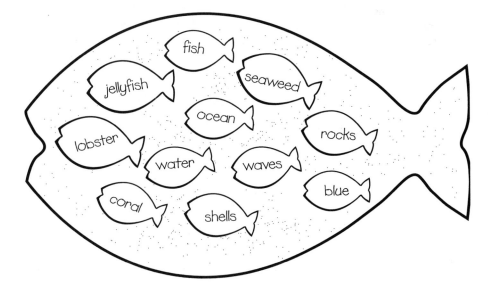

FIGURE 4.1 A Displayed Word Treasury

- Arrange cards according to the alphabetical order of their words
- Make up a sentence using some of the words on cards they are given
- Make up a story using all the words on the cards they are given

Students in the upper grades can do the following:

- Find cards whose words are synonyms, antonyms, or homonyms
- Find cards whose words belong to the same word family or have the same root
- Find cards whose words have prefixes or suffixes
- Find cards with compound or derived words
- Make up a story using all the words on the cards they are given

Using Charts and Diagrams

Charts and diagrams are good ways to awaken the students' interest in words, to expand their vocabularies, and to help them retell and analyze stories. Among the many such word-building devices you can choose from, the most popular are semantic maps or spiderwebs, Venn diagrams, flowcharts, and tree diagrams. By using their creative imaginations, teachers can arrange the information so that it is not only useful but also interesting to the students. For example, a train can offer a compelling way to show how the various elements of a story are linked. The engine can be labeled TITLE and AUTHOR; the cars in turn can be labeled SETTING, CHARACTERS, PROBLEM, MAJOR EVENTS, SOLUTION, and ENDING (see Figure 4.2). Of course, many other designs can also be used.

As a follow-up to the reading, these graphic devices are an excellent preparation for students' activities for creative expression. However, if you believe that the students will not be able to comprehend a certain story unless they are already familiar with the vocabulary or concepts, you might want to start out with one of the semantic maps or diagrams.

FIGURE 4.2 A Diagram for Story Analysis

Wide reading is probably the best way to develop one's word stock. It is by repeatedly coming across words in context that we gradually and effortlessly determine their meaning and thus make them a part of our active vocabularies. We must not allow vocabulary building to take on such importance that it comes between the students and what they read or interferes with their enjoyment of a book as a literary work. Nor should we permit our own semantic bent to stand in the way of the magical encounter between children and books. Yet if we can share with the students our interest in the meaning of words and our delight at discovering their richness and variety, we will go a long way toward helping them develop into well-rounded individuals who are at home with their language.

Semantic Maps and Tables.   Semantic maps can take many different forms, depending on the subject they deal with. It is a good idea to vary the format from time to time to show the students that they are dealing with a device that is useful for the task at hand, not a construct that is carved in stone. This will encourage them to give fresh, thoughtful answers and will keep their interest in the activity high.

Drawing on the students' previous knowledge, you might want to prepare and discuss a semantic map before the reading begins. A prereading semantic map can help the students realize that they are approaching a book with previous knowledge based on their experience. It can also help to awaken a sense of community in the classroom as the students come to see that the collective knowledge of the entire group is greater than that of any of its members. Afterward, you might turn the class's attention back to the drawing, both to determine which of the elements mentioned do in fact appear in the book and to add information gained from the reading.

If the map is prepared on a large sheet of paper, it can be kept in view and referred to often.

EXAMPLES

For the Lower Grades (K–3)

- Ada, Alma Flor. 2001. *Daniel's Mystery Egg.* Illustrated by Brian Karas. San Diego, CA: Harcourt.

- Ada, Alma Flor. 1989. *Who's Hatching Here?* Illustrated by Viví Escrivá. English translation by Bernice Randall. Miami, FL: Alfaguara. (Also in Spanish: *¿Quién nacerá aquí?*)

- Ada, Alma Flor. 1993. *A Rose with Wings.* Illustrated by Viví Escrivá. English translation by Rosalma Zubizarreta. Miami, FL: Alfaguara. (Also in Spanish: *Rosa alada.*)

These three books talk about animals born from eggs and the metamorphosis some of them experience. Before reading, invite the students to make semantic

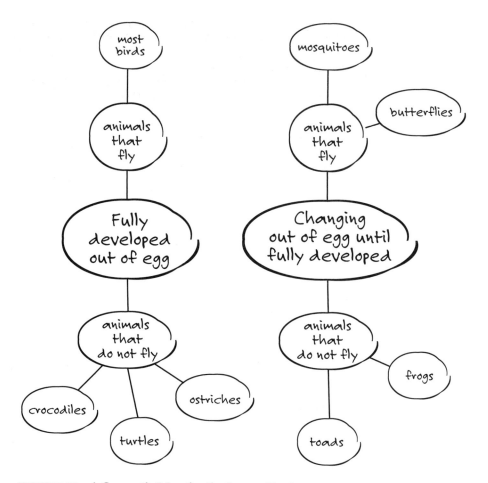

FIGURE 4.3   A Semantic Map for the Lower Grades

maps of what they know about animals that are born from eggs. A simple one could divide them into two main groups and a second level of subgroups (see Figure 4.3).

For the Upper Grades (4 and up)

- Jean Craighead George. 1972. *Julie of the Wolves.* New York: Harper and Row. (Also in Spanish: 1986. *Julia y los lobos.* Madrid, Spain: Alfaguara.)

Like many Eskimos, Miyak has two names; her Christian name is Julie. And like many Eskimos, Miyak must choose between the traditional values of her culture and the new values of the European invaders. Lost in the tundra, Miyak survives only with the help of a pack of wolves, which she patiently observes and imitates. One day, Miyak is horrified to see the leader of the wolf pack shot and killed by a hunter in an airplane. Learning that the hunter is her own father forces Miyak to make a most difficult decision.

The prereading semantic map might take the form of the one in Figure 4.4. The postreading table might include the information given in Figure 4.5 (p. 100).

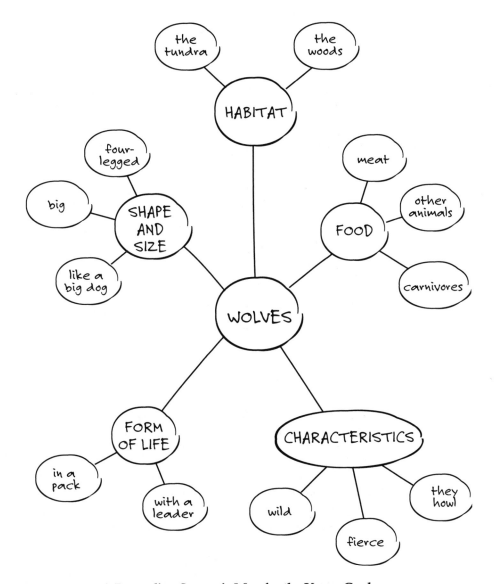

FIGURE 4.4   A Prereading Semantic Map for the Upper Grades

WHAT WE KNOW NOW ABOUT WOLVES

Communication

They have a form of language.

They communicate through gestures and growling.

To lie on their back letting others see the white of their stomach means to surrender and to ask forgiveness or to be afraid.

To bite another's chin signifies asking for protection and affection.

To bite another's muzzle is a way to reinforce authority.

Relationships

They live in packs.

The adults protect the young ones.

The young ones are respectful of the chief.

The chief does not tolerate in the pack anyone who cannot contribute or anyone who harms a pup.

Couples live together all year.

Attitudes

They are generally shy.

Food

Large animals: caribou (especially the old and infirm)

Small animals: lemmings

Adults keep food in their stomach and regurgitate it for the pups.

The male brings large pieces of meat, including a whole caribou leg, to feed the mother while she stays in the den nursing the pups.

Food is shared with all members of the pack.

Human contact

If their den is visited by humans, they abandon it.

FIGURE 4.5   A Postreading Semantic Table for the Upper Grades

Narrative Story Guides.   The students might be better able to retell a story if they have a structured way to analyze it. Besides, using narrative story guides will help them to understand that stories have an internal organization and will give them a foundation for narrating their own stories in an organized way later on (see Figure 4.6 on p. 102 and Figure 4.7 on p. 103).

Again, it is important to vary the format from time to time to keep the process from becoming routine.

EXAMPLES

For the Lower Grades (K–3)

- Rosa-Casanova Sylvia. 1997. *Mama Provi and the Pot of Rice.* Illustrated by Robert Roth. New York: Atheneum.

Lucy is sick with chicken pox, and her Puerto Rican grandmother, Mama Provi, climbs eight flights of stairs to bring her granddaughter some *arroz con pollo.* On each floor, one of the neighbors is very happy to add a particular delicacy to Lucy's meal, sometimes in exchange for some of Mama Provi's rice. At the end, Mama Provi and Lucy will sit down to a tremendous feast.

In preparation for filling their study guides, the students could make a list with four columns for the floors, the apartment numbers, the names of the neighbor, and what they contributed to the meal:

Floor	Apartment	Neighbor	Contribution
2nd	2B	Mrs. Landers	crusty white bread
3rd	3E	Señor Rivera	black beans
4th	4G	Mrs. Bazzini	fresh green salad
5th	5A	Mrs. Johnson	collard greens
6th		Mrs. Woo	a pot of tea
7th	7C	Mrs. Kelly	apple pie

and on every floor, the contribution of goodwill and nice neighborly feelings!

For the Upper Grades (4 and up)

- Borton de Treviño, Elizabeth. 1989. *El Güero: A True Adventure Story.* Pictures by Leslie W. Bowman. New York: Farrar, Straus and Giroux.

The Newbery Award winner author of *I, Juan de Pareja* tells the boyhood adventures of her father-in-law in the late 1800s. Exiled to Baja California by Mexico's dictator Porfirio Díaz, the family of Judge Cayetano Treviño struggles to survive the harsh frontier life at a time when the border between the two Californias is a land of unrest.

After reading the book, students can analyze the story line. They can divide the book in the major sections that are frequent in many stories: setting the stage, conflict, and resolution:

Setting the Stage

- Life in Mexico
- Trip to Baja California

STORY GUIDE

Student's name: ....

Title of the book: .... Friend Frog ....

There once was .... a field mouse ....

There was a problem. The problem was that .... Field Mouse wanted
a friend. He wanted to be Frog's friend . But he couldn't
croak, nor jump, nor swim like Frog.

The problem got solved when .... Field Mouse saved Frog's life. ....

The story ends when .... Frog and Field Mouse listen to Field Mouse's
grandfather tell them stories of the meadow and the pond.

The book was written by .... Alma Flor Ada ....
and illustrated by .... Lori Lohstoeter ....

What I liked the most was .... when Field Mouse tells Frog to
jump and she jumps into the water and saves her life.

FIGURE 4.6   A Narrative Story Guide for the Lower Grades

STORY GUIDE

Student's name: María Isabel Salanzar López

Title of the book: How Tía Lola Came to ~~Visit~~ Stay

Author: Julia Álvarez

Places where the story takes places Mainly in Vermont, a little in New York

Major characters Miguel, his sister Juanita, his mother and father, who are divorced, Tía Lola

Conflict Miguel is worried that his mother's aunt, Tía Lola, who has come visiting from the Dominican Republic will embarrass him in front of his friends. Tía Lola doesn't speak English, dresses in very bright colors and looks completely out of place in Vermont. She also insists on kissing everyone instead of shaking hands.

Goals of the protagonist Initially to make his parents live together again. Later to create a baseball team. Finally, to make sure that, after visiting the Dominican Republic, Tía Lola comes back to stay.

Major events Miguel and Juanita's visit to New York; Miguel's birthday party; his mother's surprise birthday party; their trip to the Dominican Republic.

Ending Miguel understands he has to accept his parents' divorce, and can still love them both; he discovers that he is both American and Dominican and can enjoy being both and learns that his place is with family, all his family.

FIGURE 4.7 **A Narrative Story Guide for the Upper Grades**

The Conflict

■ Surviving in the frontier

■ Judge Treviño is thrown into jail.

The Solution

■ El Güero's friends help him communicate with his father.

■ El Güero sets out to obtain justice for his father.

■ Justice is achieved. El Güero sets out to fulfill his destiny.

They can also use as a guide the one described in Figure 4.7, or a similar one devised by you.

■ Ada, Alma Flor. 1988. *Encaje de piedra.* Illustrations by Kitty Lorefice de Passalia. Buenos Aires, Argentina: Editorial Guadalupe.

This story, winner of the Martha Salotti Gold Medal, is set in the Middle Ages, while the magnificent cathedral of Burgos is being built. The whole life of the city revolves around the construction, which employs hundreds of workers. The workers are grouped in guilds, and there is sometimes severe antagonism between the guilds, which are jealous of each other's earnings. The masons depend on the carpenters to be able to do their work. Therefore, if the carpenters get behind, the masons might find themselves without work. A situation like this created the animosity felt by the father of one of the protagonists, Ana, toward the father of the other protagonist, Marcos. The situation is further compounded by the fact that Marcos and his family are seen as "foreigners": They are from Galicia, the northwestern area of Spain, and therefore speak another language, Galician instead of Castillian.

Both children await with great expectation the arrival of the famous glassmakers from France who will make the stained glass windows. Then a robbery occurs. Who will discover the truth?

A story guide for this story could look like this:

Beginnings

■ Friendship of Marcos and Ana

■ Animosity of Lope Núñez, Ana's father, toward Pero Fáñez, Marcos's father

■ Arrival of the highly regarded French glassmakers

Conflict

■ Marcos begins to work as apprentice to the glassmakers.

■ Being a girl, Ana cannot join him. But she hangs out and listens to the speech of the foreigners and begins to understand their language.

■ She is hired to work as a maid for the wife of one of the French artisans, and her knowledge of French increases.

Major Development

- An important robbery of the bishop's treasure has taken place.
- A conversation in French overheard by Ana holds the clues to the mystery.
- Ana is caught out in a storm and hurt by a falling tree.
- Marcos's family finds and rescues her, but she remains unconscious for many days.

Ending

- No one suspects the highly regarded French.
- Ana's information allows Marcos to unravel the mystery and recover the stolen jewels.

Narrative Cubes.   The activity of creating a narrative cube might be carried out by cooperative groups. Indeed, the greater the student participation in deciding on the contents of the cube, the more interesting the activity. As with most other activities, it will be helpful if you model this one when you introduce it. From then on, the students can take over.

What is involved is creating a cube on each of whose sides the students write or draw something related to the story. It can be made of cardboard or any available box covered with white paper. The cube should, of course, be large enough that the students can draw their answers on the sides and, if possible, add some writing as well. There is no set formula for what appears on the cube. The students might write or draw answers to given questions, or they might make up their own questions. Figures 4.8 and 4.9 (p. 106) give examples of narrative cubes.

The manual aspect of the activity might be useful in itself. It might, for example, keep part of the class engaged in a meaningful task while you work with a small group.

Interacting with books, whether by being read to, by reading independently, or by responding to them, either orally on in writing, will enhance students' language abilities. Once again, we want to emphasize that strong language development is one of the best predictors of academic success, because so much of academic growth is based on strong reading skills, and language development is the basis for effective reading. But let's remember also that academic success is only one of the results we want for our children; good social skills, such as the ability to interact harmoniously with others, to build lasting interpersonal relationships, to discover and foster the best of other human beings and oneself, are also important goals. Every single one of them is aided by the ability to use language effectively. Having an awareness of the other person's feelings and concerns, being able to express truthfully what one feels and thinks, having the capacity to identify the common ground in arguments and to recognize revealing subtleties and nuances—all these can grow from interaction with books.

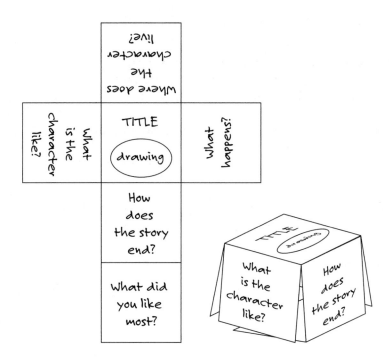

FIGURE 4.8   A Narrative Cube for the Lower Grades

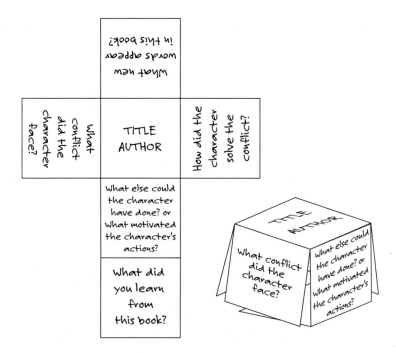

FIGURE 4.9   A Narrative Cube for the Upper Grades

5 PROMOTING DISCOVERY AND RESEARCH

Besides entertainment, a literary work offers a wide range of learning opportunities. Some of this learning derives from the facts given in the book and some from the personalities, beliefs, and attitudes modeled in it. Moreover, as an artistic creation, the work invites its reader to discover the various aesthetic devices that are employed. The reader can also feel motivated to go beyond the book—to look at reality with a new interest and with new viewpoints as offered by the book or to investigate or research more about a given aspect of the book. Promoting these responses will contribute to the overall education of the students.

Discoveries within the Book

Students will be able to make these discoveries on their own, once they learn how to analyze the books they read. The purpose of literary analysis is, of course, to enhance the reader's enjoyment of a work, not to diminish it.

The Setting.   Although every narrative occurs in a certain time and place, their importance varies from work to work. You might encourage the students to discuss the setting with these questions in mind:

- Does the narrative occur in a real or imaginary time and place?
- Does the setting create a special background (physical or psychological) against which the action occurs?
- Is the setting essential, or could it be changed without affecting the narrative in a fundamental way?
- Is the setting familiar? If not, how does it differ from the one the students know?

EXAMPLES

For the Lower Grades (K–3)

- Lattimore, Deborah Nourse. 1994. *Frida María: A Story of the Old Southwest.* New York: Harcourt. (Also in Spanish: *Frida María: Un cuento del sudoeste de antes.*)

Frida María loves to ride horses. But this disturbs her mother, who would like Frida María to behave in the way that at the time was considered appropriate for a young lady.

Invite the students to pay attention to the powerful illustrations and to discover in them details that place the setting in old Spanish-speaking California. Guide the students in analyzing the importance of the setting for the story. *Would this story be likely today where you live? Why or why not? What kind of family is Frida María's? Would her mother have treated her differently if she had not been such a fine lady? Would Frida María have had the opportunity to ride the race if she had had an older brother? Did the fiesta atmosphere help Frida María win her mother's approval?*

For the Upper Grades (4 and up)

- Ryan, Pam Muñoz. 1999. *Riding Freedom.* Illustrated by Brian Selznick. New York: Scholastic.

The protagonist of this book spent much of her life hiding the fact that she was a woman by dressing as a man to have freedom she would otherwise not have had. As such, she was the first woman to cast a vote in national elections, at a time women were not allowed to vote.

During the discussion about the book, call the students' attention to the opening paragraphs. Ask: *What effect do these initial paragraphs of the story have in creating a climate for the narration? What feelings do they evoke? How do they prepare us for what comes next?*

Talk about the setting and the time: *Would a girl of today have to change her dress in order to move as freely as a boy? Is this true where the students live? In other parts of the world?*

The Author's Point of View.   The way in which the characters, events, and ideas are revealed plays a very important part in shaping a narrative or a poem. The students' enjoyment of reading will be increased if they understand that a story can be told either in the third person (that is, from the point of view of an author who sees all, hears all, and knows all) or in the first person (from the more limited point of view of one person who knows only what he or she sees, hears, feels, or is told by others).

Their enjoyment of reading will be increased if they understand as well that a story can be told in either the past or present tense. Being able to distinguish among various points of view will, of course, be invaluable to the students as they begin writing their own stories.

After a book or a poem has been read either by you or by the students themselves, lead a discussion that centers on these questions:

- Is the narrative (or poem) written in the third or first person? How can we tell?
- Does the narrator (or poet) speak directly to the reader, using the second person? Again, how can we tell?
- Does the action take place in the present or in the past?

EXAMPLES

For the Lower Grades (K-3)

- Ada, Alma Flor. 2002. *I Love Saturdays y domingos.* Illustrated by Elivia Savadier. New York: Atheneum.

Explain to the students that when books talk about the authors' real life, they are usually written in the first person. We know they are true, and we expect the author to be speaking about himself or herself using "I." Then make the children aware that this is a fictional book but that it is written in the first person. *Does that help make the book feel more real to them than if it were written in the third person?*

For the Upper Grades (4 and up)

- Stanek, Muriel. 1989. *I Speak English for My Mom.* Illustrated by Judith Friedman. Niles, IL: Albert Whitman.

Like many children whose parents are recent immigrants, Lupe must translate for her mother, who is just beginning to learn English. With realistic text and illustrations, the book explores some of the hardships, but also the satisfactions, that this responsibility can entail.

Students can discuss whether the use of the first person in the book made the narrative more real for them. Of course, it will be very important to allow them to voice their own reflections about the role of language or languages in their lives.

- Alarcón, Francisco X. 1997. *Laughing Tomatoes and Other Spring Poems/ Jitomates risueños y otros poemas de primavera.* Illustrated by Maya Christina González. San Francisco: Children's Book Press.
- Alarcón, Francisco X. 1998. *From the Bellybutton of the Moon and Other Summer Poems/Del ombligo de la luna y otros poemas de verano.* Illustrated by Maya Christina González. San Francisco: Children's Book Press.
- Alarcón, Francisco X. 1999. *Angels Ride Bikes and Other Fall Poems/Los ángeles andan en bicicleta y otros poemas de otoño.* Illustrated by Maya Christina González. San Francisco: Children's Book Press.

The point of view chosen by the author is as important in poetry as in prose. Invite your students to read these poems with attention to the ones in which the author chooses to write in the first person. *Why do they think the author makes that choice? What is the effect in the poem? Would the poem be different if written in third person?*

- Ada, Alma Flor. 1993. *Canción de todos los niños del mundo.* Boston: Houghton Mifflin. (*Canción.* Cassette. Westlake, OH: Del Sol.)

This poem is written in the second person, as one child talking to another, first pointing out the differences created by the geographical distance: *"Cuando aquí es de noche / para ti amanece./ ¿Vivimos muy lejos, / no te lo parece?..."* ["While here is nightime, / for you the day breaks. /We live too far away./ Don't you agree with me?..."] Then it moves on to discover the similarities between all children of the world, who study, play, learn, and dream.

After reading or singing the poem, have the students consider that it is written using the first and second person. *How would it be different if it were written in the third person? Why do they think the poet chose the point of view of one child talking to another?*

Characterization. One of the benefits of good literature is that it enlarges and enriches the sphere of human relations. In creating well-defined characters with their own personalities, the author deepens our understanding of ourselves and others. Freed from the bonds of the here and now, we develop emotional ties to those characters, who, though the product of the author's imagination, somehow take on lives of their own as part of the humanizing impulse we all share.

Children are comforted and validated by characters who face the same problems as they do and who, like them, struggle to make sense of reality. Moreover, they are exposed to and come to understand new feelings, emotions, attitudes, and values.

Give the students whatever help they need to discover the richness and diversity of the characters they read about. Distinguish between a protagonist, or main character, and a secondary character, among other reasons because it is a way of reminding the students that they are protagonists, not merely secondary characters, in their own lives.

The activities related to this area of discovery are many and varied. The students might, for example, write a letter to a storybook character, make a drawing of the character for inclusion in a gallery of their favorites, or write an account of one day in the character's life in journal form.

EXAMPLES

For the Lower Grades (K–3)

- Dorros, Arthur. 1995. *Abuela.* Illustrated by Elisa Kleven. New York: Dutton. (Also in Spanish with the same title.)
- Dorros, Arthur. 1995. *Isla.* Illustrated by Elisa Kleven. New York: Dutton. (Also in Spanish with the same title.)

In *Abuela,* watching birds in the park with her grandmother makes Rosalba imagine that they can fly over the city of New York. In *Isla,* it is the grandmother's stories about her beloved Puerto Rico that stir Rosalba's imagination.

Invite the students to find clues about Rosalba and her grandmother from both books. They will find them in the illustrations as well as in the text. *Where do they live? What do they like to do together? Can you tell whether they like being with each other? Do you see signs of affection? What language does the grandmother speak? Can Rosalba also speak Spanish? Where did the grandmother come from? How did she arrive in New York? Are they close to their family?* The students' responses can take the form of a characterization table like the one shown in Figure 4.10.

- Garay, Luis. 1997. *Pedrito's Day.* New York: Orchard.

This book gives a detailed account of one day in Pedrito's life. Through his actions, we get a clear picture of Pedrito—not only what he does, but also how he feels.

What is Abuela like?	She has white hair. She is happy. She dresses with very vivid colors. She is kind and loves her granddaughter.
Where does she live?	She lives in New York, but she used to live in Puerto Rico.
What languages does she speak?	We know she speaks Spanish. We suspect she speaks some English too.
What does she like?	Going to the park
	Adventures, like sailing in the park
	The Statue of Liberty
	Remembering her beautiful island
	Spending time with her granddaughter and telling her stories

FIGURE 4.10 A Characterization Table

The extraordinary illustrations contribute to make Pedrito and his world very clear to us. Invite the students to imagine having a conversation with Pedrito once he gets the bike he dreams of having.

For the Upper Grades (4 and up)

- Ada, Alma Flor. 1990. *The Gold Coin.* Illustrated by Neil Waldman. English translation by Bernice Randall. New York: Atheneum. (Also in Spanish: 1992. *La moneda de oro.* León, Spain: Everest.)

Juan is a thief in pursuit of doña Josefa's gold. He follows this old healer through the countryside, determined to force her to give him the many gold coins he believes she has. She becomes an obsession in his mind as he discovers that wherever she goes, she is able to bring some comfort to a sick person as well as a gold coin.

Throughout the book, doña Josefa speaks only a couple of phrases, yet we know who she is by the reactions of all the other characters to her actions. She is a well-developed but unchanging personality. On the other hand, Juan undergoes a major transformation as a result of his quest for the gold.

After reading the book, students will be able to describe doña Josefa as they see her and the earlier and later Juan. Because the book purposefully does not use adjectives to describe the moral character of the protagonists but lets the narrative allow for the reader's interpretation, it would be very interesting to see which adjectives the students use to describe them.

Creating collectively a list of adjectives to describe moral character can enrich the activity. The list can later be used to describe characters from other stories:

Which of these adjectives would apply to doña Josefa, to Juan at the beginning of the story, and to Juan at the end of the story?

benevolent	hardworking	quiet
brave	honest	responsible
careful	kind	selfish
courageous	loving	selfless
friendly	magnanimous	supportive
generous	obsessed	tenacious
giving	patient	trustworthy, etc.

abnegado	*compasivo/a*	*paciente*
amistoso/a	*cuidadoso/a*	*persistente*
benevolente	*dadivoso/a*	*prudente*
bondadoso/a	*despredido/a*	*responsable*
callado/a	*egoísta*	*tenaz*
cariñoso/a	*generoso/a*	*trabajador/a*
confiable	*honesto/a*	*valiente, etc.*
consciente	*obsesionado/a*	

Literary Devices. A literary work derives much of its charm from the special devices it employs, and so recognizing them adds to the reader's enjoyment. It is a good idea to take every opportunity to familiarize the students with such qualities of written work, because besides being able to identify literary devices in their future reading, they can use them in their own creative writing. Care must be taken, however, not to turn the act of reading into a guessing game in which the students are so intent on identifying the author's literary devices that they lose interest in—and thus enjoyment of—in the work as a whole.

These are some of the many literary devices to which you might direct the students' attention: rhyme; alliteration; rhythm; repetitions; choice of characters' names; characterization based on repeated words or phrases, gestures, or attitudes; comparison and contrast; the element of surprise; imagery and figures of speech; and realistic details used to buttress fantasy.

Discoveries beyond the Book

After reading a book, the students are likely to turn to their immediate surroundings with renewed interest. Indeed, books are an excellent way to put us more closely in touch with reality.

Some books may make the students more attentive to the uses of language. Others, having shown them the immense variety of the world around them, may make the students eager to explore that world firsthand. Choose some of the many activities that will lead them to recognize and act on such incentives. In doing so, you will instill in them one of the most worthwhile habits of good readers: looking to books as a source of enrichment and support.

EXAMPLES

For all grades

- Ancona, George. 1993. *Pablo Remembers: The Fiesta of the Day of the Dead.* New York: Lothrop, Lee and Shephard. (Also in Spanish: *Pablo recuerda: La Fiesta del Día de los Muertos.*)
- Ancona, George. 1995. *Earth Daughter: Alicia of Ácoma Pueblo.* New York: Simon & Schuster.
- Ancona, George. 1997. *Mayeros: A Yucatec Maya Family.* New York: Lothrop, Lee and Shephard.
- Ancona, George. 1998. *Fiesta Fireworks.* New York: Lothrop, Lee and Shephard.
- Ancona, George. 1998. *Barrio: José's Neighborhood.* San Diego, CA: Harcourt.
- Ancona, George. 1998. *Let's Dance.* New York: Morrow Junior Books.
- Ancona, George. 1999. *Charro. The Mexican Cowboy.* New York: Harcourt.
- Ancona, George. 2000. *Cuban Kids.* New York: Marshall Cavendish.
- Ancona, George. 2001. *Harvest.* New York: Marshall Cavendish.
- Ancona, George. 2002. *Viva Mexico! The People.* New York: Marshall Cavendish.

George Ancona's excellently researched books, illustrated by the author with artistic photographs, can offer students of all grades the opportunity to discover information about the Latino culture and the culture of Latin America.

Once the students have had the opportunity to enjoy any of the books, it will be important to encourage them to learn more about the reality presented in the book. *Do they know anyone from the place described in the book? Someone of the same profession? Have they participated in similar celebrations to those depicted? What further questions do they have? What else would they like to know? Can their parents and relatives share some experiences similar to those in the book? Where else can they obtain additional information?*

Research

Research activities are similar to those of discovery. However, instead of being concerned mainly with making the students more aware of the world around them, they call for a concerted effort to obtain information to supplement that provided in the books. The possibilities for research are virtually limitless. To a large extent, they depend on the students' age and level of maturity, the interdisciplinary connections you want to make, and the subject matter being studied now or planned for the future.

EXAMPLES

For the Lower Grades (K–3)

- Schwalm, Claudia. 1998. *Being Bilingual Is Fun!* Alameda, CA: Cultural Connections Publishing.

This book explores the joy of being bilingual, with photographs of children from various cultures and short and bright captions.

- Lachtman, Ofelia Dumas. 1995. *Pepita Talks Twice/Pepita habla dos veces.* Houston, TX: Piñata Books.

Many bilingual children in the United States have been made ashamed of speaking a home language that is different than English. In their desire to blend in with the rest, they many times stop speaking their home language. This unconscious decision can have very negative consequences. Later on in life, the students may discover that they have lost the ability to speak it and, with that, not only the multiple advantages derived from being bilingual but also the possibility for fully benefiting both from their cultural heritage and from full communication and interaction with relatives. In some dramatic cases, one or both parents have never developed full fluency in English, and they may therefore be unable to have truly meaningful conversations with their child.

After reading these books, children can research answers to such questions as these:

What are the names of some of the languages in the world?

Where are they spoken?

What are the benefits of speaking more than one language?

How many languages do the students in the class and their families speak? Which are they?

What feelings do children in the class who speak more than one language have about their languages?

For the Upper Grades (4 and up)

Books that touch on the history and the culture of Latinos can help Latino students discover additional sources of information about their heritage. They can help students of other backgrounds develop an understanding of the richness of the culture of peoples who contributed significantly to the development of the society of the United States even before there were speakers of any other European language, including English, in this land.

A few titles that can serve this purpose are listed here. They are only a starting point.

Books on Hispanic Art, Outside and Inside the United States
These books on the extraordinary artistic richness of the Hispanic world include reproductions of paintings from various periods and countries in Latin America and Spain as well as Latino artists. Classical artists, well-known contemporary painters, and anonymous art from the people are included.

- Ada, Alma Flor, and F. Isabel Campoy. 2000. *Artist's Easel.* Miami, FL: Alfaguara. Collection Gateways to the Sun. (Also in Spanish: *Caballete.*)
- Ada, Alma Flor, and F. Isabel Campoy. 2000. *Blue and Green.* Miami, FL: Alfaguara. Collection Gateways to the Sun. (Also in Spanish: *Azul y verde.*)
- Ada, Alma Flor, and F. Isabel Campoy. 2000. *Brush and Paint.* Miami, FL: Alfaguara. Collection Gateways to the Sun. (Also in Spanish: *Brocha y pincel.*)
- Ada, Alma Flor, and F. Isabel Campoy. 2000. *Canvas and Paper.* Miami, FL: Alfaguara. Collection Gateways to the Sun. (Also in Spanish: *Lienzo y papel.*)

Books on Latin American History and Art
- García, Guy. 1995. *Spirit of the Maya: A Boy Explores His People's Mysterious Past.* Photographs by Ted Wood. New York: Walker.

Vibrant pictures of a young Lacando boy complement the exploration of the extraordinary monuments of his Mayan ancestors.

- Presilla, Maricel E. 1996. *Mola: Cuna Life Stories and Art.* New York: Henry Holt.

Astonishing photographs of molas, the embroidery art of the Cuna women of the San Blas Islands in Panama, are accompanied by brief poetic text that allows us to see how the molas are indeed a depiction of Cuna life and dreams.

- Presilla, Maricel E., and Gloria Soto. 1996. *Life around the Lake: Embroideries by the Women of Lake Pátzcuaro.* New York: Henry Holt.

Photographs of the embroidery of the women of Lake Pátzcuaro depict both the daily activities and the special celebrations of this community of fishermen and artisans.

6 PROMOTING CREATIVE WRITTEN EXPRESSION

Literature is a form of art, so what better way to promote creative expression? In the case of children's literature, most good books combine literary text with artistic illustrations, thus stimulating their readers both linguistically and visually.

Children's books will have accomplished one of their main purposes if they motivate the students to express themselves in writing. They will have accomplished even more if they lead the students to understand that writing can be as easy and as much fun as reading.

In talking with the students about books, point out that behind every book is an author, a person who has experienced or imagined something he or she wants to share with others. Point out as well that because the students experience and imagine things, they too can be authors.

Letters

The students might write to some of the authors and illustrators of books they have read. Their letters, sent in care of the publishers, will of course be more interesting if they include brief comments on the text or art. The students might also write to publishers, both to say which of the publisher's books they liked and to suggest subjects they would enjoy reading about. Many books carry the publisher's address on the copyright page. For those that do not, two useful annual directories can be found at the reference desk of almost every public library: *Literary Market Place* for U.S. publishers and *International Literary Market Place* for publishers in other countries.

A nearby public library might welcome letters from the students. Perhaps the class would like to invite a librarian to come to speak about and show children's books and, in turn, invite the students to visit the library. An interest in books might also lead to an exchange of letters with students in another class at your school, in another local school, or in other places.

Few letters in Spanish are as well written, as sincere, and as brimming with ideas and poetic statements as José Martí's letters to a young girl named María Mantilla. You can find them either in the special edition listed in the Bibliography at the end of this book or in a collection of Martí's works. Reading several of these letters aloud would show the class how one can not only feel things but also share such feelings with others.

Their reading might lead the students to write a very different kind of letter: letters to storybook characters. Students might, for instance, tell certain characters what they like and dislike about them, or they might invite characters from the books they are reading come to class. To prepare the visitors for the things they would see, the students could describe how present-day life in the United States is different from the characters' lives, or they might write letters in which certain characters tell others why they behaved as they did. For Spanish-speaking students who have read Nellia Bosnia's wonderful book *Arturo y Clementina*, Arturo is a case in point: The turtle might ask Clementina's forgiveness for his insensitivity and tell her how he plans to change so that they can be happy together. Another letter of apology is in order from Hansel and Gretel's parents. And Cinderella and Snow White might each write thank you letters, one to her fairy godmother and the other to the seven dwarfs.

You might want to enlarge on this activity. If so, have the students exchange the first letters they have written so that other students, acting as the recipients, can answer them.

For Intermediate Grades (3–5)

- Ada, Alma Flor. 1993. *Dear Peter Rabbit.* Illustrated by Leslie Tryon. New York: Atheneum. (Also in Spanish: *Querido Pedrín.*)

Well-loved storybook characters meet in this book written entirely in letters. After reading the book, have students select other characters and tell a story through letters written by them.

Journals

Ideally, all the students are making daily entries in their journals. One way to promote or reinforce this activity is to read aloud a book published in diary form. For Spanish-speaking students, portions of the moving book *Corazón* by Edmundo d'Amicis might be appropriate. Good examples in English are, for intermediate level students, *Are You There God? It's Me, Margaret* by Judy Blume and, for older students, *Isabel: Jewel of Castilla* by Carolyn Meyer (Collection The Royal Diaries) and the *Diary of Anne Frank.*

Stories

Turning students into authors of their own stories is one of the main reasons for using children's literature in the classroom. It is therefore essential to provide both the means and the opportunity for the students to write, revise, and make clean copies of original stories.

This activity, like all others, runs the risk of becoming routine unless you are careful to introduce variety. Sometimes the students will appreciate your providing guidelines on which to pattern their stories; at other times, you would do well to give them only encouragement, allowing them to follow their own creative impulses.

New Stories Based on Another Book Structure.   Drawing on a story they have read as the basis for writing one of their own is a useful device for students of all ages. Be sure, however, to allow for a great deal of variety in plot and organization.

For the Lower Grades (K–3)

- Ada, Alma Flor. *Strange Visitors.* Illustrated by Viví Escrivá. English translation by Bernice Randall. Miami, FL: Alfaguara. (Also in Spanish: *Una extraña visita.*)

This predictable story centers on the days of the week. The students will have no trouble using its simple structure as a model for their own stories. They can substitute many different kinds of characters: from fairy tales, from the circus, from the community, from the world of animals.

New Stories with Well-Known Characters.   A starting point for a story could be incorporating characters students have met in other books. Whether they work independently or in cooperative groups, they might start by choosing the characters and listing some of their qualities, or they might first decide on a setting and imagine all the familiar characters who might fit into it. If they select the ocean, for example, they can incorporate the little fish in Leo Leonni's *Swimmy* (*Nadarín*), the octopus in *José el gran ayudante* by Robert Kraus, the barnacle in Alma Flor Ada's *Bernice the Barnacle* (in Spanish, *Más poderoso que yo*), and the turtle in *A Chance for Esperanza* (*La oportunidad de Esperanza*).

Companion Stories for Picture Books without Text.   Student writers will find an excellent motivator in the picture book without text. Having the basic structure and story line before them, they can set about creating the missing text. Encourage students to provide details, to interpret the character's feelings, and to add anecdotes and any other material they think appropriate. The following examples have titles in Spanish, but because there is no texts in the books, they can be used equally well with English-speakers. Any of the books of M. Anno could also be effectively used.

EXAMPLES

For the Lower Grades (K–3)

- Felix, Monique. 1981. *Historia de una ratita encerrada en un libro.* Caracas, Venezuela: Maria di Mase.

In this charming wordless book, a tiny rat becomes trapped inside a book. After many unsuccessful attempts to escape, she begins to gnaw at a page. When the page becomes loose, she uses it to build a paper airplane. Flying to the illustration on the next page, she lands in a wheat field, and so on.

    Besides being delighted by the ingenious plot and lovely drawings, the students will see that through reason and persistence, one can overcome difficulties. They might want to offer variations on this moral in their own stories, or they might prefer to create more adventures for the tiny rat.

For the Upper Grades (4 and up)

- Baum, Willi. 1989. *La expedición.* San Francisco: Iaconi Books.

In this extraordinary wordless book, a European captain and his men destroy the temple that overlooks the island on which they have just landed. When they return to their ship to load the spoils from the temple, they are surprised to see that their own smokestacks have disappeared from the ship and have been set on the base of the destroyed temple.

Students of all ages will enjoy this book. Their analysis of its basic premises might lead to a discussion about conquest and colonization or about any other form of domination.

To prepare for writing their own text for the book, which they can do independently or in cooperative groups, it can be useful to have them stop at each page of the book and describe what the characters are feeling or saying.

Sequels and Prequels.   To encourage the students to write, you might suggest that their stories be forward-looking or backward-looking extensions of ones they already know. If a new work carries the action of an existing novel, motion picture, or television show into the future, it is called a *sequel.* If it portrays events that led up to the action in the existing work, it may be called a *prequel,* a term that has come into use in recent years.

Stories Told from a Different Viewpoint.   One of the tenets of transformative education is that students should be guided to understand that reality can be interpreted in various ways, depending on the perspective of each person involved in an event. In the search for alternatives that free one to view reality as something that is open to change, analyzing the viewpoints of several characters can be very useful.

Once the students realize that a story can seem quite different if it is told from different narrators' viewpoints, they can retell it from a new viewpoint: their own. To get them started, you might ask questions along these lines: *What might the story of Cinderella be like if it were told by her stepmother or stepsisters? How do you think the witch in the Hansel and Gretel story felt? What might have made her behave the way she did? What do you think the story of the hare and the tortoise be if the hare told it?*

Real-Life Stories.   Reading realistic fiction or autobiographical narrative can inspire the students to think about their own lives. In the process, they are sure to find experiences worth recounting and feelings worth exploring.

EXAMPLES

For the Lower Grades (K–3)

- Pérez, Amada Irma. 2000. *My Very Own Room/Mi propio cuartito.* Illustrated by Maya Christina González. San Francisco: Children's Book Press.

In this real-life story, the author shares how she used to dream about having her own space, separate from her five little brothers, and how with creativity, cooperation, enthusiasm, and love, her family made her dream come true.

The authenticity of this very simple story lends itself to helping children realize that they also have real stories to tell. All episodes of our lives are important, no matter how small they might seem, and they all can be beautifully told.

For the Upper Grades (4 and up)

- Ada, Alma Flor. 1994. *Where the Flame Trees Bloom*. Illustrated by Antonio Martorell. New York: Atheneum. (Also in Spanish: 2000. *Allá donde florecen los framboyanes*. Miami, FL: Alfaguara.)
- Ada, Alma Flor. 1998. *Under the Royal Palms*. New York: Atheneum. (Also in Spanish: 2001. *Bajo las palmas reales*. Miami, FL: Alfaguara.)
- Mohr, Nicholasa. 1994. *In My Own Words: Growing Up inside the Sanctuary of My Imagination*. New York: Julian Messner/Simon & Schuster.
- Ortiz Cofer, Judith. 1990. *Silent Dancing: A Partial Remembrance of a Puerto Rican Childhood*. Houston, TX: Arte Público Press.
- Soto, Gary. 1992. *Living up the Street: Narrative Recollections*. New York: Dell.

After the students have read one or several of these autobiographical books, invite them to select one moment of their lives that they would like to recount. That memory can make a book unto itself, or it could be the beginning of a collection of vignettes.

Stories about Real People.   Realistic fiction also provides good models and inspiration for stories whose characters are based on real people. Some students might prefer to write factual accounts of people they know very well, with very little, if any, fiction.

EXAMPLES

For the Lower Grades (K–3)

- Ada, Alma Flor. 2002. *I Love Saturdays y domingos*. Illustrated by Elivia Savadier. New York: Atheneum.
- Anaya, Rudolfo. 1995. *The Farolitos of Christmas*. Illustrated by Edward González. New York: Hyperion.
- Anaya, Rudolfo. 1997. *Farolitos for Abuelo*. Illustrated by Edward González. New York: Hyperion.
- Córdova, Amy. 1997. *Abuelita's Heart*. New York: Simon & Schuster.
- Torres, Leyla. 1998. *Liliana's Grandmothers*. New York: Farrar, Straus and Giroux. (Also in Spanish: *Las abuelas de Liliana*.)
- Nodar, Carmen Santiago. 1992. *Abuelita's Paradise*. Illustrated by Diane Paterson. Morton Grove, IL: Albert Whitman. (Also in Spanish: *El paraíso de abuelita*. Translated by Teresa Mlawer.)

For the Upper Grades (4 and up)

- Alarcón, Francisco X. "Matriarch" In: A. F. Ada, V. Harris, and L. B. Hopkins. 1993. *A Chorus of Cultures*. Carmel Valley: Hampton Brown.

After reading one or more of these books or poems, the students might describe a noteworthy experience they have had with their own grandparents, parents, or other family members. Encourage them to use various literary forms (narrative, description, dialogue, letters) and to illustrate their stories.

Creating Books

Once the students have discovered the world of books and the joy of reading stories, they can easily be motivated to create their own books. They might begin by deciding on a topic and making a list of characters. Then, if they are working in groups, each student might dictate a part of the story. If text is written on chart paper or the chalkboard, you might transcribe it and reproduce it, giving each student a copy to illustrate, or the students might copy it themselves. Depending on the age of the students and the length of the story, each page might contain only one sentence or perhaps a paragraph or two.

For a class book, all the students join in illustrating the pages. For individual books, each student works on his or her own illustrations. Binding and laminating the books or placing the pages in plastic page protectors will extend their life, especially if they are to be used time and time again. You might also consider giving copies of student-produced books to the school and public libraries with the request that they be catalogued as part of the collections.

Point out to the students that most books contain the following:

- A cover, with the title and names of the author and illustrator
- A title page, which repeats the cover information and adds the name of the publishing house (which they can all create) and the year of publication
- A dedication, that is, a brief message from the author to another person or persons as a sign of honor and affection
- Information about the author and the illustrator

As an aid for very young students and for others who have not had much bookmaking experience, you might prepare and distribute sample title and "about the author" pages (see Figure 4.11 on p. 122 and Figure 4.12 on p. 123).

Big Books. Besides being attractive, oversize storybooks, known as "big books," are very appropriate for group reading. Encourage the students to produce such books and to read them, in small groups, to other classes. Two students hold the oversized book open while the third reads the text and discusses the illustrations. If the students are going to read the books to younger children or to English-learners, they might want to make charts showing the meaning of certain words or describing the characters.

Title: A birth in the sea

Author and Illustrator: Camille Rosa Zubizarreta

Milliken School, Santa Cruz

2nd grade

FIGURE 4.11   A Sample Title Page Form

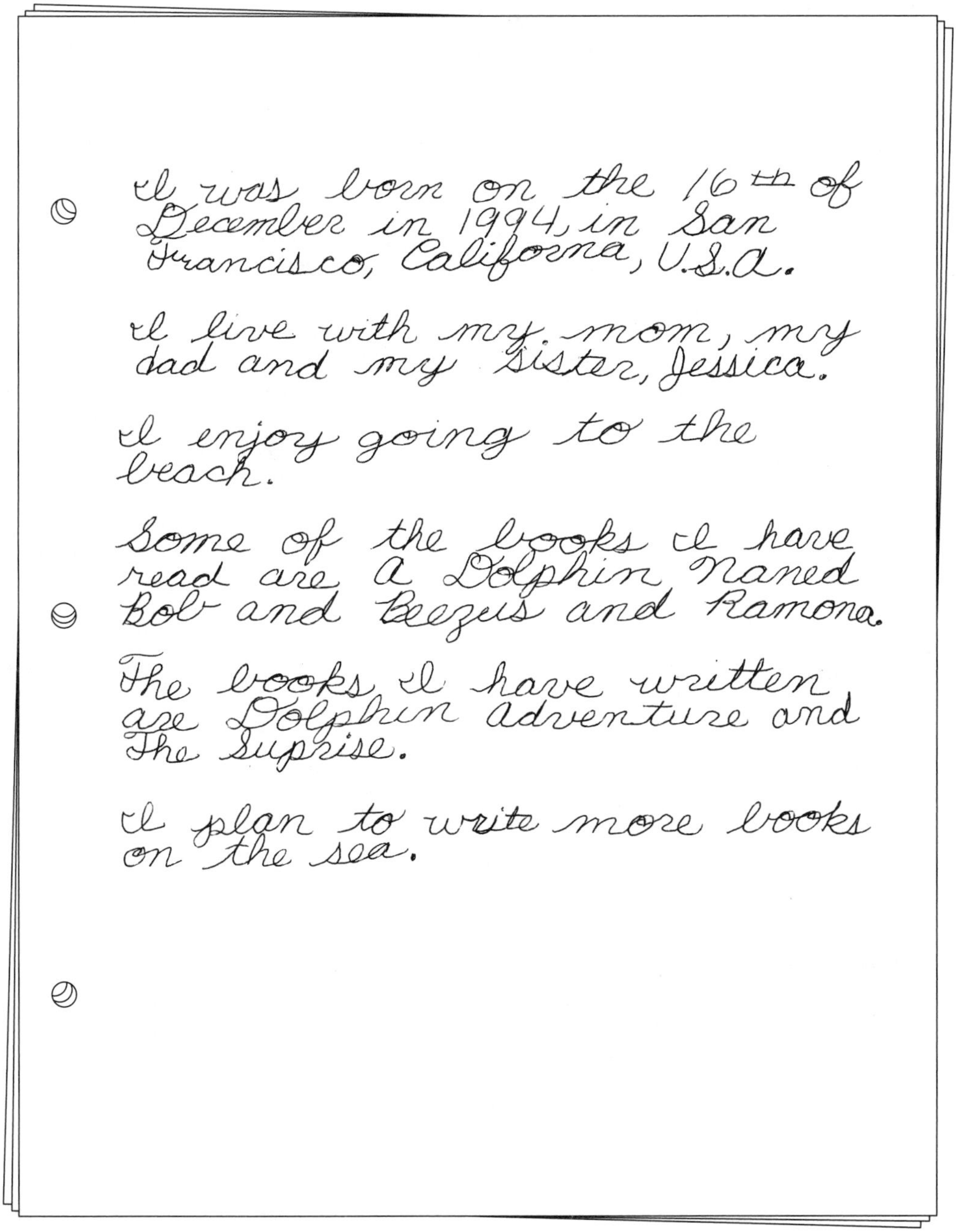

I was born on the 16th of December in 1994, in San Francisco, California, U.S.A.

I live with my mom, my dad and my sister, Jessica.

I enjoy going to the beach.

Some of the books I have read are A Dolphin Named Bob and Beezus and Ramona.

The books I have written are Dolphin Adventure and The Suprise.

I plan to write more books on the sea.

FIGURE 4.12 A Sample "About the Author" Page

EXAMPLES

For the Lower Grades (K–3)

■ Campoy, F. Isabel. 2002. *Todas las buenas manos.* Illustrated by Yuyi Morales. Orlando, FL: Harcourt.

This book, whose title means "All the good hands," celebrates many different people who work to sustain our daily life.

Students can determine whose are the good hands that sustain their own lives and create a similar book showing their gratitude to those people.

Theme-Related Formats.   Variety in the size and formats of the students' books will help to keep interest high. Some members of the class might want to pick up a certain element in a book they have read and carry it over to the design or even the shape of the books they are creating. As Figure 4.13

FIGURE 4.13   Theme-Related Storybook Formats

shows, among the themes that lend themselves to such a visual treatment are the following:

Fruits and vegetables: apple, pear, tomato, strawberry, pineapple
Animals: bear, cat, bird, whale, fish, turtle
Toys: car, train, boat, plane, skate
Characters: clown, witch, wizard, fairy, firefighter, cowboy

A wide range of topics and literary forms, ranging from realistic descriptions of everyday life to pure fantasy, can find their way into these books. You might suggest the following titles as story motivators:

All we know about... Each student tells in one sentence, paragraph, or page whatever he or she knows about a given animal, fruit, game, place, etc.

The extraordinary adventure of...

A counting book of... Each page shows the same characters—let's say from one to ten—doing different things. For example, one monkey eating, two monkeys running, three monkeys sleeping, four monkeys jumping, and so on; or counting from one to seven with the colors of the rainbow: one red flower; two flowers: red and pink; three flowers: red, pink, and orange; four flowers: red, pink, orange, and yellow; and so on.

My favorite... Each student writes and illustrates a book about an animal he or she would like to have, describing among other things the kind of animal it would be, what it would eat, and how the student would care for it and, giving free rein to fantasy: the adventures they would have together, the places they would go, the friends they would meet, and so on.

My mother (father, sister, brother)... Students create a human figure, with a circle for the face, a square for the body, and smaller rectangles for the limbs. On the square body, they paste their book of several pages describing the person they have chosen to write about. The book can also take the form of an accordion, opening lengthwise.

Flap Books.   In a flap book, all the pages of a student book are trimmed to the same geometric shape—a square, rectangle, or circle, for example. The book is then attached to a large posterboard cutout. A circular book might have as its backing the body of a clown or a whale; a square book, a railroad car, or a circus tent; and a rectangular book, an elephant, or a boat (see Figure 4.14, p. 126).

Accordion Books.   As its name suggests, an accordion book is made by taping together several pieces of cardboard so that they can be opened and closed like the folds of an accordion. The pages of the student's book are then

FIGURE 4.14 Flap Books

pasted onto the cardboard panels, one page per panel. The first panel might carry a colorful illustration. For an even livelier book, all the panels might be cut to a special shape (Figure 4.15).

Spin-and-Look Books. To present a succession of images, a wheel on which various pictures have been drawn is fastened to the inside cover of the book, with a bit of the wheel protruding beyond the outer edge of the cover. Each time the wheel is turned, a different picture appears in a small window cut out in the cover (see Figure 4.16).

Movable Books. In a movable book, a retractable element is held in place by a fastener attached to the inside of the back cover. The element, which can be pulled out at will, might be part of a person or animal pictured on the

FIGURE 4.15   Accordion Books

FIGURE 4.16   Spin-and-Look Books

FIGURE 4.17   Movable Books

FIGURE 4.18   Pop-Up Books

front of the book: for instance, a rabbit's ears, a cat's tail, a giraffe's head and feet (see Figure 4.17).

Pop-Up Books.   A guaranteed child pleaser, the pop-up book is easy to make. Its essential requirement is a firm base made of posterboard or heavy paper. As Figure 4.18 shows, first a page is folded in half, cutouts are made where indicated by the heavy lines, and the paper is folded back along the dotted lines. Second, the page is opened to provide a base, or support, for the pop-up element. Third, characters, story props, or other illustrative elements are glued to the base so that when the book is opened, a three-dimensional scene is revealed.

7 PROMOTING CREATIVE VISUAL EXPRESSION

Illustrators complement children's books in a very important way. Besides awakening the students' interest in reading, good artwork helps to develop their aesthetic sense. Just as storybooks can motivate students to write, book illustrations can encourage them to express themselves through a wide range of visual forms.

Analysis of Illustrations

Help the class to realize that the pictures in books employ various media. Besides arousing their curiosity about and interest in all kinds of artwork, the discovery is likely to make them more adventuresome when they illustrate their own books.

Show the students books with various kinds of illustrations, and invite them to think about the different media used. Relate book illustration to the visual arts. Make students aware of the pictorial richness of the Latino world. In the bibliography of Latino authors included at the end of the book, you will find a section on art with reference to books by Carmen Lomas Garza and Amado Peña as well as the art series of the collection *Gateways to the Sun/Puertas al sol* published by Alfaguara.

As you speak to your students of great artists of the Hispanic world— Diego Velazquez, Goya, Picasso, Frida Kahlo, Diego Rivera, Fernando Botero, and Judith Baca, to name some among so many—you can also make them aware of the Latino artists who devote their talent to illustrating books for children: Felipe Dávalos, Lulú Delacre, David Díaz, Viví Escrivá, Asun Balzola, Pablo Torrecilla, Susan Guevara, Daniel Moretón, Simón Silva, and Leyla Torres are some among them.

Puppet Making

Puppetry is an artistic activity that encompasses both visual and dramatic expression. Nowadays, puppets can be made with such a wide range of materials that the students will be able to explore their creativity in many ways. Encourage them to find library books showing how to design, construct, dress, and operate puppets. At the same time, urge them to give free rein to their imagination.

Older students can investigate the history of puppetry and its varied manifestations throughout the world.

Masks

Like puppets, masks blend visual art with theater. Students are certain to enjoy making masks of storybook characters they have read about. This project will also give them an opportunity to reflect critically on the characters' most distinctive features.

Masks have a long history of symbolism and have played important cultural roles. Older students can do research on the topic, looking at the different uses of masks across cultures or focusing on the masks used in the rituals of the indigenous cultures of the Americas. This research will give an added dimension to the masks they create.

Murals

An important part of the Hispanic tradition, murals are an excellent way to depict the plots of stories the students have read. This art form offers a wide range of choices. In a horizontal mural, one event is ordinarily shown after another in a straight line. In a circular mural, the space is divided into segments, like slices in a pie; here, the plot can also be presented sequentially, or else each segment can be devoted to a different character or to a close-up of a particular event. As the students gain skill and confidence, they can add another dimension to their murals, whether horizontal or circular. To convey a good deal of information about a story, they might use several segments, showing the setting in one segment, the action in another, and the characters in yet another. Encourage the class to experiment and vary the forms of their murals according to the nature of the story.

Posters

Because posters give the written word great visual impact through their eye-catching art, they are a popular as well as effective means of visual expression. The students can limit their illustrative elements to drawings, they can use collage and mixed-media techniques, or they can explore other forms. They should keep the text brief, usually no longer than a single word or sentence or perhaps a short rhyme. In any case, they should bear in mind that the purpose of a poster is to capture the attention of passersby.

Student-made posters can serve several purposes. They might, for example, do one of the following:

- Promote a certain book by drawing attention to the originality of the plot
- Publicize an author's or illustrator's work by showing several of their books
- Compare several books written by different authors but dealing with the same theme

The students might ask the appropriate authorities for permission to display the posters prominently at the school or another location in the community. If they do this, poster making becomes a culminating activity, in which language is used for a purpose in a real-life situation outside the classroom.

8 PROMOTING DRAMATIC EXPRESSION

By interacting with books, students become acquainted with new characters and situations and vicariously share those characters' experiences. The importance of encouraging students to perceive themselves as protagonists of their own lives as well as the need for them to develop their creativeness to the fullest has already been pointed out. Drama in the classroom makes it possible to carry storybook characters' feelings and emotions to a more active plane and to explore the characters' experiences more directly than reading alone can do.

As with all other activities, encourage variety in the dramatic presentations. These may range from informal role-playing by the students, either before the whole class or in small groups, to a large-scale performance before students in other classes, parents, and even other members of the community.

Story Dramatization

Virtually every story lends itself to dramatization, which can be improvised or written down. If improvised, students act out events in a familiar story, making up the dialogue as they go along. If written, they might dictate the dialogue, which you would transcribe on chart paper. This dialogue would later be used in a dramatic reading or in a play whose parts have been memorized.

The first step in guiding the students to produce a script is to have them discuss the story and then decide on the number of acts or scenes into which it should be divided. For example, if the play is based on the well-known story of the tortoise and the hare, these might be the five acts:

I. The tortoise and the hare meet and decide to have a race.
II. They look for a judge.
III. The hare falls asleep in the woods, and the tortoise overtakes him.
IV. The hare awakens and speeds to the finish line.
V. The tortoise wins the race.

The next step is the actual writing of the script, which might turn out to be something like this:

ACT I   THE HARE AND THE TORTOISE

Hare: How very slow you are, Turtle! You'll never get anywhere moving so slowly!

Tortoise: Shall we run a race?

Hare: A race between you and me? You're crazy! Ho, ho, ho!

Encourage the students to make all the suggestions they want and to continue editing the script until they are satisfied with it. They can give the finished script a dramatic choral reading or memorize it for a production.

Very young students will find it easier to handle their parts if you use different colors to write, underline, or highlight the characters' names and perhaps their lines as well. When the time comes for the dramatic reading, you can assign a certain color to a particular student or a group.

The performance itself need not be complicated; a simple set and a few props are enough to set the stage. Children have vivid imaginations, and theater goes a long way toward stimulating them.

Puppet Shows

Telling a story with puppets is a good way to give the students' dramatic activities a bit of variety. There are almost no limits to the ways in which puppet shows can be put on. To make a simple backdrop, the class might attach a yardstick or broomstick to each end of a piece of butcher paper on which they have drawn a mural; two students then stretch the mural between them while the action goes on in front of it. There are, of course, many other ways of building a puppet theater, from tacking two sheets to a table with an opening left for manipulating the puppets to making a stage inside a box.

The puppets, too, can take many forms. Probably the simplest to make and operate are those that fit over the hand, but even they can be created in a number of different ways.

The student puppeteers might follow a written script or present an impromptu performance. Either way, a puppet show is very much like a play. (See the previous section entitled "Story Dramatizations.")

Monologues

You might consider monologue, another dramatic activity that is quite simple yet can do much to develop the students' self-confidence and ability to get their ideas, feelings, and presence across to others. Ask everyone in the class to present a monologue as if he or she were a character in a story. The character's words or thoughts should, of course, be presented orally, but allow older students to write them out if they are still hesitant to perform before the whole class, or allow them to perform in front of a small group.

Start by asking the students to discuss what their monologues will deal with. They might do this in small groups or all together. A character might introduce himself and then talk about his appearance, experiences, thoughts on a given subject, opinion of other characters, and so on. The Little Red Hen, for example, is likely to stress the importance of cooperation; the Turtle, in the story about the hare and the tortoise, the value of perseverance.

The students' age and the books they have read will undoubtedly shape their monologues. If several or all class members are familiar with the same books, you might ask someone to present a monologue without saying who the character is. It will then be up to the rest of the class to identify the character.

Dialogues

Carrying the monologue one step further, you might encourage the students to engage in a dialogue in which several students come together to express the thoughts of different characters in one or more books.

To replace a dialogue with a debate, all you have to do is propose a topic or have the students propose it and then ask the students to present opposing sides of the question. In doing so, the debaters use the arguments one would expect a certain character to utter. For example, the three little pigs would each in turn extol the virtues of straw, wood, and brick as a building material to prove that he or she had made the wisest choice. An example of a real debate carried on in a fourth-grade class about the book *My Name Is María Isabel* is found in the section entitled "The Transformative Language Arts Classroom" in Chapter 1.

Interviews

Dramatic expression can also take the form of an interview. The interviewee can be a character from a story or the author of a book. The questions can be generated individually or in cooperation, and they can be asked by one interviewer or by the class. You might experiment with different formats to add variety to the process and to discover what works best with your own students.

All the creative activities proposed in this chapter can contribute to the basic goal of ensuring that all students have an opportunity to explore different intelligence modalities, to discover their many hidden talents, and to strengthen their expressive abilities. From this wide repertoire, you will be able to choose appropriately in each circumstance what is best suited to the moment. Many times, the process will be as empowering as the product and provide ample moments for critical reflection as well as of joy.

9 HOME–SCHOOL INTERACTION

Strong bonds between home and school are essential if the educational process is to be effective. A school that validates a student's home life and shows an appreciation for his or her parents or caregivers goes a long way toward building the student's sense of identity and self-esteem. So also do parents who take a lively interest in what goes on in their children's education.

Although there is much talk about parental involvement in schools, much too frequently the reality is far from the stated goals. Except for truly affluent schools where there may be very active PTA organizations, the most frequent reason working-class parents come to school is to be informed of disciplinary or academic difficulties of their children. They also come to hear the school tell them what the school is doing, for example on open house nights, and occasionally to see their children perform. When their collaboration is requested, it is usually to solicit their assistance with fund-raising or field trips. Although it is true that federally funded programs require a parent advisory council, much too often these parents only serve in a rubber-stamp capacity. There are exceptions to this picture, but they are few and far between.

Some schools have developed programs for parent education. Although these programs can be very beneficial, they are seldom designed to include the parents as equal partners in the education of their children. Yet anything less than the recognition of parents as the first and most constant educators of their children threatens the foundations of the family.

There are two basic ways to involve parents in their children's schooling. The first calls for direct interaction and dialogue between the school and parents, leading to a joint plan of action. The second centers on activities promoted by the teacher but carried on at home by parents and their children. Far from being mutually exclusive, these two approaches are most effective if followed simultaneously.

Family–School Interaction

Teachers and parents alike stand to gain a great deal from a dialogue in which parents are encouraged to reflect critically on their relationship with their children and on how they might help the school raise the level of its programs to the benefit of those children (Ada, 1988; Ada & Campoy, 1998b, 1998c; Ada & Smith, 1998; Ada & Zubizarreta, 2001; Auerbach, 1990, 2002; Balderas, 1993; Keis, 2002a, 2002b; McCaleb, 1994; Murillo, 1987; Patrón, 1988; Reichmuth, 1988). All such exchanges of views must of course be based on the conviction that what make us most human are our abilities to learn, to increase our understanding, and to solve the problems that confront us.

Finding ways to involve working-class parents and, in particular, language minority parents in school programs has been a long-standing concern for a number of reasons. Some are socioeconomic: Many parents work long hours, including graveyard shifts, depend on public transportation, and have younger children to care for. Others are sociopsychological: Many parents either did not have the opportunity to go to school for very long or did not do well academically and therefore associate the school with some degree of shame or failure, and many are intimidated by an unfamiliar language and new attitudes that don't make them feel welcome. The school can overcome these barriers by inviting parents to take part in a process whose importance is emphasized by conducting the dialogue in the parents' first language and by making it easier for the parents to attend.

School–parent interaction can deal with a wide range of subjects and include a wide range of activities. Given the nature of this book, I will focus on one model, which centers on parental involvement through the use of children's literature and has in turn inspired other similar programs.

Family Literature Programs

In 1986, the *Programa de Literatura Familiar: Padres, Niños y Libros* (Family Literature Program: Parents, Children and Books) was initiated in 1986 in Watsonville, California, with the support of Alfonso Anaya, then the bilingual director for the Pájaro Valley School District. A detailed description, together with the testimonials of participating parents has been published (Ada, 1988), and the success of the program has inspired many replications throughout California and elsewhere (Ada & Zubizarreta, 2001; Keis, 2002a, 2002b; Zubizarreta, 1996).

The main purpose of the program is to promote in parents and children the practice of reading together and interacting together in a reflective dialogue about books. The fact that many of the parents in the initial program and other similar programs have had little schooling and reduced literacy exposure has in no way limited their participation. On the contrary, the parents are delighted with the opportunity to interact with high-quality books.

Reading at home is beneficial for children's academic growth. Meaningful interaction with parents and daily conversations about meaningful topics also result in more academic gain for children, regardless of the economic conditions or previous schooling of the parents. Stronger bonds between school and home give children greater assurance at school. Besides, knowing that their parents have a high regard for the learning process makes the children more eager to do well in their schoolwork.

The benefits of the program are by no means limited to the children. Many parents have told us how much they themselves have gained. They are more comfortable coming to school and interacting with teachers and administrators. They have acquired skills that make it easier for them to participate in groups and speak in public. And having discovered that the public library contains treasures that are easily accessible, they have begun reading themselves.

Depending on the number of parents who are expected, one or more facilitators are needed to run a family literature program. Usually, the time is divided between a general session and small-group sessions, each chaired by a facilitator. Some of the parents have eventually assumed the role of facilitator.

One of the most important elements of the process is that the meetings are conducted in the parents' first language. If there are both English-speaking and Spanish-speaking parents in a school, we recommend holding separate meetings so that the parents can express themselves fully. We have conducted similar meetings with speakers of many other languages—Chinese, Vietnamese, Laotian, and Tagalog—with the assistance of interpreters. The purpose in doing so has been to model and share the process. Although every one of those meetings has been very rewarding and satisfying for me, the ideal situation is that the speaker be someone from the parents' culture, speaking in the home language.

General Sessions.   At the first general session, the parents are told what the program hopes to achieve. Then the meeting is opened for a discussion of broad topics such as these:

- Parents are the first, the best, and the most reliable teachers of their children.
- Education constantly requires negotiation of meaning and values clarification, for which one's first language is most appropriate.
- Using a home language other than English does not hinder the acquisition of English in the children but actually facilitates it. If children become strong speakers of the home language, they will have many skills to transfer into English, and their English acquisition will be stronger.
- Affection, not violence or punishment, is conducive to learning. At the same time, affection helps to develop children's self-esteem and maintain their mental health. Besides acquiring deep psychological scars, abused children are more likely to go on being mistreated by others throughout their lives.
- Schoolwork is based on reading, so the better readers children become and the more they enjoy reading, the greater are their chances of success in school.
- In talking at home with parents, children develop listening abilities and enrich their language skills, which are important tools for school success.

The topics taken up at the general sessions should reflect the needs of the community. Parents, as well as teachers and school administrators, therefore decide on the agendas.

Every opportunity is taken to encourage discussion by all those present, not only remarks by the facilitator. Children's books are distributed at the end of the general session. If the parents will be divided into small groups, it might be a good idea to have three or four titles available so that the parents can choose the one they would like to discuss and, if possible, take home.

Including the exchange of views on topics of broad interest and the book distribution, the general session—the first part of the meeting—usually lasts about an hour.

Whenever space and facilitators are available, the second part of the meeting is conducted in small groups. If it is not possible to break into groups, the activities described below are carried on with the whole group.

Small Groups.   When conditions allow for small groups, the second part of the meeting is conducted in that fashion. If several picture books are being introduced, there will be one group at least per book. The teacher or other person who serves as facilitator will have read the book to be discussed ahead of time and will have prepared a list of talking points to guide the creative dialogue that will follow the reading, as described below. Each group session begins with an oral reading of the book by the facilitator. If this reading is done dramatically, parents who cannot read will find it easier to recall the story and retell it with the help of the illustrations. Parents who can read will also benefit, because this initial oral reading serves as a model for reading to children.

The postreading discussion is based on the creative reading process, whose phases were described in Chapter 1 and expanded on in "The Creative Dialogue" section in this chapter. (For a detailed guide and specific questions to facilitate the dialogue for several picture books effectively used with parents see *Transformative Family Literacy: Engaging in Meaningful Dialogue with Spanish-Speaking Parents* by R. Zubizarreta, 1996. The questions, of course, can be adapted to any language.)

All the parents should be made to feel that their opinions count and thus be encouraged to take part. Indeed, one of the assumptions of this program is that the use of literature invites parents to participate freely, without fear of misspeaking or of betraying ignorance on a given point. If parents disagree, the facilitator need not take sides but instead can encourage constructive dialogue in which everyone feels entitled to express his or her view. By helping the parents see the logic of the various positions, the facilitator will give them enough confidence to continue the discussion.

After taking part in the group discussion, the members are invited to join in producing a book of their own. They begin by dictating the text, which the facilitator writes on large sheets of paper. At the next meeting, they are given copies of these sheets, which by now are in book form.

Although no constraints are placed on these books, it is sometimes a good idea to offer certain suggestions. This will make it possible to produce a book in the limited time available; in addition, it will show the parents that a high value is placed on them as individuals and on their cultural heritage. These are some of the topics and formats we have used successfully:

- *From yesterday to tomorrow/Del ayer al mañana:* A collection of riddles, sayings, rhymes, lullabies, and tongue twisters makes parents aware of the folklore they know and proud to share it with their children.
- *The good and bad in my life/Lo bueno y lo malo:* A compilation of good and bad aspects of the participants' own lives serves as the basis for a discussion of what can be done to improve one's reality.
- *What I want for my children's future and how I will help them to reach these goals/Lo que quiero para el futuro de mis hijos y cómo voy a ayudarlos a conseguirlo:* Like the previous book, this is a book of contrasts. It helps both to set goals and to find ways to achieve them.
- *A moment that changed my life/Cuando mi vida cambió:* This book leads to useful reflection as the group compiles and shares its oral history.

Besides becoming authors in their own right, working in cooperative groups during the meetings, the parents are asked to encourage their children to produce books at home. Then, at the next meeting, the parents are invited to read or show their children's work. Ideally, the facilitator sees to it that the books are photocopied for distribution to all the group members.

The project that has been summarily described here has been carried on by me and by F. Isabel Campoy in numerous settings throughout the United States, sometimes as a program in which we have been continuously involved, sometimes as a kickoff session. The tenets of the project have been adopted and expanded by Richard Keis of Independence, Oregon. The *Familias y Libros*/Families and Books program that he has developed regularly brings authors, illustrators, and folksingers to meet with parents, who have first been introduced to books and tapes authored by the visiting artist. In turn, parents write their own books, which are published and distributed at the following meeting. (For more on that exciting project, see Keis, 2002a, 2002b.)

Parent–Child Interaction through Homework

Although parents are not always able to visit the school to discuss their children's education, teachers can enlist parental involvement by designing activities to be carried out at home.

It has been proposed that out-of-school assignments should be interesting and that the name *homework* be changed to *funwork* (Enright & McCloskey, 1988). I agree that these tasks should be as interesting and enjoyable as possible, and I further propose that they not be additional schoolwork to be done at home, but truly be "home" work, activities that can be done only at home because they require the student's interaction with the family. On a daily basis, teachers can brainstorm with the students questions that they can ask at home to continue exploring the issues presented in class.

The following pages describe activities that the students might undertake with their parents or caregivers during or after reading certain books. It is not a matter of parents helping their children with their schoolwork, but rather of children and parents joining in activities that everyone will find rewarding. Though they need not be complex, the activities ought to be meaningful, taking into account the reality of the home and the community.

For detailed explanation on how to foster the development of books written by or about family members, see *Authors in the Classroom* (Ada & Campoy, 2003).

The Family History Revisited.   There is no more solid basis on which to build education and develop one's personality than a positive self-image. Indeed, fostering every child's self-esteem should be the first priority of the learning process, yet it is difficult for children to take pride in themselves if they question the values of their families and communities.

By learning about their family history, the students can better understand their roots and thus come to feel identified with and linked to their family and community.

A Closer Look at Family, Friends, and Community. The students can come to the realization that their families and friends are protagonists in their own lives and, as such, are as important and interesting as the protagonists in the books they read. By comparing the attitudes and feelings of both sets of protagonists, the students can arrive at a fuller understanding and appreciation of those around them.

It might be a good idea to have the students form cooperative groups to draw up plans for making the comparison: What can they ask their family and friends so as to understand them better?

Reading Together at Home. Every reading program should include among its top priorities encouraging parents and children to share books at home. Try to find the best way to communicate this notion to parents, whether by meeting with them personally, in one of your telephone conversations, by letter, or by some other means. Some teachers send home cassettes on which they have recorded brief messages. Another idea is to have the students make posters depicting the joy of reading with their parents, to be taken home and displayed prominently as a reminder. Like all other activities I have suggested, this one will benefit from variety. On the other hand, because the idea is to create a habit, a certain amount of consistency is in order.

The books that are selected for reading and discussion by the students and their parents should deal with subjects such as good communication and family relations. By portraying understanding and tenderness on the part of the adult characters, the books can also subliminally model parental roles.

EXAMPLES

For All Grades

- Kurusa. 1985. *Streets Are Free*. Illustrated by Monika Doppert. Translated from the Spanish by Karen Englander. Copenhagen, Denmark: Annik. (Also in Spanish: *La calle es libre*. 1983. Caracas, Venezuela: Ekaré/Banco del Libro.)

A group of children living in the slum areas surrounding Caracas meet to decide how they can get a playground. After a series of disappointments and false promises from the authorities, they achieve their goal through their own efforts with the help of the community.

This book shows the need for people to get together and talk if they are to arrive at fruitful decisions. With its realistic pictures and its clear message, this book can help lay the groundwork for community action.

To make sharing books at home a habit, the students might either have to borrow books from the classroom or school library or have to accompany their parents to the public library. Consider giving the students a log, on heavy paper or in a folder, so that they can list all the books they read with their parents, a relative, or a caregiver. This person will sign the last column. Then, perhaps once a week, invite the students to share with their classmates a book they have read at home with their parents. The form for young students might be very simple, like the one shown in Figure 4.19 (p. 142). For older students, you might prepare a weekly or monthly calendar along the lines of the one shown in Figure 4.20 (p. 143).

Another possibility is to create some kind of display in which the titles of the books read by the students and their parents can be attractively shown.

Sharing and Connecting with Books Read in Class.   Another activity, which might supplement rather than replace the one just described, is to ask the students to share with their parents the books they read in class. They can take a copy of each book home and read it to their parents, or if not enough copies are available for them to take home, they can tell the story to their parents.

Encourage the students to decide in advance what questions they will ask their parents. The questions they draw up, perhaps in cooperative groups, might be along these lines:

- What did they like most about the story? What did they like least?
- Has something similar ever happened to them?
- Do they know anyone who resembles the main character?
- What would they have done if they had been in the character's place?
- What conclusion did they draw from the story?

Another possibility is to have the students read their parents only half the book or retell only half of the story and then ask their parents to predict the ending. The students might also ask their parents to make up a sequel or continuation. Of course, the students will be better able to carry out reading-related activities at home if they have already experienced them in class.

Authoring Books Together.   Once the students have practiced making books in class, you might ask them to undertake a similar project at home. Write the parents a note pointing out that it is essential that the book be a cooperative effort. You might even have the students write not only their own names on the cover but also those of family members who help them so that the adults will see that such assistance is appropriate.

Depending on the students' age, they might create the illustrations and dictate the text to parents or older siblings, or they might do the writing themselves and ask for help in producing the book. In either case, be sure to emphasize that developing the story line or researching the content can be a joint effort.

If the goals set forth in this book are to be met, every classroom should have a collection of student-made books. Many of these books will be produced by individual students, whether working at school or at home. Others

BOOKS I READ AT HOME AND WHO READS WITH ME

Date:	Title:	Who reads with me:
Oct. 15	The Upside Down Boy	Mom
Oct. 21	With Love, Little Red Hen	Dad
Nov. 3	Mama Provi and the Pot of Rice	Mom
Nov. 10	My Very Own Room	Mom

FIGURE 4.19   A Reading Log for the Lower Grades

BOOKS I READ AT HOME AND WHO READS WITH ME

My name: _Gloria_

Family members or friends who read with me:
Rebecca

Sunday	Monday	Tuesday	Wednesday	Thursday	Friday	Saturday
Spindle's End	Spindle's End	Rose Daughter	Rose Daughter	Rose Daughter		

FIGURE 4.20   A Reading Log for the Upper Grades

will be collaborative efforts, some enlisting the participation of parents. For instance, each student might prepare one or two pages at home with their parents' help; then the whole class together would assemble the pages into a book.

A Recipe Book.   This activity might start with reading a book that contains recipes or refers to cooking. Some examples are the following:

- Reiser, Lynn. 1998. *Tortillas and Lullabies/Tortillas y cancioncitas.* Illustrated by "Corazones valientes." New York: Greenwillow Books.
- Tenorio-Coscarelli, Jane. 1998. *The Tamale Quilt.* Murrieta, CA: 1/4 Inch Design.
- Balzola, Asun. 1986. *Santino el pastelero.* Barcelona: Destino.

Then you would tell each student to ask someone at home to provide a recipe for a favorite dish. Make it clear that the recipe need not be complicated. It might be for a main dish, a salad, a dessert, or even juice or flavored water. The only requirement is that the family member like whatever it is.

The student's next tasks are to write down the recipe (perhaps with help from a family member), to illustrate the dish, and to write down the name of the person who provided the recipe and how he or she learned it.

The recipes will be grouped by category and organized into a book.

A Book of Family Experiences.   Have the students follow the same steps as for the recipe book, but in this case, the objective is to collect anecdotes or experiences from family members.

Providing opportunities for both worlds of the child—home and school—to learn about each other and, through that knowledge, to develop respect and appreciation will enrich all involved: students, families, and teachers.

10 CULMINATING ACTIVITIES

According to the tenets of Transformative Education as set forth in Chapter 1 of this book, education ought not to be limited to the classroom. Instead, it must recognize that students are social beings, members of their families and the community at large, whose lives are works in progress. However much these individuals benefit by the learning process, they are not defined only by what goes on in school.

If it is to be a vital force, then, education must avoid empty ritual. Students must be freed from reading and language arts activities that are mere academic exercises or practice of discrete, isolated skills. On the contrary, reading and language arts must be a part of the students' very lives, helping them to better understand reality and to begin shaping it to their needs. Every book and every unit within a study plan should be considered to have achieved its objective only when it goes beyond the limits of the classroom and somehow enables the students to interact creatively with the world around them.

The interaction can be with students in other classes or other schools, with community groups, and with the students' own families. It can take many forms and have many purposes. The students might, for example, acquaint others with books they have read and enjoyed; publish their own books; invite family and community members to school for theatrical performances; or use the mass media—radio, television, newspapers, and magazines—to bring their ideas and artistic creations before large numbers of people. The only limit on these activities would be those that you set.

Plays and Puppet Shows

An extremely worthwhile activity is to encourage the students to present a play, a dramatic reading of a story, or a puppet show, using their own scripts.

One of the greatest benefits of such a project is the cooperation and camaraderie it fosters. Each class member should be given an assignment, and it will soon become clear that the performance cannot succeed unless everyone does his or her share. Another benefit is the self-confidence and selfesteem the students develop as they become accustomed to performing in public and receive recognition for a job well done. That the theater promotes many forms of creative expression and a wide range of skills goes without saying. The multiple benefits of theatrical activities were discussed in the section entitled "Plays and Dramatic Games" in Chapter 3.

We all know that what the audience sees and hears is vital, yet numerous activities must be carried on out of sight and earshot to ensure the success of the performance. In the real-life atmosphere of a production, students can undertake these activities with a clear sense of their importance.

Publicity. The students can publicize the performance in various ways. They can make posters and place them in strategic locations in the school and the community, they can place ads in the school newspaper and perhaps local ones as well, they can set up a telephone bank, and they can tape one or more announcements for broadcast over the school's public address system and perhaps even over local radio and television stations.

Encourage the members of the publicity committee to discuss these different channels of communication and to decide on the ones that are best suited for the task at hand.

Scenery and Stage Properties. The set and props need not be elaborate. They should, however, be well thought out and carefully constructed so as to help create a magical world in which the performance can take place. Give the students a great deal of freedom in constructing the backdrops, from drawing colorful scenes on the chalkboard to hanging real curtains at the back of the stage. A backdrop can be drawn on a transparency with colored markers and then projected onto the stage. Let the students use their imaginations as well in making the various movable props used to enhance the setting.

Costumes and Makeup. The students who are in charge of costumes and makeup have important backstage roles. If the performers' clothing is elaborate, the wardrobe crew will probably have to seek the help of adults who are willing to do the actual fitting and sewing, a task that requires both diplomacy and coordinating skills. After obtaining the costumes, this crew must care for them and be sure they are available when needed during the performance. The makeup artists, too, are likely to call on adults when the time comes to fit the performers with wigs and to apply greasepaint, powder, and the like.

A Poster Gallery

You might encourage the students to establish and operate a gallery for the display of posters on children's books and children's book characters, subject matter, authors, and illustrators. They might even take responsibility for approaching the administration of the school or the community center that is chosen as the gallery site both to explain the nature of the project and to obtain permission to carry it out.

The students will then have to make decisions about the operation of the gallery. They will be concerned with, among other things, how many posters or other visuals will ordinarily be on display, for how long (a week, two weeks, a month, or another suitable period of time), and the content of the material. The displays might, for example, present lively reports on books read by the entire class, by small groups, or by individual students; provide background on the lives and work of the authors and illustrators of those books; and, for special occasions, deal collectively with a number of books on certain topics.

Sharing Books

The class might build an activity around sharing books they have read and enjoyed or perhaps those they have made themselves. In such a project, the students would seek out other students in their school or other schools, residents of retirement or nursing homes, and other interested groups.

You and the class might decide on an each-one-reach-one approach; that is, every student in the project reads to another person. Or you might prefer group readings, in which four or five students read either chorally or sequentially. This arrangement is especially appropriate if the students have joined in telling a story by means of an illustrated big book.

A Classroom Library

With your encouragement, the students might establish a classroom library consisting of commercially published children's books, books they have made themselves, or a combination of the two.

At the outset, they will have to agree on a number of policy matters. For example, who will be allowed to borrow books? For how long? How can the library be certain that its books will be returned on time? How can a check be made on the location of the books at any given moment?

The class will have to assign the various tasks involved in operating the library. Will students take turns as head librarian? Who will prepare the catalog cards and how—by hand or in a computer? Will the cards list only the titles and authors of the books, or will the illustrators and the subjects be listed as well? Who will actually check out the books? Who will see that they are returned on time? Will a special committee be formed to recommend new books for the library, or will the class as a whole propose and vote on new titles to add to the collection?

Classroom Publishing

The students are likely to welcome the opportunity to establish a publishing house in the classroom. Modeling their work on that of professionals in the publishing industry, they will soon be producing their own books.

First, they will probably want to choose a name for the "firm," then decide what kinds of books to publish (stories, poems, plays, picture books, etc.). If they want to publish related material in separate series, they might give these collections special names.

To staff the publishing house, the class will have to be divided into several groups. One group will decide which books to publish, another will be in charge of editing the texts, another will ensure that appropriate illustrations are included, another will be responsible for printing and binding, another will handle the publicity, and still another will see that the books reach their readers. Ideally, every student should be involved in all these activities at one time or another.

A goal of the classroom publishing house should be to distribute copies of the books to the students' families and friends, to the school library, and to the public library. To this end, the students should write letters explaining the project and enlisting outside cooperation. For example, librarians might be asked to catalog the books as the first step toward including them in their libraries' permanent collections, and authors and commercial publishers of children's books might be asked to send the class samples of their work in exchange for student-produced books.

Literary Circles

Gatherings of people who are bound by a common interest in literature and the arts are far from new. In the seventeenth and eighteenth centuries, the aristocracy regularly held salons in which fashionable guests mingled with outstanding writers and artists of the time. Toward the end of the nineteenth century, the tradition of *tertulias literarias,* as they are called in Spain and Latin America, took a democratic turn as ordinary citizens congregated in cafes when authors and critics could be counted on to make their appearance. The discussion centered on the latest books, plays, and works of art, along with other cultural and political topics of the moment.

Today, the desire to exchange information and views on literature and the arts is still strong. Indeed, it has led to the formation of many more or less structured groups or circles within cultural organizations, clubs, and schools.

You might encourage the students to meet informally for a discussion of their own favorite books. These literary circles, or *tertulias literarias,* might take place for a few minutes at the end of the day or for a longer period at the end of the week. Or you might decide on a topic for the week (anything from bears to ghosts, ecology, divorce, or death in the family). Students who have read one or more books on the subject will be urged to discuss how the topic is treated in the books and then to answer questions from their classmates. This can be a good way to give the class an opportunity to talk about emotionally charged subjects, because the fact that they are dealt with in books lessens the personal threat that they could otherwise pose.

Whatever the culminating activities and whether chosen singly or combined, they should have the goal of transcending the boundaries of the classroom and facilitating student involvement in real-life, authentic projects. They will be beneficial to all if they are carried out with enthusiasm and everyone is invited to take part joyfully and creatively.

11 AN AUTHOR'S VISIT OR AUTHOR'S STUDY

The students' interest in literature is stimulated when they are aware of the people behind the creation of the books: the authors, illustrators, and translators. An author's visit (and, of course, this applies to an illustrator or a creative translator as well) is one of the most effective ways to develop this awareness in children.

The benefits of this activity are such that it deserves to be extended for a period of several weeks or months. For this reason, rather than including it as just one more of the culminating activities, it has been given its own chapter, albeit a brief one. In writing it, I have drawn extensively on the many times I have visited schools as an author and the wonderful creative activities with which teachers had prepared their students for these visits.

The main objectives of an author's visit are to convey children the following messages:

- Good books are fun and can be great friends to everyone; all we need to do is find those appropriate for each moment.
- Language belongs to all of us, and we can use it creatively to enhance our lives.
- Cultures are fascinating, and we can learn about them in books; by learning about other people, we can develop better relationships with them.
- Every child has the potential and the right to become the person he or she wants to be.
- There are multiple ways to express one's creativity and ideas, and these are worth exploring. The process will be full, and the final product will give us great satisfaction.
- Books are works of art but are also the product of the efforts of many people. There are many professions within the publishing industry, as within the production of all things around us. There are many ways of being useful and productive in life.
- We all have stories to tell. We all have known someone worth writing about. We all can be authors.

Because it is not always possible to have an author visit the classroom in person, the ideas given here could be applied to an author's study involving a simulated visit when one of the students, or perhaps another teacher in the school or a librarian, takes on the role of the author.

Even if the author is not going to visit the classroom, you can let her or him know that you are engaging in an author's study with your class. Some authors will be willing to send you their photo and some informative material to add to what you may have already obtained from publishers or the Internet. Certainly, most authors will be delighted to have you share the results of the project and pictures and samples of the students' work.

Selecting the Author

You might want to be the one to choose the author(s) to invite or to study. If you prefer to have the students make the choice, it will be important for them to become familiar with some works of the authors from among whom they will choose.

If you select more than one author to study during the year, it will be important that women as well as men be represented. You might also want to take this opportunity to make sure students get to know wonderful authors to whom they may not otherwise be exposed, authors who represent diverse cultures. The Bibliography at the end of the book will provide you with names of the most relevant Latino authors.

Preparing for the Visit or Study

The quality of the visit or study will be greatly enhanced by advanced preparations made by the teachers. Some suggestions are as follows:

- Prepare an exhibit of the author's books to display in the classroom and/or the school library.
- Create a bulletin board or wall display with book covers, photos of the author, quotes or sayings from the author, and so on.
- Read to, and with, the students as many of the author's books as possible.
- Encourage students to borrow books by the author from the school and public library and share them at home.

Turning the Focus on the Children

Explain to the students that the author (illustrator or translator) has made an effort to share her or his talents with them. Invite the students to prepare their own creations as a response to the books they have read so that they can share them with the author, whether in person or by mail.

The responses from the children can take many forms, some of which have been discussed in the previous chapter:

- Visual arts creations: posters, murals, dioramas of favorite moments in the story, painted T-shirts with characters or scenes from a book, masks of the characters, mobiles, etc.
- Verbal creations: poems, debates, interviews
- Musical creations: songs, dances
- Dramatic creations: plays, readers' theater

Facilitating Interaction

If the students are prepared for the dialogue with the author or whoever is representing the author, the communication will be more fluid. Learning to question is a very important part of learning to think and reflect. Encourage interesting questions, different for each child or each cooperative group. Encourage the students to assist in designing creative welcome banners or displays to greet the author(s) at the school and/or classroom. Have the children create their own original name tags, with very visible letters. This way, the author or visitor can refer to each child by name.

Becoming Authors

Turn the author's visit into a meeting of authors by encouraging the students to create their own books, perhaps following some of the suggestions given in the previous chapters.

Making the Visit or Study a Whole-School Event

Have the students organize one or more of the following:

- A students' or young authors' book fair, at which original books from all children in the school will be displayed
- A schoolwide display of students' art created in response to the author's work.
- A classroom doors gallery. Every class decorates their classroom door in response to one of the author's books.
- Keep the whole experience joyful. Have fun!

This project should continue to reinforce the idea that learning is joyful. As an author, I have had extraordinarily good moments during author's visits. I have been touched by the ingenuity of the teachers and the imagination of the children. It has been fun, for example, to listen to children impersonating me, see the ways they have drawn me, or read the "autobiographies" they have written of me, particularly when they have made use of the dedications in my books to make stories about my friends and relatives or when they have interpreted the scenes of many of my books of fantasy as being real episodes of my life.

I will always remember the little girl who, touching me, said, "Ah, but you're real. I thought you were like Little Red Riding Hood!" But I particularly hold dear the memory of a little kindergartner in Salem, Massachusetts, who thanked me so profusely that I wanted to know which book she had liked so much. Her explanation held quite a lesson. She said, "I'm thanking you for your video. You told us you also needed to learn to crawl." I said no such thing in the video she had seen, but it does show some baby pictures. For her, that meant I also had to learn how to crawl—and that gave her a message of hope.

That's the message authors' visits and authors' studies can convey: We all started as children. Anything anyone they admire has done, *they* can do. And this is why it is also so important that teachers reveal themselves to their students as the children they were, as the students they were. Children have not had a model for growing up, because there is no time in childhood to witness that. It is up to us, the adults in their lives, to give them the message of reassurance and hope.

12 EVALUATION

One of the paradoxes that teachers face is that many academic decisions are made by people outside of the classroom, often even outside of the area of education, and are forced on teachers without taking into account their teaching preferences, their educational training, and their experience.

Among the decisions that are informed by political and even economic pressure, no example is more flagrant than that of standardized testing. Yet corporations and businesses—the workplaces that many of today's students must soon join as productive members—repeatedly point out the need to prepare young people for a changing world. It is a world that demands the ability to reason; to make informed decisions; to engage in creative problem solving; to be able to answer new questions as they arise; and to retrieve, process, and manipulate data.

The role of the United States in the world market is centered in three areas: (1) the development of high technology; (2) the communication industry, ranging from movies to music, with every possible sort of publication in between; and (3) higher learning, whether by bringing international students to this country or educating throughout the world. Every one of these fields requires high levels of independent thinking. Educating children to fill positions of leadership in this society or to hold professional positions will require much more than teaching isolated skills that can be tested by standardized measures.

It is already very evident that there is a major drop in students' results in the standard tests at the fourth-grade level, when language becomes more cognitively demanding and the depth of the reasoning processes increases. It is therefore essential to develop ways of evaluating how what students do in school prepares them to develop to their fullest potential. At the same time, we should bear in mind that students who participate fully in the interactive and critical activities proposed here rather than being "taught to the test" quite possibly will also perform very well in those tests (for more on this subject, see Mayer, 1988; Knepper, 2001).

If evaluation is to be truly useful, of course, it cannot merely quantify schoolwork but must be an educational process in itself. It will allow the students to see for themselves which skills they have acquired and which activities have been most effective in promoting learning and in furthering their development; moreover, it will suggest to the teacher how his or her teaching methods might be improved in the future.

End-of-Project Reflections

Involving the students in reflection about their own learning process can be one of the most valuable learning activities. Just as the old fable proposes that better than giving someone a fish is teaching them to fish, in the learning process "to learn how to learn" should be the ultimate goal, a far richer one than learning any specific content.

At the end of a unit or a project, it is an excellent idea to give the students the time and space to reflect on the questions that follow and to answer them. Depending on the age of the students, you might want to have them brainstorm the questions in a group and answer orally or in writing. But although you can follow different processes and vary the language as you see appropriate, the ultimate goal should be that each child becomes responsible for his or her individual reflections and answers. One of the most important benefits of this activity for the group is to see the diversity of answers, which will correspond, of course, to the diversity found among themselves as among any group of human beings.

The questions are as follows:

- What was the most important thing you learned?
- How is what you learned important for you?
- What helped you learn?
- What did others learn from you? How did you help others learn?
- What questions do you still have? What is not clear?
- What else would you like to learn about this topic?
- How do you feel about the project you just completed?

These seven questions facilitate the whole reflective process. The answers will be very revealing to the teacher.

Reader's Journals

It is a good idea to encourage students to keep individual journals in which they record all the books they read or listen to. The type of entry will, of course, depend on the students' age and repertoire of skills.

The journals of the younger students, perhaps those in kindergarten or first grade, are likely to consist of drawings and book titles. For books you read to the class, a page in a journal that is titled, for example, "The books my teacher read to me" might look something like the one shown on Figure 4.21 (p. 154), with the title of the book written in by you beforehand or copied from models you provide. If the students can read and write, with perhaps some help from you, their journal pages will probably be quite similar. The journals themselves, however, might be given a title like "Books I Have Read."

Whether they read on their own or have books read to them, first and second graders can be expected to provide more information in their journals. On each page, they might give the title of the book, the date they started reading, and a drawing or brief comment about something they liked in the book. An example appears in Figure 4.22 (p. 155).

By the time the students are in fourth, fifth, and sixth grades, their journals will be more sophisticated. Each entry might give not only the title and the author of the book, but also the period when the book was read, a brief statement about the characters, and perhaps some personal comments. An example appears in Figure 4.23 (p. 156).

A Class Reading Log

With your encouragement, the class might keep track of their reading activities. The log would record, among other items, the books the students read; trips to the school library, the public library, or both; and letters written to and received from authors and illustrators.

In time, other information might be included in the log, for example, the results of a survey undertaken by class members to determine which authors, titles, and subjects are most popular. Trends in reading habits—hopefully, showing an increase in the number of books the students read on their own—would probably be of interest as well.

Reading and "Real Life"

It would be worthwhile to ask the students what impact, if any, their reading has had on their lives. For example, have the books they have read, together with the classroom dialogues and activities in which they have taken part,

FIGURE 4.21 **A Reader's Journal Page for Very Young Students**

Title of the book: Friend Frog

Date: May 5, 2002

Something I like in this book: Frog and Field Mouse
became good friends.

FIGURE 4.22   **A Reader's Journal Page for Beginning Readers**

Date I started the book: October 5, 2004

Date I finished the book: October 16, 2004

Book title: The Gold Coin

Author: Alma Flor Ada

Characters: Juan, doña Josefa, the girl and others

Setting: Latin American countryside

Something special about the book: I liked that Juan was able to change.

He stop being greedy and became generous, like doña Josefa. I think

the book tells us we can all learn and become better.

FIGURE 4.23   A Reader's Journal Page for Students in the Upper Grades

shed light on a puzzling subject? Helped them in another subject? Made it easier for them to get along with others?

The answers might be written, oral, or drawn as pictures. If they are oral, you will probably want to tape-record them or take notes as the students speak. Whatever form the answers are in, be sure the process is as natural and nonthreatening as possible, preferably part of another activity. You might suggest that the students either deal with the subject in separate notebooks or set aside special sections in their journals, perhaps under the headings "Books and I" and "Books and my life."

The students need not write their comments immediately after reading a book but instead whenever a connection between the book and their own lives comes up. To help them see these connections, you might draw up and discuss with them a list of possibilities. These are some of the items you might include:

- Places I know that are like those in the book
- A person I know who resembles a character in the book
- Times when I have felt like one of the characters in the book
- Things in the book that I would like to do
- Places in the book that I would like to visit someday
- Something I learned from reading the book and want to remember

The students should understand that being able to read is a human right but that, because many people throughout the word are unable to read, it is also a privilege to be treasured. They should also understand that all children ought to be provided with lovely books written especially for them yet many do not have access to them. This right, too, carries with it a privilege and an opportunity that should be fully enjoyed, not wasted.

If the students are enabled to feel that reading and group dialogue help them better understand themselves and their relationship to others and better appreciate universal feelings and values, they may well come to see themselves as advocates of reading. So this might be a good time to talk with them about how they can convey to others their friendship with books. Happily, by the very act of sharing their love of reading and their interest in what they have read, they will become even better readers.

I hope that all magical encounters between children and books will lead to ever-broadening experiences and ever greater opportunities. May you who facilitate that magical encounter have the joy of seeing it bloom.

HISPANIC PROVERBS AND SAYINGS

A buen hambre, no hay pan duro.
[When we're hungry, no bread is too hard.]

In case of need, one should not be too choosy about accepting what one can get.

A caballo regalado, no se le mira el colmillo.
[Don't look a gift-horse in the mouth.]

Don't demand too much of something you receive free or at little cost.

A Dios rogando y con el mazo dando.
[Praying to God but continuing to work.]

While you're waiting for assistance or good luck, move things along on your own.

A mal tiempo, buena cara.
[Face bad weather with a smiling face.]

A positive attitude will go far in overcoming difficulties.

A quien madruga, Dios lo ayuda.
[The early bird gets the worm.]

If you want to make things happen, get up early; that is, do something for yourself.

**Camarón que se duerme,
se lo lleva la corriente.**
[The sleeping shrimp will be carried away by the water's current.]

Keep on your toes if you hope to achieve your goals.

Dime con quien andas y te diré quién eres.
[Tell me who is your friend, and I will tell you who you are.]

Friends always influence us, whether for good or bad.

Donde las dan, las toman./
El que la hace, la paga./
Quien siembra vientos, recoge tempestades.
[If one sows winds, one gathers storms.]

Treat others as you would like them to treat you.

El que mucho abarca, poco aprieta.
[There is just so much one can hold onto.]

If one tries to do more than one's time and ability allow, one will probably end up doing a poor job.

El que mucho habla, yerra./
En boca cerrada no entran moscas.
[Flies won't enter a closed mouth.]

It's important to think before one speaks; otherwise, one is likely to say something foolish.

En casa del herrero, cuchillo de palo.
[The blacksmith's knife is made of wood.]

People too busy working away from home often fail to give their family or home the same attention they give their work.

Haz bien y no mires a quién.
[Be ready to help everyone, no matter who they may be.]

Treat everyone only one way: well.

Hoy por ti, mañana por mí.
[Today is your turn, tomorrow will be mine.]

Be generous on helping others, for someday you may need their help.

La ambición rompe el saco.
[A bag too full will break.]

Greed does not bring happiness.

Más sabe el diablo por viejo que por diablo.
[The devil knows more because he is old than because he is the devil.]

Wisdom comes with age and experience.

Más vale pájaro en mano, que ciento volando.
[A bird in the hand is worth more than a hundred in the bush.]

Settle for something you can count on rather than hope that something better will come along.

No hay mal que dure cien años,
ni cuerpo que lo resista.
[Nothing bad lasts a hundred years. Nor would anyone survive it.]

All bad things eventually come to an end.

No por mucho madrugar
amanece más temprano./
Poco a poco se anda lejos.
[The sun doesn't rise earlier, just because we get up. A
step at a time will cover a long distance.]

Don't be in a hurry; little by little, you
will get things done right.

Quien a buen árbol se arrima,
buena sombra le cobija.
[A good tree gives a good shade.]

Choose your friends carefully if you
want their support.

Quien bien siembra, bien recoge.
[Sow good deeds, and you will reap goodness.]

Doing what is right brings rewards.

Quien mal anda, mal acaba.
[He who goes in a bad direction will reach a bad
destination.]

Negative actions lead to negative
consequences.

Quien tiene tejado de vidrio,
no le tire piedras al vecino.
[If you have a glass roof, don't throw stones to your
neighbor's roof.]

Don't be quick to criticize others,
because you also are far from perfect.

Quien ve las barbas de su vecino arder,
ponga las suyas en remojo.
[If the beard of your neighbor is on fire, make sure to
soak yours in water.]

Learn from the experiences of others.

Vísteme despacio, que voy de prisa.
[Dress me slowly, I'm in a hurry.]

Go slowly if you want things to come
out right the first time and not waste
extra time redoing them.

STORY BEGINNINGS AND ENDINGS

SOME WAYS TO BEGIN A STORY

Allá por el tiempo de mi tatarabuela…

[When my great-grandmother was a child…]

Cuentan los que lo vieron, y así me lo dijeron…

[Those who saw it say that…]

En el País de Irás y No Volverás…

[In the land of no return…]

En la Tierra del Olvido, donde de nada nadie se acuerda, había…

[In the land where all is forgotten and no one remembers, there once was…]

En tiempos de Mari Castaña…

[In the times of Old Mother Chestnut…]

En un país muy lejano…

[In a faraway land…]

Ésta era una vez…

[Once upon a time…]

Érase lo que se era, y el mal que se vaya, y el bien que se quede…

[Let it be as it may, and let all things bad disappear and all good things remain…]

Hace mucho, pero mucho tiempo…

[A very long time ago…]

Para saber y contar y contar para aprender…

[To know in order to tell and to tell in order to know…]

¿Quieren que les cuente un cuento?

[Shall I tell you a story?]

Una vez, érase que se era…

[Once upon a long time…]

In addition, this folklore-inspired story beginning is appropriate for the classroom:

Les voy a contar lo que pasó
   en un lugar muy lejano
   cerca del cielo.
   Ustedes, como oyentes buenos,
   escúchenme calladitos,
   sentaditos en el suelo.

[I am now going to tell you what happened
in a faraway land
very close to the sky.
As the good listeners you are,
listen to me very quietly
as you sit on the floor.]

SOME WAYS TO END A STORY

…así pasaron muchos años
   hasta que este cuento
   se perdió entre castaños.

[…and many years have passed
since this story
got lost among the chestnut trees.]

…cuento contado
   de la chimenea al tejado.

[… a story finished
from the chimney to the roof.]

…entre por el sano
   salga por el roto
   y el que quiera venga
   y me cuente otro.

[…let it enter where it's whole
and exit where it's torn.
And anyone is welcome
to tell me another one.]

…este cuento se entró
   por un caminito plateado
   y salió por otro dorado.
   Y el tuyo no ha empezado.

[…this story entered
by a silver path;
it exited by a golden one.
And where is yours? When will it start?]

…esto es verdad y no miento
   como me lo contaron
   se los cuento.

[…this is true. I tell no lies.
I just tell it
as they told me.]

…fueron muy felices
   y comieron perdices
   y a mí no me dieron
   porque no quisieron.

[… they lived happily ever after,
eating partridges for lunch,
and gave me none
because they chose not to.]

…se acabó el cuento,
   se lo llevó el viento
   y se fue volando
   por la mar adentro.

[…this is the end of the story
the wind has carried it away;
it left flying
to the deep blue sea.]

…y Colorín Colorado
   este cuento se ha acabado.

[…and little bird of many colors
this is the end of my tale.]

…y se acabó lo que se daba.

[…and this is all there was!]

…zapatito roto,
   cuéntame tú otro.

[…little torn shoe
now it's your turn to tell me one.]

If after telling a story, you want your students to return to their seats, you might say:

…y aquí se rompió una taza
   y cada quien para su casa.

[…and now that the cup is broken,
let everyone return home.]

LITERATURE FOR CHILDREN AND ADOLESCENTS BY LATINA AND LATINO WRITERS

This bibliography constitutes an effort to offer to the reader a sampling of what Latino authors and illustrators are creating and publishing in the United States. It does not aim to be all encompassing, nor does it intend to exclude; it is meant only to be representative.

In a very few instances, books by non-Latinos have been included when the authors have written from a profound depth of understanding of the Latino culture and the books have gained great acceptability among Latinos.

To make this bibliography of greatest use to the reader, the titles have been grouped according to genre, language, and appropriate occasion, purpose, and setting. The following list gives the categories used. Books are grouped in the bilingual category when the text appears in English and Spanish in the same book.

When separate editions in English and Spanish exist, the English edition has been listed and a note added as to existence of a Spanish edition.

When there are several books in Spanish that have not yet been translated into English, a separate category for Spanish titles appears.

1. **Nursery Rhymes and Oral Folklore: Riddles, Rhymes, Songs, etc.**
   Bilingual Anthologies
   Anthologies in Spanish

2. **Poetry**
   Anthologies in English
   Anthologies in Spanish
   Bilingual Poetry by a Single Author
   Poetry by a Single Author in English
   Poetry by a Single Author in Spanish

3. **Theater**
   Bilingual Anthologies
   Anthologies in English
   Anthologies in Spanish
   Collections of Plays by a Single Author in English and Spanish
   Individual Plays in English
   Individual Plays in Spanish

4. **Art**
   Art Anthologies in English and Spanish
   Bilingual Books about Individual Artists
   Books about Individual Artists in English

5. **Biography**
   Biography Collections in English and Spanish
   Individual Biographies in English and Spanish

6. **Autobiographical Narrative**
   Bilingual Autobiographical Picture Books
   Autobiographical Picture Books in English and Spanish
   Autobiographical Narrative in English and Spanish

7. **Folktales and Legends**
   Bilingual Folktales and Legends
   Folktales and Legends in English and in Spanish
   Bilingual Original Folktales
   Original Folktales in English and Spanish

8. **Fantasy**
   Bilingual Fantasy Picture Books
   Fantasy Picture Books in English and in Spanish

9. **Contemporary Realistic Fiction**
   Bilingual Realistic Picture Books—U.S. Setting
   Realistic Picture Books in English and Spanish—U.S. Setting
   Bilingual Realistic Picture Books—Latin American Setting
   Realistic Picture Books in English and Spanish—Latin American
     Setting
   Realistic Narrative in English and Spanish—U.S. Setting
   Realistic Narrative in English—Latin American Setting

10. **Historical Fiction by Latino and Non-Latino Authors**

1. NURSERY RHYMES AND ORAL FOLKLORE: RIDDLES, RHYMES, SONGS, ETC.

Bilingual Anthologies

Ada, Alma Flor, and F. Isabel Campoy (Eds.). 2003. *Pio Peep.* Illustrated by Viví Escrivá. New York: Hyperion.

Delacre, Lulú (Ed.). 1989. *Arroz con Leche: Popular Songs and Rhymes from Latin America.* Selected and illustrated by Lulú Delacre. New York: Scholastic.

Delacre, Lulú (Ed.). 1990. *Las Navidades: Popular Christmas Songs from Latin America.* Selected and illustrated by Lulú Delacre. New York: Scholastic.

Frasconi, Antonio. 1961. *The Snow and the Sun/La nieve y el sol. A South American Folk Rhyme in Two Languages.* Woodcuts by Antonio Frasconi. New York: Harcourt Brace & World, Inc.

González, Ralfka, and Ana Ruiz (Eds.). 1995. *Mi primer libro de dichos/My First Book of Proverbs.* Selected and illustrated by R. González and A. Ruiz. Emeryville, CA: Children's Book Press.

Jaramillo, Nelly Palacio (Ed.). 1994. *Grandmother's Nursery Rhymes/Las Nanas de Abuelita.* Illustrated by Elivia. New York: Henry Holt and Company.

Orozco, José Luis (Ed.). 1994. *De Colores and Other Latin-American Folk Songs for Children.* Illustrated by Elisa Kleven. New York: Dutton Children's Books.

Orozco, José Luis (Ed.). 1997. *Diez deditos: Ten Little Fingers and Other Play Rhymes and Action Songs from Latin-America.* Illustrated by Elisa Kleven. New York: Dutton Children's Books.

Anthologies in Spanish

Ada, Alma Flor (Ed.) 1992. *El cuento del gato y otras poesías favoritas.* Carmel, CA: Hampton-Brown.

Jiménez, Emma Holguín, and Conchita Morales Puncel (Eds.). 1969. *Para chiquitines: Cancioncitas, versitos y juegos meñiques.* Illustrated by Gilbert T. Martínez. Glendale, CA: Bowmar.

2. POETRY

Anthologies in English

Ada, Alma Flor, and F. Isabel Campoy (Eds.). 2000. *Dreaming Fish.* Collection Gateways to the Sun. Miami, FL: Alfaguara.

Ada, Alma Flor, and F. Isabel Campoy (Eds.). 2000. *Flying Dragon.* Collection Gateways to the Sun. Miami, FL: Alfaguara.

Ada, Alma Flor, and F. Isabel Campoy (Eds.). 2000. *Laughing Crocodiles.* Collection Gateways to the Sun. Miami, FL: Alfaguara.

Ada, Alma Flor, and F. Isabel Campoy (Eds.). 2000. *Singing Horse.* Collection Gateways to the Sun. Miami, FL: Alfaguara.

Ada, Alma Flor, Violet J. Harris, and Lee Bennet Hopkins (Eds.). 1993. *A Chorus of Cultures: Developing Literacy through Multicultural Poetry.* Carmel, CA: Hampton-Brown.

Mora, Pat (Ed.). 2001. *Love to Mamá: A Tribute to Mothers.* Illustrated by Paula S. Barragán. New York: Lee & Low.

Anthologies in Spanish

Ada, Alma Flor (Ed.). 1992. *Caballito blanco y otras poesías favoritas.* Carmel, CA: Hampton-Brown.

Ada, Alma Flor (Ed.). 1992. *Cinco pollitos y otras poesías favoritas.* Carmel, CA: Hampton-Brown.

Ada, Alma Flor (Ed.). 1992. *Días y días de poesía.* Carmel, CA: Hampton-Brown.

Ada, Alma Flor, and Francisca Isabel Campoy (Eds.). 1996. *Dulce es la sal.* Orlando, FL: Harcourt Brace & Company.

Ada, Alma Flor, and Francisca Isabel Campoy (Eds.). 1996. *Gorrión, gorrión.* Orlando, FL: Harcourt Brace & Company.

Ada, Alma Flor, and Francisca Isabel Campoy (Eds.). 1996. *Huertos de coral.* Orlando, FL: Harcourt Brace & Company.

Ada, Alma Flor, and Francisca Isabel Campoy (Eds.). 1996. *Nuevo día.* Orlando, FL: Harcourt Brace & Company.

Ada, Alma Flor, and Francisca Isabel Campoy (Eds.). 1996. *La rama azul.* Orlando, FL: Harcourt Brace & Company.

Ada, Alma Flor, and Francisca Isabel Campoy (Eds.). 1996. *Ríos de lava.* Orlando, FL: Harcourt Brace & Company.

Ada, Alma Flor, and Francisca Isabel Campoy (Eds.). 1996. *El verde limón.* Orlando, FL: Harcourt Brace & Company.

Ada, Alma Flor, and F. Isabel Campoy (Eds.). 1998. *El camino de tu risa. Música amiga 9.* Illustrated by Ulises Wensell. Westlake, OH: Del Sol.

Ada, Alma Flor, and F. Isabel Campoy (Eds.). 1998. *Canción y alegría. Música amiga 3.* Illustrated by Ulises Wensell. Westlake, OH: Del Sol.

Ada, Alma Flor, and F. Isabel Campoy (Eds.). 1998. *Canta la letra. Música amiga 2.* Illustrated by Ulises Wensell. Westlake, OH: Del Sol.

Ada, Alma Flor, and F. Isabel Campoy (Eds.). 1998. *Caracolí. Música amiga 6.* Illustrated by Ulises Wensell. Westlake, OH: Del Sol.

Ada, Alma Flor, and F. Isabel Campoy (Eds.). 1998. *Con ton y son. Música amiga 5.* Illustrated by Ulises Wensell. Westlake, OH: Del Sol.

Ada, Alma Flor, and F. Isabel Campoy (Eds.). 1998. *Corre al coro. Música amiga 4.* Illustrated by Ulises Wensell. Westlake, OH: Del Sol.

Ada, Alma Flor, and F. Isabel Campoy (Eds.). 1998. *Do, re, mi, ¡sí, sí! Música amiga 8.* Illustrated by Ulises Wensell. Westlake, OH: Del Sol.

Ada, Alma Flor, and F. Isabel Campoy (Eds.). 1998. *¡Qué rica la ronda! Música amiga 1.* Illustrated by Ulises Wensell. Westlake, OH: Del Sol.

Ada, Alma Flor, and F. Isabel Campoy (Eds.). 1998. *Sigue la música. Música amiga 7.* Illustrated by Ulises Wensell. Westlake, OH: Del Sol.

Ada, Alma Flor, and F. Isabel Campoy (Eds.). 1998. *El son del sol. Música amiga 10.* Illustrated by Ulises Wensell. Westlake, OH: Del Sol.

Ada, Alma Flor, and F. Isabel Campoy (Eds.). 2000. *Antón Pirulero.* Colección Puertas al Sol. Miami, FL: Alfaguara.

Ada, Alma Flor, and F. Isabel Campoy (Eds.). 2000. *Chuchurumbé.* Colección Puertas al Sol. Miami, FL: Alfaguara.

Ada, Alma Flor, and F. Isabel Campoy (Eds.). 2000. *Mambrú.* Colección Puertas al Sol. Miami, FL: Alfaguara.

Ada, Alma Flor, and F. Isabel Campoy (Eds.). 2000. *Pimpón.* Colección Puertas al Sol. Miami, FL: Alfaguara.

Bilingual Poetry by a Single Author

Ada, Alma Flor. 1997. *Gathering the Sun: An Alphabet in Spanish and English.* Translated by Rosa Zubizarreta. Illustrated by Simón Silva. New York: Lothrop. New edition: Harper Collins, 2001.

Alarcón, Francisco X. 1997. *Laughing Tomatoes and Other Spring Poems/Jitomates risueños y otros poemas de primavera.* Illustrated by Maya Christina González. San Francisco: Children's Book Press.

Alarcón, Francisco X. 1998. *From the Bellybutton of the Moon and Other Summer Poems/Del ombligo de la Luna y otros poemas de verano.* Illustrated by Maya Christina González. San Francisco: Children's Book Press.

Alarcón, Francisco X. 1999. *Angels Ride Bikes and Other Fall Poems/Los ángeles andan en bicicleta y otros poemas de otoño.* Illustrated by Maya Christina González. San Francisco: Children's Book Press.

Alarcón, Francisco X. 2001. *Iguanas in the Snow and Other Winter Poems/Iguanas en la nieve y otros poemas de invierno.* Illustrated by Maya Christina González. San Francisco: Children's Book Press.

Mora, Pat. 1994. *The Desert Is My Mother/El desierto es mi madre.* Illustrated by Daniel Lechón. Houston, TX: Piñata Books.

Poetry by a Single Author in English

Anaya, Rudolfo. 2000. *Elegy on the Death of César Chávez.* Illustrated by Gaspar Enríquez. El Paso, TX: Cinco Puntos Press.

Castillo, Ana. 2000. *My Daughter, My Son, the Eagle, the Dove: An Aztec Chant.* Illustrated by Susan Guevara. New York: E. P. Dutton.

Mora, Pat. 1996. *Confetti: Poems for Children.* Illustrated by Enrique O. Sánchez. New York: Lee & Low.

Soto, Gary. 1992. *Neighborhood Odes.* Illustrated by David Díaz. San Diego, CA: Harcourt Brace Jovanovich. New edition: 1995. *Canto familiar.* Illustrated by Annika Nelson. San Diego, CA: Harcourt Brace Children's Books, 1995. (Although the title is in Spanish the poems are in English.)

Soto, Gary. 1995. *New and Selected Poems.* San Francisco: Chronicle Books.

Soto, Gary. 1997. *Junior College.* San Francisco: Chronicle Books.

Poetry by a Single Author in Spanish

Ada, Alma Flor. 1988. *A la sombra de un ala*. Illustrated by Ulises Wensell. Madrid, Spain: Escuela Española.

Ada, Alma Flor. 1990. *Abecedario de los animales*. Illustrated by Viví Escrivá. Madrid, Spain: Espasa-Calpe.

Ada, Alma Flor. 1993. *Canción de todos los niños del mundo*. Boston: Houghton-Mifflin.

Ada, Alma Flor. 1987. *Una vez en el medio del mar*. Illustrated by Ulises Wensell. Madrid, Spain: Escuela Española.

Freire de Matos, Isabel. 1968. *ABC de Puerto Rico*. Illustrated by Antonio Martorell. Sharon, CN: Troutman Press.

Galarza, Ernesto. (No date). *Chogorrón*. Colección Mini-Libros. San José, CA: Editorial Almadén.

Galarza, Ernesto. (No date). *Más poemas párvulos*. Colección Mini-Libros. San José, CA: Editorial Almadén.

Galarza, Ernesto. (No date). *Poemas párvulos*. Colección Mini-Libros. San José, CA: Editorial Almadén.

Galarza, Ernesto. (No date). *Poemas Pe-que Pe-que Pe-que-ñitos*. Colección Mini-Libros. San José, CA: Editorial Almadén.

Galarza, Ernesto. (No date). *Rimas tontas*. Colección Mini-Libros. San José, CA: Editorial Almadén.

Galarza, Ernesto. (No date). *Zoo-Fun*. Colección Mini-Libros. San José, CA: Editorial Almadén.

Galarza, Ernesto. (No date). *Zoo-Risa*. Colección Mini-Libros. San José, CA: Editorial Almadén.

Martí, José. 1997. *Los zapaticos de rosa*. Illustrated by Lulú Delacre. New York: Lectorum.

3. THEATER

Bilingual Anthologies

Carlson, Lori Marie (Ed.). 1999. *You're On! Seven Plays in English and Spanish*. New York: Morrow Junior Books.

Rosenberg, Joe (Ed.). 1995. *¡Aplauso! Hispanic Children's Theatre*. Houston, TX: Arte Público Press.

Anthologies in English

Vigil, Ángel. 1996. *¡Teatro! Hispanic Plays for Young People*. Englewood CO: Teacher Ideas Press/Libraries Unlimited Inc.

Anthologies in Spanish

Ada, Alma Flor, Francisca Isabel Campoy, and Alberto Castilla (Eds.). 1996. *Acto final*. Orlando, FL: Harcourt Brace.

Ada, Alma Flor, and Francisca Isabel Campoy (Eds.). 1996. *Actores y flores.* Orlando, FL: Harcourt Brace.

Ada, Alma Flor, and Francisca Isabel Campoy (Eds.). 1996. *Saludos al público.* Orlando, FL: Harcourt Brace.

Collections of Plays by Single Authors in English and Spanish

Ada, Alma Flor, and Francisca Isabel Campoy. 1996. *Escenas y alegrías.* Orlando, FL: Harcourt Brace.

Ada, Alma Flor, and Francisca Isabel Campoy. 1996. *Primer acto.* Orlando, FL: Harcourt Brace.

Ada, Alma Flor, and Francisca Isabel Campoy. 1996. *Risas y aplausos.* Orlando FL: Harcourt Brace.

Castañeda, Omar. 1991. *Dance of the Conquest.* Illustrated by Véronique Fontaine. Kane Publishing.

Individual Plays in English

Ada, Alma Flor. 2001. *Serafina's Birthday.* Illustrated by Claudia Legnazzi. In A. F. Ada and F. I. Campoy (Eds.). *Roll 'N' Role.* Miami, FL: Alfaguara.

Ada, Alma Flor. 2001. *Goldie Hen.* Illustrated by Felipe Ugalde. In A. F. Ada and F. I. Campoy (Eds.) *Top Hat.* Miami, FL: Alfaguara.

Ada, Alma Flor. 2001. *Puss in Boots.* Illustrated by Gabriel Gutiérrez. In A. F. Ada and F. I. Campoy (Eds.). *Curtains Up!* Miami, FL: Alfaguara.

Ada, Alma Flor, 2001. *Christmas Presents.* Illustrated by Claudia de Teresa. In A. F. Ada and F. I. Campoy (Eds). *Top Hat.* Miami, FL: Alfaguara.

Ada, Alma Flor, and F. Isabel Campoy. 2001. *The Friendly Ant.* Illustrated by Felipe Ugalde. In A. F. Ada and F. I. Campoy (Eds.). *Roll 'N' Role.* Miami, FL: Alfaguara.

Belpré, Pura. 1999. *Tropical Memories.* English translation by Lori Marie Carlson. In Lori Marie Carlson (Ed.). *You're On! Seven Plays in English and Spanish.* New York: Morrow Junior Books.

Campoy, F. Isabel. 2001. *Charlotte's Bicycle.* Illustrated by Fabricio Vanden Broeck. In A. F. Ada and F. I. Campoy (Eds.). *Top Hat.* Miami, FL: Alfaguara.

Campoy, F. Isabel. 2001. *The Little Lamb That Wanted to Be a Buzzard.* Illustrated by Felipe Dávalos. In A. F. Ada and F. I. Campoy (Eds.). *Rat-A-Tat-Cat.* Miami, FL: Alfaguara.

Campoy, F. Isabel. 2001. *Jenny Hen.* Illustrated by María Eugenia Jara. In A. F. Ada and F. I. Campoy (Eds.). *Roll 'N' Role.* Miami, FL: Alfaguara.

Campoy, F. Isabel. 2001. *The Rainbow's Nap.* Illustrated by Rosario Valderrama. In A. F. Ada and F. I. Campoy (Eds.). *Curtains Up!* Miami, FL: Alfaguara.

Campoy, F. Isabel. 2001. *The Three Little Goats.* Illustrated by Gloria Calderas. In A. F. Ada and F. I. Campoy (Eds.). *Rat-A-Tat-Cat.* Miami, FL: Alfaguara.

Castedo, Elena. 1999. *Luck.* In Lori Marie Carlson (Ed.). *You're On! Seven Plays in English and Spanish.* New York: Morrow Junior Books.

Hijuelos, Oscar. 1999. *Christmas Fantasy.* In Lori Marie Carlson (Ed.). *You're On! Seven Plays in English and Spanish.* New York: Morrow Junior Books.

Ruiz, Denise. 1999. *Jump In.* In Lori Marie Carlson (Ed.). *You're On! Seven Plays in English and Spanish.* New York: Morrow Junior Books.

Soto, Gary. 1997. *Novio Boy: A Play.* San Diego, CA: Harcourt.

Soto, Gary. 1999. *These Shoes of Mine.* In Lori Marie Carlson (Ed.). *You're On! Seven Plays in English and Spanish.* New York: Morrow Junior Books.

Individual Plays in Spanish

Ada, Alma Flor. 2001. *El cumpleaños de Serafina.* Illustrated by Claudia Legnazzi. In A. F. Ada and F. I. Campoy (Eds.). *Teatrín de Don Crispín.* Miami, FL: Alfaguara.

Ada, Alma Flor. 2001. *Gallinita Dorada.* Illustrated by Felipe Ugalde. In A. F. Ada and F. I. Campoy (Eds.). *Escenario de Polichinela.* Miami, FL: Alfaguara.

Ada, Alma Flor. 2001. *La gata con botas.* Illustrated by Gabriel Gutiérrez. In A. F. Ada and F. I. Campoy (Eds.). *Tablado de Doña Rosita.* Miami, FL: Alfaguara.

Ada, Alma Flor. 2001. *Regalos de Navidad.* Illustrated by Claudia de Teresa. In A. F. Ada and F. I. Campoy (Eds). *Escenario de Polichinela.* Miami, FL: Alfaguara.

Ada, Alma Flor, and F. Isabel Campoy. 1996. *Caperucita roja.* In A. F. Ada and F. I. Campoy (Eds.). *Primer Acto.* Orlando, FL: Harcourt.

Ada, Alma Flor, and F. I. Campoy. 1996. *La Cucarachita Martina.* In A. F. Ada and F. I. Campoy (Eds.). *Escenas y alegrías.* Orlando, FL: Harcourt.

Ada, Alma Flor, and F. Isabel Campoy. 1996. *La cuchara de palo.* In A. F. Ada and F. I. Campoy (Eds.). *Actores y flores.* Orlando, FL: Harcourt.

Ada, Alma Flor, and F. Isabel Campoy. 1996. *La gallinita roja.* In A. F. Ada and F. I. Campoy (Eds.). *Primer acto.* Orlando, FL: Harcourt.

Ada, Alma Flor, and F. Isabel Campoy. 1996. *El gallo de boda.* In A. F. Ada and F. I. Campoy (Eds.). *Risas y aplausos.* Orlando, FL: Harcourt.

Ada, Alma Flor, and F. Isabel Campoy. 1996. *Pedro Pollito.* In A. F. Ada and F. I. Campoy (Eds.). *Escenas y alegrías.* Orlando, FL: Harcourt.

Ada, Alma Flor, and F. Isabel Campoy. 1996. *Pedro Pollito.* Illustrated by Claudia Legnazzi. In A. F. Ada and F. I. Campoy (Eds.). *Teatro del Gato Garabato.* Miami, FL: Alfaguara.

Ada, Alma Flor, and F. Isabel Campoy. 1996. *El ratón Pérez.* In A. F. Ada and F. I. Campoy (Eds.). *Escenas y alegrías.* Orlando, FL: Harcourt.

Ada, Alma Flor, and F. Isabel Campoy. 1996. *El sol.* In A. F. Ada and F. I. Campoy (Eds.). *Risas y aplausos.* Orlando, FL: Harcourt.

Ada, Alma Flor, and F. Isabel Campoy. 1996. *Los tres cerditos.* In A. F. Ada and F. I. Campoy (Eds.). *Risas y aplausos.* Orlando, FL: Harcourt.

Ada, Alma Flor, and F. Isabel Campoy. 1996. *Los tres osos.* In A. F. Ada and F. I. Campoy (Eds.). *Primer acto.* Orlando, FL: Harcourt.

Ada, Alma Flor, and F. Isabel Campoy. 2001. *Amiga hormiga.* Illustrated by Felipe Ugalde. In A. F. Ada and F. I. Campoy (Eds.). *Teatrín de Don Crispín.* Miami, FL: Alfaguara.

Ada, Alma Flor, and F. Isabel Campoy. 2001. *Amigos.* Illustrated by Nancy Tobin. In A. F. Ada and F. I. Campoy (Eds.). *Escenas y alegrías.* Orlando, FL: Harcourt.

Ada, Alma Flor, and F. Isabel Campoy. 2001. *El árbol.* In A. F. Ada and F. I. Campoy (Eds.). *Actores y flores.* Orlando, FL: Harcourt.

Belpré, Pura. 1999. *Remembranzas tropicales.* In Lori Marie Carlson (Ed.). *You're On! Seven Plays in English and Spanish.* New York: Morrow Junior Books.

Campoy, F. Isabel. 1996. *Amistad, divino tesoro.* In A. F. Ada and F. I. Campoy (Eds.). *Saludos al público.* Orlando, FL: Harcourt.

Campoy, F. Isabel. 1996. *Busco un socio para mi negocio.* In A. F. Ada and F. I. Campoy (Eds.). *Saludos al público.* Orlando, FL: Harcourt.

Campoy, F. Isabel. 1996. *La Cenicienta—versión desempolvada.* In A. F. Ada and F. I. Campoy (Eds.). *Ensayo general.* Orlando, FL: Harcourt.

Campoy, F. Isabel. 2001. *La bicicleta de Cheta.* Illustrated by Fabricio Vanden Broeck. In A. F. Ada and F. I. Campoy (Eds.). *Escenario de Polichinela.* Miami, FL: Alfaguara.

Campoy, F. Isabel. 2001. *El borreguito que quería ser buitre.* Illustrated by Felipe Dávalos. In A. F. Ada and F. I. Campoy (Eds.). *Teatro del Gato Garabato.* Miami, FL: Alfaguara.

Campoy, F. Isabel. 2001. *La gallina Josefina.* Illustrated by María Eugenia Jara. In A. F. Ada and F. I. Campoy (Eds.). *Teatrín de Don Crispín.* Miami, FL: Alfaguara.

Campoy, F. Isabel. 2001. *La siesta del arco iris.* Illustrated by Rosario Valderrama. In A. F. Ada and F. I. Campoy (Eds.). *Tablado de Doña Rosita.* Miami, FL: Alfaguara.

Campoy, F. Isabel. 2001. *Los tres cabritillos.* Illustrated by Gloria Calderas. In A. F. Ada and F. I. Campoy (Eds.). *Teatro del Gato Garabato.* Miami, FL: Alfaguara.

Castedo, Elena. 1999. *La buena suerte.* In Lori Marie Carlson (Ed.). *You're On! Seven Plays in English and Spanish.* New York: Morrow Junior Books.

Hijuelos, Oscar. 1999. *Fantasía de Navidad.* In Lori Marie Carlson (Ed.). *You're On! Seven Plays in English and Spanish.* New York: Morrow Junior Books.

Ruiz, Denise. 1999. *Saltando.* In Lori Marie Carlson (Ed.). *You're On! Seven Plays in English and Spanish.* New York: Morrow Junior Books.

Soto, Gary. 1999. *Estos zapatos míos.* Translated by Osvaldo Blanco. In Lori Marie Carlson (Ed.). *You're On! Seven Plays in English and Spanish.* New York: Morrow Junior Books.

4. ART

Art Anthologies in English and Spanish

Ada, Alma Flor, and F. Isabel Campoy. 2000. *Artist's Easel.* Miami, FL: Alfaguara. Collection Gateways to the Sun. (Also in Spanish: *Caballete.*)

Ada, Alma Flor, and F. Isabel Campoy. 2000. *Blue and Green.* Miami, FL: Alfaguara. Collection Gateways to the Sun. (Also in Spanish: *Azul y verde.*)

Ada, Alma Flor, and F. Isabel Campoy. 2000. *Brush and Paint.* Miami, FL: Alfaguara. Collection Gateways to the Sun. (Also in Spanish: *Brocha y pincel.*)

Ada, Alma Flor, and F. Isabel Campoy. 2000. *Canvas and Paper*. Miami, FL: Alfaguara. Collection Gateways to the Sun. (Also in Spanish: *Lienzo y papel*.)

Presilla, Maricel E. 1996. *Mola: Cuna Life Stories and Art*. New York: Henry Holt.

Presilla, Maricel E., and Gloria Soto. 1996. *Life around the Lake: Embroideries by the Women of Lake Pátzcuaro*. New York: Henry Holt.

Bilingual Books about Individual Artists

Alba, Juanita. 1995. *Calor*. Illustrations of Amado Peña. Waco,TX: WRS.

Lomas Garza, Carmen. 1994. *A Piece of My Heart: The Art of Carmen Lomas/Pedacito de mi corazón*. Laguna Gloria Art Museum, 1991; The New Press, 1994.

Lomas Garza, Carmen. 1999. *Magic Windows. Ventanas Mágicas: Cut Paper Art and Stories*. Spanish translation by Francisco X. Alarcón. San Francisco: Children's Book Press.

Lomas Garza, Carmen. 1999. *Making Magic Windows: Creating Papel Picado/Cut-Paper Art*. San Francisco: Children's Book Press.

Books about Individual Artists in English

Peña, Amado. 1995. *Peña on Peña*. Waco, TX: WRS.

5. BIOGRAPHY

Biography Collections in English and in Spanish

Ada, Alma Flor, and F. Isabel Campoy. 2000. *Paths: José Martí. Frida Kahlo. César Chávez*. Miami, FL: Alfaguara. Collection Gateways to the Sun. (Also in Spanish: *Caminos*.)

Ada, Alma Flor, and F. Isabel Campoy. 2000. *Smiles: Pablo Picasso. Gabriela Mistral. Benito Juárez*. Miami, FL: Alfaguara. Collection Gateways to the Sun. (Also in Spanish: *Sonrisas*.)

Ada, Alma Flor, and F. Isabel Campoy. 2000. *Steps: Rita Moreno. Fernando Botero. Evelyn Cisneros*. Miami, FL: Alfaguara. Collection Gateways to the Sun. (Also in Spanish: *Pasos*.)

Ada, Alma Flor, and F. Isabel Campoy. 2000. *Voices: Luis Valdez. Judith F. Baca. Carlos J. Finlay*. Miami, FL: Alfaguara. Collection Gateways to the Sun. (Also in Spanish: *Voces*.)

Individual Biographies in English and Spanish

Mora, Pat. 1997. *Tomás and the Library Lady*. Illustrated by Raúl Colón. New York: Alfred A. Knopf. (Also in Spanish: *Tomás y la señora de la biblioteca*.)

6. AUTOBIOGRAPHICAL NARRATIVE

Bilingual Autobiographical Picture Books

Corpi, Lucha. 1997. *Where Fireflies Dance/Ahí donde bailan las luciérnagas.* Illustrated by Mira Reisberg. San Francisco: Children's Book Press.

Delgado, María Isabel. 1996. *Chave's Memories/Los recuerdos de Chave.* Illustrated by Yvonne Symank. Houston, TX: Piñata Books.

Herrera, Juan Felipe. 1995. *Calling the Doves/El canto de las palomas.* Illustrated by Elly Simmons. San Francisco: Children's Book Press.

Herrera, Juan Felipe. 2000. *The Upside Down Boy/El niño de cabeza.* Illustrated by Elizabeth Gómez. San Francisco: Children's Book Press.

Lomas Garza, Carmen. 1990. *Family Pictures: Cuadros de familia.* Spanish translation by Rosalma Zubizarreta. San Francisco: Children's Book Press.

Lomas Garza, Carmen. 1996. *In My Family/En mi familia.* Spanish translation by Francisco X. Alarcón. San Francisco: Children's Book Press.

Pérez, Amada Irma. 2000. *My Very Own Room/Mi propio cuartito.* Illustrated by Maya Christina González. San Francisco: Children's Book Press.

Autobiographical Picture Books in English and Spanish

Ada, Alma Flor. 1995. *Barquitos de papel.* Illustrated by Pablo Torrecilla. Beverly Hills, CA: Laredo Publishing.

Ada, Alma Flor. 1995. *Barriletes.* Illustrated by Pablo Torrecilla. Beverly Hills, CA: Laredo Publishing.

Ada, Alma Flor. 1995. *Días de circo.* Illustrated by Pablo Torrecilla. Beverly Hills, CA: Laredo Publishing.

Ada, Alma Flor. 1995. *Pin, pin, sarabín.* Illustrated by Pablo Torrecilla. Beverly Hills, CA: Laredo Publishing.

Ada, Alma Flor. 1993. *Pregones.* Illustrated by Pablo Torrecilla. Beverly Hills, CA: Laredo Publishing.

Brusca, María Cristina. 1991. *On the Pampas.* Henry Holt. (Also in Spanish: *En la pampa.* Buenos, Aires, Argentina: Editorial Sudamericana.)

Brusca, María Cristina. 1991. *My Mama's Little Ranch on the Pampas.* Henry Holt.

López, Loretta. 1997. *The Birthday Swap.* New York: Lee & Low. (Also in Spanish: *¡Qué sorpresa de cumpleaños!*)

Autobiographical Narrative in English and Spanish

Ada, Alma Flor. 1994. *Where the Flame Trees Bloom.* Illustrated by Antonio Martorell. New York: Atheneum. (Also in Spanish: 2000. *Allá donde florecen los framboyanes.* Miami, FL: Alfaguara.)

Ada, Alma Flor. 1998. *Under the Royal Palms. A Childhood in Cuba.* New York: Atheneum. (Also in Spanish: 2000. *Bajo las palmas reales: Una niñez en Cuba.* Miami, FL: Alfaguara.)

Ada, Alma Flor. 2003. "My Abuelita, My Paradise." In Bonnie Christensen, *Across the River and through the Woods: Stories about Grandmothers.* New York: HarperCollins.

Belpré, Pura. 1996. *Firefly Summer.* Houston, TX: Piñata Books.

Galarza, Ernesto. 1971. *Barrio Boy.*

Jiménez, Francisco. 1997. *The Circuit: Stories from the Life of a Migrant Child.* Albuquerque, NM: University of New Mexico Press.

López, Arcadia H. 1992. *Barrio Teacher.* Houston, TX: Arte Público Press.

Mohr, Nicholasa. 1994. *In My Own Words: Growing Up inside the Sanctuary of My Imagination.* New York: Julian Messner/Simon & Schuster.

Ortiz Cofer, Judith. 1990. *Silent Dancing: A Partial Remembrance of a Puerto Rican Childhood.* Houston, TX: Arte Público Press.

Soto, Gary. 1990. *A Summer Life.* New York: Bantam Doubleday.

Soto, Gary. 1992. *Living up the Street: Narrative Recollections.* New York: Dell.

7. FOLKTALES AND LEGENDS

Bilingual Folktales and Legends

Ada, Alma Flor. 1995. *Mediopollito/Half-Chicken.* Translated by Rosalma Zubizarreta. Illustrated by Kim Howard. New York: Doubleday.

Ada, Alma Flor. 1997. *The Lizard and the Sun/La lagartija y el sol.* Translated by Rosa Zubizarreta. Illustrated by Felipe Dávalos. New York: Doubleday.

Anzaldúa, Gloria. 1995. *Prietita and the Ghost Woman/Prietita y la Llorona.* Illustrated by Christina González. San Francisco: Children's Book Press.

González, Lucía M. 1994. *The Bossy Gallito/El gallo de bodas.* Illustrated by Lulú Delacre. New York: Scholastic.

Loya, Olga. 1997. *Momentos mágicos/Magic Moments: Tales from Latin American Told in English and Spanish.* Little Rock, AK: August House Publishers.

Mohr, Nicholasa 1995. *The Song of El Coquí and Other Tales of Puerto Rico/La canción del Coquí.* Illustrated by Antonio Martorell. New York: Viking.

Volkmer, Jane Anne. 1990. *Song of the Chirimía: A Guatemalan Folktale/La música de la chirimía: Folklore guatemalteco.* Minneapolis: Carolrhoda Books.

Zubizarreta, Rosalma. 1991. *The Woman Who Outshone the Sun: The Legend of Lucia Zenteno/La mujer que brillaba aún más que el sol.* Illustrated by Fernando Olivera. San Francisco: Children's Book Press.

Folktales and Legends in English and in Spanish

Ada, Alma Flor. 1993. *The Rooster Who Went to His Uncle's Wedding.* Illustrated by Kathleen Kuchera. With a preface by Tomie de Paola. New York: Putnam. (Also in Spanish: *El gallo que fue a la boda de su tío.*)

Ada, Alma Flor. 1999. *The Three Golden Oranges.* Illustrated by Reg Cartwright. New York: Atheneum.

Ada, Alma Flor, and Francisca Isabel Campoy. 1996. *Ecos del pasado.* Orlando, FL: Harcourt Brace.

Ada, Alma Flor, and Francisca Isabel Campoy. 1996. *Imágenes del pasado.* Orlando, FL: Harcourt Brace.

Anaya, Rudolfo. 1984. *The Legend of la Llorona.* Berkeley, CA: Tonatiuh-Quinto Sol.

Anaya, Rudolfo. 1999. *My Land Sings: Stories from the Río Grande.* Illustrated by Amy Córdova. New York: Morrow Junior Books.

Belpré, Pura. 1932. *Pérez and Martina: A Puerto Rican Folktale.* Illustrated by Carlos Sánchez. New York: Frederick Warne.

Belpré, Pura. 1969. *Oté: A Puerto Rican Folk Tale.* Illustrated by Paul Galdone. New York: Pantheon.

Belpré White, Pura. 1991. *Pérez y Martina.* New York: Viking.

Bernier-Grand, Carmen T. 1994. *Juan Bobo.* Illustrated by Ernesto Ramos Nieves. New York: HarperCollins.

Brusca, María Cristina, and Tona Wilson. 1992. *The Blacksmith and the Devils.* New York: Henry Holt.

Brusca, María Cristina, and Tona Wilson. 1993. *The Cook and the King.* New York: Henry Holt.

Brusca, María Cristina, and Tona Wilson. 1995. *When Jaguars Ate the Moon and Other Stories about Animals and Plants of the Americas.* Illustrated by María Cristina Brusca. New York: Henry Holt.

Brusca, María Cristina, and Tona Wilson. 1995. *Pedro Fools the Gringo and Other Tales of a Latin American Trickster.* Illustrated by María Cristina Brusca. New York: Henry Holt and Company.

Campoy, F. Isabel. 2002. *Rosa Raposa.* Illustrated by Jose Aruego and Ariane Dewey. New York: Harcourt.

Delacre, Lulú. 1996. *Golden Tales: Myths, Legends, and Folktales from Latin America.* New York: Scholastic. (Also in Spanish: *De oro y esmeraldas: Mitos, leyendas y cuentos populares de Latinoamérica.*)

González, Lucía M. 1997. *Señor Cat's Romance and Other Favorite Stories from Latin America.* Illustrated by Lulú Delacre. New York: Scholastic.

Madrigal, Antonio Hernández. 1997. *The Eagle and the Rainbow: Timeless Tales from México.* Illustrated by Tomie de Paola. Golden, CO: Fulcrum.

Mora, Francisco X. 1992. *The Legend of the Two Moons.* Fort Atkinson, WI: Highsmith Press.

Mora, Pat. 1995. *The Race of Toad and Deer.* Illustrated by Maya Itzna. New York: Orchard.

Palacios, Argentina. 1993. *The Llama's Secret: A Peruvian Legend.* New York: Troll. (Also in Spanish: *El secreto de la llama. Leyenda peruana.*)

Pitre, Félix. 1995. *Paco y la bruja.* Illustrated by Christy Hale. New York: Lodestar.

Tafolla, Carmen. 1993. *El coyotito y la viejita.* Illustrated by Matt Novak. Boston: Houghton Mifflin.

Bilingual Original Folktales

Zubizarreta, Rosalma. 1991. *The Woman Who Outshone the Sun: The Legend of Lucía Zenteno/La mujer que brillaba aún más que el sol: La leyenda de Lucía Zenteno.* Illustrated by Fernando Olivera. San Francisco: Children's Book Press.

Original Folktales in English and in Spanish

Ada, Alma Flor. 1991. *The Gold Coin.* Illustrated by Neil Waldman. Translated by Bernice Randall. New York: Atheneum. (Also in Spanish: 1991. *La moneda de oro.* León, Spain: Everest.)

Mohr, Nicholasa. 1996. *Old Letivia and the Mountain of Sorrows.* Illustrated by Rudy Gutiérrez. New York: Viking. (Also in Spanish: *La vieja Letivia y el monte de los pesares.*)

8. FANTASY

Bilingual Fantasy Picture Books

Brusca, María Cristina, and Tona Wilson. 1995. *Three Friends: A Counting Book (Tres amigos: Un cuento para contar).* New York: Henry Holt.

Mora, Pat. 1998. *Delicious Hullabaloo/Pachanga deliciosa.* Illustrated by Francisco X. Mora. Houston, TX: Arte Público Press.

Salinas, Bobbi. 1998. *The Three Pigs/Los tres cerdos: Nacho, Tito, and Miguel.* Spanish version by Amapola Franzen and Marcos Guerrero. Oakland, CA: Piñata Publications.

Fantasy Picture Books in English and in Spanish

Ada, Alma Flor. 1993. *Dear Peter Rabbit.* Illustrated by Leslie Tryon. New York: Atheneum. (Also in Spanish: *Querido Pedrín.*)

Ada, Alma Flor. 1993. *The Empty Piñata.* Illustrated by Viví Escrivá. English translation by Rosa Zubizarreta. (Originally in Spanish: *La piñata vacía.*) Miami, FL: Alfaguara.

Ada, Alma Flor. 1993. *A Rose with Wings.* Illustrated by Viví Escrivá. English translation by Rosa Zubizarreta. (Originally in Spanish: *Rosa alada.*) Miami, FL: Alfaguara.

Ada, Alma Flor. 1993. *The Unicorn of the West.* Illustrated by Abigail Pizer. New York: Atheneum. (Also in Spanish: *El unicornio del oeste.*)

Ada, Alma Flor. 1994. *¿Quién cuida al cocodrilo?* Illustrated by Viví Escrivá. Madrid, Spain: Espasa-Calpe.

Ada, Alma Flor. 1996. *Jordi's Star.* Illustrated by Susan Gaber. New York: Putnam.

Ada, Alma Flor. 1998. *The Malachite Palace.* Illustrated by Leonid Gore. Translated by Rosa Zubizarreta. New York: Atheneum.

Ada, Alma Flor. 1998. *Yours Truly, Goldilocks.* Illustrated by Leslie Tryon. New York: Atheneum.

Ada, Alma Flor. 2000. *Friend Frog.* Illustrated by Lori Lohstoeter. New York: Harcourt.

Ada, Alma Flor. 2001. *Daniel's Mystery Egg.* Illustrated by Brian Karas. San Diego, CA: Harcourt.

Ada, Alma Flor. 2001. *With Love, Little Red Hen.* Illustrated by Leslie Tryon. New York: Atheneum.

Anaya, Rudolfo. 2000. *Roadrunner's Dance.* Illustrated by David Díaz. New York: Hyperion.

Cadilla, Carmen Alicia. 1975. *Los amigos del Tío Santiago.* Illustrated by Ernesto Ramos Nieves. Bronx, NY: CANBEE. Northeast Center for Curriculum Development.

Canetti, Yanitzia. 2000. *Completamente diferente.* Illustrated by Ángeles Peinador. León, Spain: Everest.

Deedy, Carmen Agra. 1991. *Agatha's Feather Bed: Not Just Another Wild Goose Story.* Illustrated by Laura L. Seeley. Atlanta, GA: Peachtree Publishers.

Deedy, Carmen Agra. 1993. *Tree Man.* Illustrated by Douglas J. Ponte. Atlanta, GA: Peachtree Publishers.

Deedy, Carmen Agra. 1994. *The Library Dragon.* Illustrated by Michael P. White. Atlanta, GA: Peachtree Publishers.

Deedy, Carmen Agra. 1995. *The Last Dance.* Illustrated by Debrah Santini. Atlanta, GA: Peachtree Publishers.

Delacre, Lulú. 1988. *Nathan's Fishing Trip.* New York: Scholastic.

Delacre, Lulú. 1989. *Time for School, Nathan.* New York: Scholastic.

Delacre, Lulú. 1990. *Nathan and Nicholas Alexander.* New York: Scholastic.

Delacre, Lulú. 1991. *Nathan's Balloon Adventure.* New York: Scholastic.

Delacre, Lulú. 1991. *Peter Cottontail's Easter Book.* New York: Scholastic.

Lee, Hector Viveros. 1996. *I Had a Hippopotamus.* New York: Lee & Low.

Miranda, Anne. 1997. *To Market, to Market.* San Diego, CA: Harcourt.

Miranda, Anne. 1999. *Monster Math.* Illustrated by Polly Powell. San Diego, CA: Harcourt.

Mora, Francisco X. 1993. *La gran fiesta.* Fort Atkinson, WI: Highsmith Press.

Mora, Pat. 1992. *A Birthday Basket for Tía.* Illustrated by Cecily Lang. New York: Macmillan.

Moretón, Daniel. 1993. *Martí and the Mango.* New York: Turtle Books.

Moretón, Daniel. 1997. *La Cucaracha Martina: A Caribbean Folktale.* New York: Turtle Books.

Soto, Gary. 1995. *Chato's Kitchen.* Illustrated by Susan Guevara. New York: Putnam. (Also in Spanish: *Chato y su cena.* Translated by Alma Flor Ada and F. Isabel Campoy.)

Soto, Gary. 1996. *The Old Man and His Door.* Illustrated by Joe Cepeda. New York: Putnam.

9. CONTEMPORARY REALISTIC FICTION

Bilingual Realistic Picture Books—U.S. Setting

Anzaldúa, Gloria. 1993. *Friends from the Other Side/Amigos del otro lado.* Illustrated by Christina González. San Francisco: Children's Book Press.

Anzaldúa, Gloria. 1995. *Prietita and the Ghost Woman/Prietita y la Llorona.* Illustrated by Christina González. San Francisco: Children's Book Press.

Bertrand, Diane González. 1996. *Sip, Slurp, Soup, Soup/Caldo, caldo, caldo.* Illustrated by Alex Pardo DeLange. Houston, TX: Piñata.

Lachtman, Ofelia Dumas. 1995. *Pepita Talks Twice/Pepita habla dos veces.* Illustrated by Alex Pardo DeLange. Houston, TX: Piñata Books.

Lachtman, Ofelia Dumas. 1998. *Big Enough/Bastante grande.* Illustrated by Enrique O. Sánchez. Spanish Translation by Yanitzia Canetti. Houston, TX: Piñata.

Rodríguez, Doris. 1994. *Diego Wants to Be/Diego quiere ser.* Fort Atkinson, WI: Highsmith.

Rodríguez, Luis J. 1999. *It Doesn't Have to Be This Way: A Barrio Story/No tiene que ser así: Una historia del barrio.* Illustrated by Daniel Gálvez. San Francisco: Children's Book Press.

Tabor, Nancy Margarita Grande. 1996. *A Taste of the Mexican Market/El gusto del mercado mexicano.* Watertown, MA: Charlesbridge.

Realistic Picture Books in English and Spanish—U.S. Setting

Ada, Alma Flor. 2002. *I Love Saturdays y domingos.* Illustrated by Elivia Savadier. New York: Atheneum.

Anaya, Rudolfo. 1995. *The Farolitos of Christmas.* Illustrated by Edward González. New York: Hyperion.

Anaya, Rudolfo. 1997. *Farolitos for Abuelo.* Illustrated by Edward González. New York: Hyperion.

Ancona, George. 1995. *Earth Daughter: Alicia of Ácoma Pueblo.* New York: Simon & Schuster.

Ancona, George. 1998. *Let's Dance.* New York: Morrow Junior Books.

Ancona, George. 2001. *Harvest.* New York: Marshall Cavendish.

Córdova, Amy. 1997. *Abuelita's Heart.* New York: Simon & Schuster.

Figueredo, D. H. 1999. *When This World Was New.* Illustrated by Enrique O. Sánchez. New York: Lee & Low.

González-Jensen, Margarita. 1994. *Tortillas.* Illustrated by René King Moreno. New York: Scholastic. (Also in Spanish: *Tortillas.*)

Martel, Cruz. 1987. *Yagua Days.* Illustrated by Jerry Pinkney. New York: Dial Books.

Mora, Pat. 1992. *A Birthday Basket for Tía.* Illustrated by Cecily Lang. New York: Macmillan.

Nodar, Carmen Santiago. 1992. *Abuelita's Paradise.* Illustrated by Diane Paterson. Morton Grove, IL: Albert Whitman. (Also in Spanish: *El paraíso de abuelita.* Translated by Teresa Mlawer.)

Palacios, Argentina. 1993. *A Christmas Surprise for Chabelita.* Illustrated by Lori Lohstoeter. Mahwah, NJ: Bridge Water Books. (Also in Spanish: *Sorpresa de Navidad para Chabelita.*)

Rodríguez, Luis J. 1997. *America Is Her Name.* Illustrated by Carlos Vázquez. Willimantic, CN: Curbstone Press. (Also in Spanish: *La llaman América.* Translated by Tino Villanueva.)

Rosa-Casanova, Sylvia. 1997. *Mamá Provi and the Pot of Rice.* Illustrated by Robert Roth. New York: Atheneum.

Soto, Gary. 1993. *Too Many Tamales.* Illustrated by Ed Martínez. New York: Putnam. (Also in Spanish: *¡Qué montón de tamales!* Translation by Alma Flor Ada and F. Isabel Campoy.)

Soto, Gary. 1997. *Snapshots from the Wedding.* Illustrated by Stephanie García. New York: G. P. Putnam's Sons.

Soto, Gary. 1998. *Big Bushy Mustache.* Illustrated by Joe Cepeda. New York: Alfred A. Knopf.

Torres, Leyla. 1993. *Subway Sparrow.* New York: Farrar, Straus, Giroux. (Also in Spanish: *El gorrión del metro.*)

Torres, Leyla. 1998. *Liliana's Grandmothers.* New York: Farrar, Straus and Giroux. (Also in Spanish: *Las abuelas de Liliana.*)

Bilingual Realistic Picture Books— Latin American Setting

Ancona, George. 1994. *The Piñata Maker/El piñatero.* New York: Harcourt.

Delacre, Lulú. 1993. *Vejigante/Masquerader.* New York: Scholastic.

Realistic Picture Books in English and Spanish—Latin American Setting

Ancona, George. 1993. *Pablo Remembers: The Fiesta of the Day of the Dead.* New York: Lothrop, Lee & Shepard. (Also in Spanish: Jorge Ancona Díaz. *Pablo recuerda: La fiesta del Día de los Muertos.*)

Ancona, George. 1997. *Mayeros: A Yucatec Maya Family.* New York: Lothrop, Lee & Shephard.

Ancona, George. 1998. *Fiesta Fireworks.* New York: Lothrop, Lee & Shepard.

Ancona, George. 1999. *Charro: The Mexican Cowboy.* New York: Harcourt.

Ancona, George. 2000. *Cuban Kids.* New York: Marshall Cavendish.

Ancona, George. 2001. *Harvest.* New York: Marshall Cavendish.

Ancona, George. 2002. *Viva Mexico! The People.* New York: Marshall Cavendish.

Castañeda, Omar S. 1993. *Abuela's Weave*. Illustrated by Enrique O. Sánchez. New York: Lee & Low. (Also in Spanish: *El tapiz de abuela*. Translated by Aída E. Marcuse.)

Garay, Luis. 1997. *Pedrito's Day*. New York: Orchard.

Lázaro León, Georgina. 1996. *El flamboyán amarillo*. Illustrated by Myrna Oliver. Río Piedras, Puerto Rico: Ediciones Huracán.

Madrigal, Antonio Hernández. 1999. *Erandi's Braids*. Illustrated by Tomie de Paola. New York: Putnam.

Madrigal, Antonio Hernández. 2000. *Blanca's Feather*. Illustrated by Gerardo Suzán. Flagstaff, AZ: Rising Moon.

Torres, Leyla. 1995. *Saturday Sancocho*. New York: Farrar, Straus and Giroux. (Also in Spanish: *El sancocho del sábado*.)

Realistic Narrative in English and Spanish—U.S. Setting

Ada, Alma Flor. 1993. *My Name is María Isabel*. New York: Atheneum. (Also in Spanish: *Me llamo María Isabel*.)

Acierno, María Armengol. 1994. *Children of Flight Pedro Pan*. New York: Silver Moon Press.

González, Gloria. 1977. *Gaucho*. New York: Alfred A. Knopf.

Martínez, Víctor. 1996. *Parrot in the Oven: Mi vida*. New York: J. Cotler Books/HarperCollins.

Mohr, Nicholasa. 1979. *Felita*. New York: Bantam.

Mohr, Nicholasa. 1986. *Going Home*. New York: Bantam.

Ryan, Pam Muñoz. 1998. *Riding Freedom*. New York: Scholastic.

Ryan, Pam Muñoz. 2000. *Esperanza Rising*. New York: Scholastic.

Silva, Simón. 1998. *Small-Town Browny: Cosecha de la Vida*. San Bernardino, CA: Arte Cachanilla.

Soto, Gary. 1990. *Baseball in April and Other Stories*. San Diego, CA: Harcourt Brace Jovanovich. (Also in Spanish: 1993. *Béisbol en abril y otras historias*. Translated by Tedi López Mills. México: Fondo de Cultura Económica.)

Soto, Gary. 1991. *Taking Sides*. San Diego, CA: Harcourt. (Also in Spanish: *Tomando partido*. Translated by Ángel Llorrente. México: Fondo de Cultura Económica.)

Soto, Gary. 1992. *Pacific Crossing*. San Diego: Harcourt. (Also in Spanish: 1997. *Cruzando el Pacífico*. Translated by Carmen Corona del Conde. México: Fondo de Cultura Económica.)

Soto, Gary. 1995. *The Cat's Meow*. New York: Scholastic. (Also in Spanish: *El maullido de la gata*. Illustrated by Joe Cepeda. Translated by Clarita Kohen. New York: Scholastic.)

Soto, Gary. 1993. *Local News*. New York: Harcourt.

Soto, Gary. 1993. *The Pool Party*. New York: Yearling.

Soto, Gary. 1993. *The Skirt*. Illustrated by Eric Velázquez. New York: Delacorte.

Soto, Gary. 1995. *Summer on Wheels*. New York: Scholastic.

Soto, Gary. 1997. *Buried Onions*. New York: Harcourt.

Realistic Narrative in English—
Latin American Setting

Becerra de Jenkins, Lyll. 1988. *The Honorable Prison.* New York: Lodestar.
Castañeda, Omar S. 1991. *Among the Volcanoes.* New York: Lodestar.
Castañeda, Omar S. 1994. *Imagining Isabel.* New York: Lodestar.

10. HISTORICAL FICTION BY LATINO
AND NON-LATINO AUTHORS

Ada, Alma Flor. 1988. *Encaje de piedra.* Illustrations by Kitty Lorefice de Passalia. Buenos Aires, Argentina. Editorial Guadalupe.

Anderson, Joan. 1989. *The Spanish Pioneers in the Southwest.* Photography by George Ancona. New York: E. P. Dutton. (Also in Spanish: *Los pioneros españoles en el suroeste.* Translated by Louis de la Haba. Orlando, FL: Harcourt.)

Borton de Treviño, Elizabeth. 1989. *El Güero: A True Adventure Story.* Pictures by Leslie W. Bowman. New York: Farrar, Strauss and Giroux.

González-Jensen, Margarita. 1993. *Botas negras.* Illustrated by Enrique O. Sánchez. New York: Scholastic.

Tripp, Valerie. 1997. *Josefina Learns a Lesson: A School Story.* New York: Scholastic. (Also in Spanish: *Josefina aprende una lección. Un cuento de la escuela.* Translated by José Moreno.)

Tripp, Valerie. 1997. *Meet Josefina. An American Girl.* New York: Scholastic. (Also in Spanish: *Así es Josefina.* Translated by José Moreno.)

REFERENCES AND
SUGGESTED READINGS

Ada, A. F. (1987). Creative education for bilingual teachers. In M. Okazawa-Rey, J. Anderson, & R. Traver (Eds.), *Teachers: Teaching and teacher education* (pp. 57–65). Harvard Educational Review. Reprint Series No. 19. Cambridge, MA: Harvard University.

Ada, A. F. (1988). The Pájaro Valley experience: Working with Spanish-speaking parents to develop children's reading and writing skills through the use of children's literature. In T. Skutnabb-Kangas & J. Cummins (Eds.), *Minority education: From shame to struggle* (pp. 223–238). Clevedon, England: Multilingual Matters.

Ada, A. F. (1991). Creative reading: A relevant methodology for language minority children. In C. Walsh (Ed.), *Literacy as praxis: Culture, language, and pedagogy* (pp. 89–102). Norwood, NJ: Ablex.

Ada, A. F. (1995). Fostering the home-school connection. In J. Frederickson (Ed.), *Reclaiming our voices: Bilingual education, critical pedagogy and praxis* (pp. 163–178). Los Angeles: California Association for Bilingual Education.

Ada, A. F. (1996a). A visionary look at Spanish language arts in the bilingual classroom. In C. Walsh (Ed.), *Education reform and social change: Multicultural voices, struggles and visions* (pp. 165–170). Mahwah, NJ: Lawrence Erlbaum Associates.

Ada, A. F. (1996b). The Transformative language arts classroom. In L. Scott (Ed.), *Promising practices: Unbearably good, teacher-tested ideas* (pp. 5–10). San Diego, CA: The Greater San Diego Council of Teachers of English.

Ada, A. F. (1997a). Linguistic human rights and education. In E. Lee, D. Menkart, & M. Okazawa-Rey (Eds.), *Beyond heroes and holidays: A practical guide to K–12 antiracist, multicultural education and staff-development* (pp. 181–184). Washington, DC: Network of Educators for the Americas.

Ada, A. F. (1997b). Contemporary trends in literature written in Spanish in Spain and Latin America. In J. V. Tinajero & A. F. Ada (Eds.), *The power of two languages: Literacy and biliteracy for Spanish-speaking students* (pp. 107–116). New York: Mac-Millan/McGraw Hill.

Ada, A. F. (1997c). Mother tongue literacy as a bridge between home and school cultures. In J. V. Tinajero & A. F. Ada (Eds.), *The power of two languages: Literacy and biliteracy for Spanish-speaking students* (pp. 158–163). New York: Macmillan/McGraw-Hill.

Ada, A. F., & Campoy, F. I. (1998a). *Comprehensive language arts.* Westlake, OH: Del Sol Publishing.

Ada, A. F., & Campoy, F. I. (1998b). *Effective English acquisition.* Westlake, OH: Del Sol Publishing.

Ada, A. F., & Campoy, F. I. (1998c). *Home school interaction with cultural or language diverse families.* Westlake, OH: Del Sol Publishing.

Ada, A. F., & Campoy, F. I. (1998d). *Música amiga.* Westlake, OH: Del Sol Publishing.

Ada, A. F., & Campoy, F. I. (1999). *Ayudando a nuestros hijos.* Westlake, OH: Del Sol Publishing.

Ada, A. F., & Campoy, F. I. (2003). *Authors in the classroom: Transformative education for teachers, students, and families.* Boston: Allyn & Bacon.

Ada, A. F., Campoy, F. I., & Zubizarreta, R. (2001). Assessing our work with parents on behalf of children's literacy. In S. R. Hurley & J. V. Tinajero (Eds.), *Literacy assessment of second language learners* (pp. 167–186). Boston: Allyn & Bacon.

Ada, A. F., & Smith, N. J. (1998). Fostering the home-school connection for Latinos. In M. L. González, A. Huerta-Macías, & J. V. Tinajero (Eds.), *Educating Latino students: A guide to successful practices* (pp. 47–60). Lancaster, PA: Technomic Publishing.

Ada, A. F., & Zubizarreta, R. (2001). Parent narratives: The cultural bridge between Latino parents and their children. In M. L. Reyes & J. J. Halcón (Eds.), *The best for our children: Critical perspectives on literacy for Latino students* (pp. 229–244). New York: Teachers College Press.

Adorno, T. W., & Horkheimer, M. (1972). *Dialectics of enlightenment.* (John Cumming, Trans.). New York: Seabury Press.

Anzaldúa, G. (1987). *Borderlands/La frontera: The new mestiza.* San Francisco: Aunt Lute Books.

Apple, M. W. (1993). *Official knowledge: Democratic education in a conservative age.* New York: Routledge.

Aronowitz, S., & Giroux, H. (1985). *Education under siege: The conservative, liberal and radical debate over schooling.* South Hadley, MA: Bergin & Garvey.

Ashton-Warner, S. (1986). *Teacher.* New York: Simon & Schuster. Touchstone.

Auerbach, E. (1989). Towards a social-contextual approach to family literacy. *Harvard Educational Review, 59*(2), 165–181.

Auerbach, E. (1990). *Making meaning, making change: A guide to participatory curriculum development for adult ESL and family literacy.* Boston: University of Massachusetts Press.

Auerbach, E. (Ed.). (2002). *Case studies in community partnerships.* Alexandria, VA: TESOL Press.

Baird, P. (2001). *Children's song-makers as messengers of hope: Participatory research with implications for teacher educators.* Unpublished dissertation. University of San Francisco: San Francisco, CA.

Baker, C. (1997). *Foundations of bilingual education and bilingualism.* Clevedon, England: Multilingual Matters.

Baker, C., & Jones, S. P. (1998). *Encyclopedia of bilingualism and bilingual education.* Clevedon, England: Multilingual Matters.

Bakhtin, M. (1981). *The dialogic imagination.* Austin: University of Texas Press.

Balderas, V. A. (1993). *Reclaiming and affirming voice and culture. Family contributions through book creation of live history and experience: A participatory research with Mexican families.* Unpublished dissertation. University of San Francisco, San Francisco, CA.

Barillas, M. R. (2000). Literacy at home: Honoring parent voices through writing. *The Reading Teacher, 54*(3), 302–308.

Belenki, M. F., Clinchy B., Goldberger, N. R., & Tarule, J. M. (1986). *Women's ways of knowing: Development of self, voice and mind.* New York: Basic Books.

Berthoff, A. E. (1981). *The making of meaning: Metaphors, models and maxims for writing teachers.* Montclair, NJ: Boynton/Cook.

Bigelow, B., Christensen, L., Karp, S., Miner, B., & Peterson, B. (Eds.). (1994). *Rethinking our classrooms: Teaching for equity and justice.* Milwaukee, WI: Rethinking Schools.

Blumenfeld, W. (Ed.). (1992). *Homophobia: How we all pay the price.* Boston: Beacon Press.

Boal, A. (1979). *Theatre of the oppressed* (Charles A. and Maria-Odilia Leal McBride, Trans.). New York: Urizan Books.

Brisk, M. E. (1998). *Bilingual education: From compensatory to quality schooling.* Mahwah, NJ: Lawrence Erlbaum Associates.

Brisk, M. E., & Harrington, M. M. (2000). *Literacy and bilingualism: A handbook for ALL teachers.* Mahwah, NJ: Lawrence Erlbaum Associates.

Carnoy, M. (1977). *Schooling in a corporate society: The political economy of education in America.* New York: David McCay.

Chomsky, N. (1989). *Necessary illusions: Thought control in democratic societies.* Boston: South End Press.

Christensen, B. (2003). *Across the river and through the woods.* New York: HarperCollins.

Clemens, S. G. (1983). *The sun's not broken. A cloud's just in the way: On child-centered teaching.* Mt. Ranier, MD: Gryphon House.

Cummins, J. (1996). *Negotiating identities: Education for empowerment in a diverse society.* Ontario, CA: CABE.

Cummins, J. (2000). *Language, power and pedagogy: Bilingual children in the crossfire.* Clevedon, England: Multilingual Matters.

Cummins, J., & Sayers, D. (1995). *Brave new schools: Challenging cultural illiteracy through global learning networks.* New York: St. Martin's Press.

Day, F. A. (1997). *Latina and Latino voices in literature for children and teenagers.* Portsmouth, NH: Heinemann.

Delgado-Gaitán, C. (1994). Sociocultural change through literacy: Toward the empowerment of families. In B. M. Ferdman, R. M. Weber, & A. Ramírez (Eds.), *Literacy across languages and cultures* (pp. 143–170). Albany: State University of New York Press.

Delgado-Gaitán, C., & Trueba, H. (1991). *Crossing cultural borders: Education for immigrant families in America.* Bristol, PA: The Falmer Press, Taylor and Francis Inc.

Delpit, L. (1995). *Other people's children: Cultural conflict in the classroom.* New York. The New Press.

Derman-Sparks, L., & the ABC Task Force. (1989). *Anti-bias curriculum tools for empowering young children.* Washington, DC: National Association for the Education of Young Children.

Derman-Sparks, L., & Phillips, C. B. (1997). *Teaching/learning anti-racism: A developmental approach.* New York: Columbia University Teachers College Press.

Enright, D. S., & McCloskey, M. L. (1988). *Integrating English.* Reading, MA: Addison-Wesley.

Fanon, F. (1967). *Black skin. White masks.* New York: Grove Press.

Ferreiro, E., & Gómez Palacio, M. (1982, 1986). *Nuevas perspectivas sobre los procesos de lectura y escritura.* Mexico City: Siglo XXI Editores.

Fishman, J. A. (1972). *The sociology of language.* Rowley, MA: Newbury House.

Fishman, J. A. (1976). *Bilingual education: An international sociological perspective.* Rowley, MA: Newbury House.

Fishman, J. A. (1989). *Language and ethnicity in minority sociolinguistic perspective.* Clevedon, England: Multilingual Matters.

Fishman, J. A. (1996). *In praise of the beloved language: A comparative view of positive ethnolinguistic consciousness.* Berlin: Mouton de Gruyter.

Frederickson, J. (Ed.). (1995). *Reclaiming our voices: Bilingual education and critical pedagogy & praxis.* Ontario, CA: California Association for Bilingual Education.

Freinet, C. (1969, 1986). *Técnicas Freinet de la escuela moderna.* Mexico City: Siglo XXI Editores.

Freinet, C. (1973, 1975). *El texto libre.* Barcelona, Spain: Editorial Laia.

Freinet, C. (1974, 1976). *El método natural de lectura.* Barcelona, Spain: Editorial Laia.

Freire, M. (1985). *A praixão de conhecer o mondo: Relatos de uma professora.* São Paolo, Brazil: Editora Paz e Terra.

Freire, P. (1970). *Pedagogy of the oppressed.* New York: Continuum.

Freire, P. (1982). *Education for critical consciousness.* New York: Continuum.

Freire, P. (1997). *Pedagogy of hope: Reliving pedagogy of the oppressed.* New York: Herder and Herder.

Freire, P., & Macedo, D. (1987). *Literacy: Reading the word and the world.* South Hadley, MA: Bergin & Garvey Publishers.

Frisbie, M. J. (1982). *The active writer.* New York: Macmillan.

Gardner, H. (1993). *Multiple intelligences.* New York: Basic Books.

Gilligan, C. (1982). *In a different voice: Psychological theory and woman's development.* Cambridge, MA: Harvard University Press.

Giroux, H. A. (1983). *Theory and resistance in education: A pedagogy for the opposition.* South Hadley, MA: Bergin and Garvey.

Giroux, H. A. (1988a). *Schooling and the struggle for public life: Critical pedagogy in the modern age.* Minneapolis: University of Minnesota Press.

Giroux, H. A. (1988b). *Teachers as intellectuals: Towards a critical pedagogy of learning.* Granby, MA: Bergin & Garvey.

Giroux, H. A., Simon, R. I., & Contributors. (1989). *Popular culture, schooling, and everyday life.* New York: Bergin & Garvey.

González, M. L., Huerta-Macías, A., & Tinajero, J. V. (Eds). (1998). *Educating Latino students: A guide to successful practices.* Lancaster, PA: Technomic Publishing.

Gordon, N. (1984). *Classroom experiences: The writing process in action.* Exeter, NH: Heinemann Educational Books.

Gramsci, A. (1971). *Selections from the prison notebooks.* (Q. Hoare and G. N. Smith, Trans.). New York: International Publishers.

Graves, D. (1982). *Children want to write....* Exeter, NH: Heinemann Educational Books.

Greene, M. (1995). *Releasing the imagination: Essays on education, the arts, and social change.* San Francisco: Jossey-Bass.

Greene, M. (1996). In search of a critical pedagogy. In P. Leistyna, A. Woodrom, & S. A. Sherblom (Eds.), *Breaking free: The transformative power of critical pedagogy.* Harvard Educational Review. Reprint Series No. 27.

Greene, M. (1998). Introduction: Teaching for social justice. In W. Ayres, J. A. Hunt, & T. Quinn (Eds.), *Teaching for social justice* (pp. xxvii–xlvi). New York: Teachers' College Press.

Gutiérrez, G. (1971). *Teología de la liberación: Perspectivas.* Lima, Perú: Editorial Universitaria.

Habermas, J. (1981). *The theory of communicative action: Reason and the rationalization of society.* Boston: Beacon Press.

Hoffman, E. (1989). *Lost in translation: A life in a new language.* New York: Penguin.

hooks, b. (1984). *Feminist theory: From margin to center.* Boston: South End Press.

hooks, b. (1989). *Talking back: Thinking feminist, thinking black.* Boston: South End Press.

hooks, b. (1994). *Teaching to transgress: Education as the practice of freedom.* New York: Routledge.

Horton, M., & Freire, P. (1990). *We make the road by walking: Conversations on education and social change.* Philadelphia: Temple University Press.

Hurley, S. R., & Tinajero, J. V. (Eds.). (2001). *Literacy assessment of second language learners.* Boston: Allyn & Bacon.

Igoa, C. (1995). *The inner world of the immigrant child.* New York: St. Martin's Press.

Johnson, D. M., & Roen, D. H. (1989). *Richness in writing: Empowering ESL students.* White Plains, NY: Longman.

Keis, R. (2002a). Building community with books: The Libros y Familias program. In E. Auerbach (Ed.), *Community partnerships* (pp. 133–146). Alexandria, VA: Teachers of English to Speakers of Other Languages Inc.

Keis, R. (2002b). Developing authorship in Latino parents. Unpublished doctoral dissertation, University of San Francisco, San Francisco, CA.

Keis, R. (Producer) and Hogg, R. (Director). (1998). *Celebrating literacy: Reflections on literacy, language and culture.* (Video). (Available from the Libros y Familias Program, 150 So. 4th St., Independence, OR 97351).

Kendall, F. E. (1996). *Diversity in the classroom: New approaches to the education of young children.* New York: Columbia University. Teachers' College Press.

Knepper, S. (2001). *Educational philosophies of successful English teachers of adolescent female students.* Unpublished dissertation, University of San Francisco, San Francisco, CA.

Kozol, J. (1985). *Illiterate America.* New York: Anchor Press/Doubleday.

Kozol, J. (1991). *Savage inequalities: Children in America's schools.* New York: Harper Perennial.

Krashen, S. (1984). *Writing-research: Theory and applications.* Elmsford, NY: Pergamon Press.

Krashen, S. (1993). *The power of reading: Insights from the researcher.* New York: Libraries Unlimited.

Krashen, S. (1999). *Condemned without a trial: Bogus arguments against bilingual education.* Portsmouth, NH: Heinemann.

Kreisberg, S. (1992). *Transforming power: Domination, empowerment and education.* New York: State University of New York Press.

Kridel, C. (1998). *Writing educational biography.* New York: Garland Publishing.

Lee, E., Menkhart, D., & Okazawa-Rey, M. (1997). *Beyond heroes and holidays: A practical guide to K–12 anti-racist, multicultural education and staff development.* Washington, DC: Network of Educators of the Americas.

Leistyna, P., Woodrom, A., & Sherblom, S. A. (1996). *Breaking free: The transformative power of critical pedagogy.* Harvard Educational Review. Reprint Series No. 27.

Levin, D. E. (1994). *Teaching young children in violent times. Building a peaceable classroom: A preschool–grade 3 violence prevention and conflict resolution guide.* Cambridge, MA: Educators for Social Responsibility.

Lorde, A. (1984). *Sister. Outsider.* New York: The Crossing Press.

Macedo, D. (1994). *Literacies of power: What Americans are not allowed to know.* Boulder, CO: Westview Press.

Marcuse, H. (1968). *An essay in liberation.* Boston: Beacon Press.

Marcuse, H. (1977). *The aesthetic dimension.* Boston: Beacon Press.

Marzán, J. (Ed.). (1997). *Luna, luna: Creative writing ideas from Spanish, Latin American and Latino literature.* New York: Teachers and Writers Collaborative.

Mayer, J. (1988). *The empowerment of ethnolinguistic minority students through an interactive pedagogy within an additive bilingual environment.* Unpublished doctoral dissertation. University of San Francisco, San Francisco, CA.

McCaleb, S. P. (1994). *Building communities of learners.* New York: St. Martin's Press.

McLaren, P. (1986). *Schooling as a ritual performance.* London: Routledge and Kegan Paul.

Memmi, A. (1965). *The colonizer and the colonized.* Boston: Beacon Press.

Merchant, C. (1980). *The death of nature: Women, ecology and the scientific revolution.* San Francisco: Harper & Row.

Moller, S. C. (2001). *Library services to Spanish speaking patrons: A practical guide.* Englewood, CO: Libraries Unlimited.

Murillo, S. (1987). *Toward improved home-school interaction. A participatory dialogue with Hispanic parents in Berkeley.* Unpublished doctoral dissertation, University of San Francisco, San Francisco, California.

Nieto, S. (1992). *Affirming diversity: The sociopolitical context of multicultural education.* New York: Longman.

Nieto, S. (1999). *The light in their eyes: Creating multicultural learning communities.* New York: Teachers College Press.

Okazawa-Rey, M., Anderson, J., & Traver, R. (Eds.). (1987). *Teachers: Teaching and teacher education.* Harvard Educational Review. Reprint Series No. 19.

Olsen, L. (1988). *Crossing the schoolhouse border: Immigrant students and the California public schools.* San Francisco: California Tomorrow.

Patrón, R. L. (1988). *Promoting family interaction and literacy through children's literature in Spanish and Spanish-speaking parents: A participatory study.* Unpublished doctoral dissertations, University of San Francisco, San Francisco, CA.

Paul, S. C. (1990). *Illuminations: Visions for change, growth and self-acceptance.* San Francisco: Harper San Francisco.

Pérez, B., & Torres-Guzmán, M. E. (1992). *Learning in two worlds: An integrated Spanish/ English biliteracy approach.* New York: Longman.

Pinkola Estés, C. (1997). *Women who run with the wolves: Myths and stories of the wild woman archetype.* New York: Ballentine Books.

Ponsot, M., & Deen, R. (1982). *Beat not the poor desk—Writing: What to teach, how to teach it and why.* Montclair, NJ: Boynton/Cook.

Poplin, M., & Weeres, J. (1992). *Voices from the inside: A report on schooling from inside the classroom.* Claremont, CA: The Institute for Education in Transformation at the Claremont Graduate School.

Ramos, J. (Ed.). (1994). *Compañeras: Latina lesbians.* New York: Routledge.

Reichmuth, S. (1988). *Hispanic parent empowerment through critical dialogue and parent-child interaction within the school setting.* Unpublished doctoral dissertation, University of San Francisco, San Francisco, CA.

Reyes M. L., & Halcón, J. J. (Eds.). (2001). *The best for our children: Critical perspectives on literacy for Latino students*. New York: Teachers College Press.

Reza, J. (2002). *Anti bias curriculum*. New York: Open Society Institute.

Rose, M. (1989). *Lives on the boundary: The struggles and achievements of America's underprepared*. London: The Free Press.

Schon, I. (1997). *Best of the Latino heritage: A guide to the best juvenile books about Latino people and culture*. Landham, MD: Scarecrow Press.

Scott, L. (Ed.). (1996). *Promising practices: Unbearably good, teacher-tested ideas*. San Diego, CA: The Greater San Diego Council of Teachers of English.

Shapiro, J. P. (1933). *No pity: People with disabilities forging a new civil rights movement*. New York: Random House.

Sherover-Marcuse, R. (1981). Towards a perspective on unlearning racism: Twelve working assumptions. *Issues in Cooperation and Power, 7*, 14–15.

Shor, I. (1980). *Critical teaching and everyday life*. Boston: South End Press.

Shor, I. (1992). *Empowering education: Critical thinking for social change*. Chicago: University of Chicago Press.

Shor, I., & Freire, P. (1987). *A pedagogy for liberation: Dialogues in transforming education*. South Hadley, MA: Bergin & Garvey.

Skutnabb-Kangas, T. (2000). *Linguistic genocide in education—or worldwide diversity and human rights*. Mahwah, NJ: Lawrence Erlbaum Associates.

Skutnabb-Kangas, T., & Cummins, J. (Eds.). (1988). *Minority education: From shame to struggle*. Clevedon, England: Multilingual Matters.

Skutnabb-Kangas, T., Phillipson, R., & Rannut, M. (Eds.). (1994). *Linguistics human rights: Overcoming linguistic discrimination*. New York: Mouton de Gruyter.

Smith, F. (1993). *Whose language? What power? A universal conflict in a South African setting*. New York: Teachers College Press.

Smith, F. (1995). *Between hope and havoc: Essays into human learning and education*. Portsmouth, NH: Heinemann.

Takaki, R. (Ed). (1987). *From different shores: Perspectives on race and ethnicity in America*. New York: Oxford University Press.

Takaki, R. (Ed). (1990). *Iron cages: Race and culture in 19th century America*. New York: Oxford University Press.

Takaki, R. (1993). *A different mirror: A history of multicultural America*. Boston: Little, Brown and Co.

Tatum, B. D. (1992). Talking about race, learning about racism: The application of racial identity development theory in the classroom. *Harvard Educational Review, 62*(1), 1–24.

Tatum, B. D. (1997). *"Why are all the black kids sitting together in the cafeteria?" and other conversations about race*. New York: Basic Books.

Tinajero, J. V., & Ada, A. F. (Eds.). (1997). *The power of two languages: Literacy and biliteracy for Spanish-speaking students*. New York: Macmillan/McGraw-Hill.

Torre, A., & Pesquera, B. M. (1993). *Building with our hands: New directions in Chicana studies*. Berkeley: University of California Press.

Vygotsky, L. (1962). *Thought and language*. Cambridge, MA: MIT Press.

Vygotsky, L. S. (1978). *Mind in society: The development of higher psychological process* (M. Cole, V. John-Steiner, S. Scribner, & E. Souberman, Trans. & Eds.). Cambridge, MA: Harvard University Press.

Wallerstein, N. (1987). Problem-posing education: Freire's method of Transformation. In I. Shor (Ed.), *Freire in the classroom: A source book*. Portsmouth, NH: Heinemann.

Walsh, C. E. (Ed.). (1991a). *Literacy as praxis: Culture, language and pedagogy*. Norwood, NJ: Ablex.

Walsh, C. E. (1991b). *Pedagogy and the struggle for voice: Issues of language, power and schooling for Puerto Ricans*. New York: Bergin & Garvey.

Walsh, C. E. (Ed.). (1996). *Education reform and social change*. Norwood, NJ: Ablex.

Wink, J. (1997). *Critical pedagogy: Notes from the real world*. Reading, MA: Addison Wesley Longman.

Wong-Filmore, L. (1991). When learning a second language means losing the first. *Early Childhood Research Quarterly, 6,* 3223–3246.

Zubizarreta, R. (1996). *Transformative family literacy: Engaging in meaningful dialogue with Spanish-speaking parents*. Westlake, OH: Del Sol.

NAME AND TITLE INDEX

SUBJECT INDEX